WHY YOU DO THE THINGS YOU DO

DR. TIM CLINTON
DR. GARY SIBCY

WHY YOU DO THE THINGS YOU DO

The Secret to Healthy Relationships

THOMAS NELSON
Since 1798

NASHVILLE   DALLAS   MEXICO CITY   RIO DE JANEIRO   BEIJING

Published in Nashville, Tennessee, by Thomas Nelson. Thomas Nelson is a trademark of Thomas Nelson, Inc.

Published in association with Yates and Yates, LLP, Literary Agents, Orange County, CA.

Thomas Nelson, Inc. books may be purchased in bulk for educational, business, fund-raising, or sales promotional use. For information, please e-mail SpecialMarkets@ThomasNelson.com.

Unless otherwise indicated, Scripture quotations used in this book are from the Holy Bible, New International Version® (NIV®). Copyright © 1973, 1978, 1984 by International Bible Society. Used by permission of Zondervan. All rights reserved.

Other Scripture references are from the following sources:

The King James Version of the Bible (KJV). Public domain.

The New King James Version® (NKJV®), Copyright © 1979, 1980, 1982, 1992 by Thomas Nelson, Inc. Used by permission. All rights reserved.

Names and details in the case studies and anecdotes included in this volume have been changed to protect the identities of those involved. Some examples are composites of actual cases.

Why You Do the Things You Do is a revised version of *Attachments*.

Cover Design: Christopher Tobias; Tobias' Outerwear for Books
Interior Design: Inside Out Design & Typesetting

Library of Congress Cataloging-in-Publication Data

Clinton, Timothy E., 1960–
    Why you do the things you do / by Tim Clinton and Gary Sibcy.
        p.cm.
    Includes bibliographical references and index.
    ISBN-13: 9-781-59145-420-5
    ISBN-10: 1-59145-420-4
        1. Interpersonal relations—Religious aspects—Christianity. I. Sibcy, Gary.
        II. Title.
BV4597.52 .C55 2002
158.2–dc21

                                                                    2002027370

Printed in the United States of America
08 09 10 11 RRD 8 7 6

Dedication

Tim: To the ones for whom my love knows no bounds: Julie and our children—Megan and Zachary. You bring such joy to my life.

And to my greater family, both the Clintons and the Rothmanns.

Gary: To Lory and our children, Jacob and Jordan, the family I love most deeply, and to my father, Gary Sibcy Sr., with love and respect.

Contents

CONTENTS

PART II: UNLOCKING THE SECRETS
TO LOVING AND LASTING RELATIONSHIPS

FOREWORD

The Secret to Loving and Being Loved

I know what it is like to feel unloved and have no emotional connection to the people who are supposed to be the most important ones in your life. That's because I spent a significant portion of my early childhood locked in a closet by my mentally ill mother. My dad was gone a lot, and when he was home, he was exhausted and barely "there."

Because of the condition of my primary relationships, I never felt loved or connected to another person in *any* relationship. At least not until I received the Lord. Then I started reading the Bible and learning about God and His ways. I came to see that He is a God who loves us more than we can imagine. I was amazed to learn that He loves even me. And although I had always lived with fear, depression, loneliness, and anxiety, God's love was powerful enough to penetrate my brokenness and take all those negative emotions away. God's love made me into a whole person.

As I got to know my heavenly Father better and better, I learned that we will never be able to find any degree of wholeness in our lives without His love. It is the air that keeps us breathing. We have to be able to take it in, and we have to know how to give it out as well. And we can better do both those essential things when we understand why we do what we do.

That's what this book will help you to do. How I wish that back in those early years I had had a book like *Why You Do the Things You Do* to help me understand why I did the things I did in my relationships and learn the secret to loving and being loved.

If you have come out of a painful, damaging, or traumatic past; if you have experienced too many empty, broken, or unfulfilling relationships; if you are tired of feeling unloved, disconnected, or lonely; then you are going to love reading this book. It will help you connect with the true Lover of your soul. It will help you experience the love and closeness you want to feel. It will teach you how to find loving, fulfilling, rich, and satisfying relationships. Reading this book will be a refreshing, encouraging, enlightening, comforting, and life-transforming experience. There is healing within its hope-filled pages. Who in the world doesn't need that?

—*Stormie Omartian*

I

RELATIONSHIPS
ARE
EVERYTHING

1

THE HEART OF THE MATTER: RELATIONSHIPS IN EVERYDAY LIVING

Why You Do the Things You Do

Anyone who goes too far alone . . . goes mad.
—JEWISH PROVERB

W here have you been?" Sandra's voice was harsh and accusing. "Do you have any idea how late you are?"

A thirty-four-year-old mother of two, Sandra had bright blue eyes and brown, highlighted hair. She was wearing her new bathing suit and a bright floral cover-up as she scolded her husband, Mike, who stood framed in the hotel-room doorway, his expression both taken aback and laced with weariness. Had they been at home in Virginia, he would have expected to be accosted at the door like this; here, though, he had expected a truce.

You see, he and Sandra were in Hawaii—a perk of Mike's success. What's more, it was February, and much of America was locked in ice and snow. Virginia had been pitched into a deep freeze, cursed by unusually icy temperatures and whipped by nail-sharp winds. Had he thought it would make a difference, Mike would have pointed out—again—that they were missing all that and that the world they were in was perfumed by orchids, hibiscus, and royal tuberoses, fragrances carried along by warm, balmy sea breezes.

They were at a luxury hotel on Poipu Beach, Kauai, an island Mike loved. He was a computer systems engineer who'd decided a decade earlier to go into computer sales—and he was good at it. Every year since then, he'd "made his numbers," and Sandra had accompanied him on one of these award trips. Last year it had been a week in Cancun, the year before some resort in the

3

Dominican Republic, and next year—according to the rumors—a seven-day Caribbean cruise.

Why isn't she happy? Mike wondered incredulously. *How can she not be happy in Hawaii? The place even* smells *happy.*

Sandra herself believed she should be happy on her vacation. But she wasn't. And the longer she'd waited for Mike, the less happy she'd become—and the angrier. After all, what good was it to be in a place like Kauai and spend it alone? Well, okay, she wasn't always alone, but she might as well be. Like this morning, when they were scheduled to go snorkeling. A boat was leaving in less than fifteen minutes. And only now did Mike show up. And he knew how much she loved to snorkel. The first time she'd gone was nearly six years ago when the award trip was to the Virgin Islands. Since then, snorkeling, when offered, had been the highlight of the trips for her. And he'd ignored all that and been late—too late for them to go. Why? Because of a stupid meeting. A hastily called thing that had already interrupted their lanai breakfast buffet and now threatened to ruin not only her afternoon but her whole Hawaii experience.

Mike recoiled. "It's not my fault."

"Sure, it's your fault," Sandra fired back, turning her back on him and stalking back into the room. "It's certainly not *my* fault."

"It's nobody's fault," Mike deflected. "It was a meeting. An important meeting. Very important, actually."

"You know how I like snorkeling with you. It gives us a chance to do something together." Then her voice turned bitter. "But I should have known you'd put your meeting first."

"My boss wanted to talk to me. It was important."

"Important," she spat. "What's important about you and the guys swapping computer-sales war stories around the silver coffee urn? Real important."

"There are rumors the company might be sold," Mike volleyed.

"There are always rumors," Sandra said. "And you're always doing this to me. Putting me second, third, or fourth to everything else. They wouldn't fire you if you had gotten up and left. You could hear about your silly rumors tonight at dinner. But you chose coffee over me."

"Coffee? Is that what you think I do? It's that meeting and a bunch more like it that got us here. Anyway," he said, taking a step or two away from her, his tone withdrawing into a don't-hurt-me-again place, "we can still go."

"No, we can't."

"Sure we can. With the meeting going so long, they delayed the departure."

"It doesn't matter."

"Doesn't matter?" He shook his head. "Of course it wouldn't matter to you. It never matters how much I do for you. Look around you. You're in Kauai, for cryin' out loud. Flowers. You love flowers. The place stinks of flowers. You know what you are? You're an ingrate."

"An ingrate?" She stepped toward him aggressively. "I should be grateful that you ruined our day together?"

Mike expelled a huge, accusing jet of air through his tightly drawn lips. "I'm done. If you don't want to go, we won't go. It's better anyway." Mike grabbed a folder from the open briefcase on his bedside table. "I'm chairing a meeting in the morning. I need to get ready for it."

"Another meeting? Why'd you bring me in the first place?"

He just waved a dismissive hand and stomped into the bathroom. He closed the door just as she stepped up to it. The door nearly hit her.

"I can't believe it. You've deserted me again. The first night we were here, you left me waiting for you in the hotel lobby. And today you left me waiting in this room, waiting for what I thought would be time for the two of us."

"Go snorkeling by yourself," he called through the door.

"No," Sandra cried to the door. "I'm too angry. Too hurt."

"Do what you want. I'm going to the Jacuzzi."

"I might be an ingrate," she said, falling against the door. "But you're an abuser. You get my hopes up and then you dash them. You smash them to smithereens. You're cruel—cruel and insensitive." She took a deep breath as if loading her emotional guns. "You're just like your father."

In the bathroom Mike was stepping into his bathing suit. The instant he heard those words, he felt Sandra's emotional fist bury itself in his stomach. Pulling up his swim trunks, he all but fell against the marble counter, thinking, *Relationships just don't work. Women just don't make sense, so how can you figure them out? No matter how hard you try to please them, nothing works. No wonder*

Dad left Mom. Mom drove him crazy just like Sandra's driving me crazy. Nothing could please Mom, and nothing pleases Sandra.

The business papers clutched in his hand like a lifeline, Mike grabbed a towel with his other hand and tossed it over his shoulder. Then he stepped from the bathroom to the hotel-room door.

"That's the way it always is, isn't it?" Sandra fired her final shot as Mike opened the door. "You go your way; I go mine. I think you enjoy deserting me."

HISTORY REPEATS ITSELF

Did you know that as many as 40 to 50 percent of today's marriages end in the brokenness of divorce? Marriages conceived in love and blessed in heaven develop severe fissures and begin to crumble. Sadly, that's been Mike and Sandra's experience—and perhaps your own as well. Have you ever felt betrayed and abandoned as Sandra does? Or felt battered and, like Mike, withdrawn into yourself? Or have you and the one you love had a fight that's been left unresolved, leaving you and the other person emotionally further apart than ever?

Mike and Sandra's trouble in paradise reminds us of trouble in Paradise with a capital *P*. Remember Adam wandering around the Garden of Eden by himself? God saw that it wasn't good for man to be alone. So He caused a deep sleep to fall on Adam, and then He gave Adam someone he could relate to—a woman, Eve. Later God would give Adam and Eve other humans to relate to—their children. Clearly, God created us to be in relationship with other people as well as with Him. But maintaining and nurturing our relationships—that's the tricky thing.

Hardwired for intimacy—just as you and I are—Adam and Eve had a perfect relationship . . . for a while. But even in Paradise things went wrong. Evil lurked. Satan tempted. Eve bit the apple. Adam caved in. Soon they were blaming each other. Their previously easy intimacy was no longer easy at all—and this was *before* their children arrived on the scene, entangling them in an entirely different set of relational challenges.

And isn't this exactly what happens today? Our relationships start out so beautifully, and the next thing we know we're hurting or being hurt by those around us, especially the ones we love the most. Why does this happen? What are we contributing to the pain? Why, in our relationships, do we do the unhelpful things we do? How can we keep this hurt from happening? And how can we repair the relationship once it has been damaged—or we've damaged it?

Teaching you those secrets is the focus of this book. You can learn why you do the things you do. And you *can* learn to build and maintain—or restore and maintain—strong, nurturing, loving relationships with the people closest to you. That's what God has intended for you all along.

The Desire for Intimacy

When God entered the Garden and called out, "Adam, where are you?" God already knew what had happened and where Adam was hiding. Yet He was inviting Adam to walk with Him—to continue to be in relationship with Him. And, as counselors, we notice that part of the story the most: not the eating-the-apple part, but God's desire for intimacy with us. The Genesis account of creation reminds us not only of the power of God's love and of love itself but also of the fact that He's given us other intimate relationships like those with our spouses, our children, our parents—people to be there for us through thick and thin—to help fill our hearts and satisfy our longing for love.

Unfortunately, so much today competes for our relationships and tears at our love. Over time our vital relationships can sour and become seriously flawed. As our relationships sour, our sense of well-being can sour as well. Filled with hurt, and maybe dealing with a sense of rejection and aloneness as well, we pull inward to protect our hearts. We begin to distance ourselves from the people we care about most. Empty and desperate, we try to fill the holes in our souls with things like work, play, or entertainment, things which may become other "lovers" that give us purpose, meaning, and value. As one wise observer noted, "Modern man is drinking and drugging himself out of awareness, or he spends his time shopping, which is the same thing."[1] Before long, we find ourselves intensifying our aloneness, magnifying our broken selves, and maybe even denying our God and causing more hurt to the people we care about most.

Why *do* we do the things we do? All of us cause pain in relationships as well as experience it—and we can't help ourselves. And we keep going back for more! The persistent human cry is for someone to love us. Our need for relationship is even more powerful than our need for food.

Understanding what you contribute (consciously and unconsciously) to your relationships and then gaining insight into what the people you care about are contributing to those relationships—this knowledge is key to unlocking the secrets to loving and lasting relationships. Providing you that key is our goal in *Why You Do the Things You Do.*

We've introduced you to Mike and Sandra, one relationship that is feeling the pressure and strain of people trying to get along. As their story unfolds in this book, we'll show you how seeds planted early and throughout their lives matured into these frightening and deeply destructive moments—and seeds like that are planted in all of us and are at work in all of us. We'll also follow Mike and Sandra—and others—as they journey toward a much better place.

Abandoned Parent, Abandoned Child

Two of those "others" are Hannah and her seven-year-old son, Darcy. He came for counseling about a month after he started second grade, a notorious time for behavior problems to surface in children. Hannah was twenty-six and blonde; she wore slacks and an untucked blue blouse. Built like a bear cub, Darcy had dark hair, wide shoulders, and busy, fast-moving hands.

Hannah was a single mother. "My divorce became final just three months ago," she said. "My ex lives in Florida now. He's training to be a police officer there. He's also got a new honey and rarely sees Darcy anymore. The girlfriend has a baby that takes all his time."

"His baby?"

She shook her head. "No, but he treats it like it is." She gave Darcy a concerned glance and went on. "I'm a nurse. In the emergency room, the ER. Like on the old TV show. I'm babbling, aren't I?" She took a deep breath to calm herself. Then she slumped. "I'm just overwhelmed. I've got people bleeding all over me during the day and sometimes half the night, and I've got Darcy screaming at me when I'm home."

"That sounds overwhelming. How does it happen that Darcy ends up screaming at you?"

"He just won't do what he's told," she explained. "I come home exhausted and ask him to pick up his toys or his dirty clothes, and he explodes." She sighed as if just thinking about it were tiring. "He's so angry all the time. He talks back, throws tantrums—even kicks things. And he argues about *everything*. It rained the other day. I asked him to put on his jacket before going out, and we ended up in a big battle. 'I don't want to wear a jacket!' he screamed. 'But it's raining,' I said. 'Who cares?' he said. He just argues to argue.

"And he argues with other adults, not just me. My next-door neighbor gets the brunt of it: 'Don't swing on that branch; it'll break,' she'll say to him. 'I'll swing if I wanna,' he yells back at her. 'Don't throw that ball so close to my house. You'll break a window.' 'I won't break no window.' 'Don't throw the ball.' And he just itches to keep throwing the ball. He's annoying me—purposely annoying me—and I'm exhausted. I'm tired from work, and then I go home and walk into this hurricane. Right away we're both yelling—but no one can hear.

"And Darcy walked over to a kindergartner the other day at school and stepped on his lunch. Mashed both the sandwich and the Twinkies. It was the third time in the last six weeks or so that he's ruined another kid's lunch. And yesterday he deliberately wrote on a little girl's white dress with a black marker— and he wrote *A-C-B*. He couldn't even get the alphabet right. That's one of the reasons we're here. The school told me I needed to have him evaluated."

Helping a Child Feel Loved and Cared For

We strongly believe that, before more structured behavioral techniques are used to help a defiant child, the parent-child relationship must first improve. Clearly—and understandably—Darcy was filled with a lot of anger. If a child is angry, if he feels unloved and uncared for, no parenting technique can make him behave. So, to help improve Hannah and Darcy's relationship, we assigned them "special times."[2]

Special time is playtime that parents intentionally invest in their child, and it is totally command free. Parents are not allowed to give their child any commands or suggestions. If you say, "Let's play army," you just blew it. A parent in command-free time is like an announcer at a horse race: You're involved in the moment together with your child. You're watching, describing, *being with*, but you're giving no commands and offering no suggestions. None. And we wanted Hannah to spend one-on-one time with Darcy for twenty to thirty minutes at a time.

In our counseling practice we have seen phenomenal results from special time. But this kind of relating can be difficult for parents who may not be used to connecting with their children during playtime. And what makes it even more difficult for parents is that they have to refrain from asking intrusive questions or giving commands. Hannah had to let Darcy take the lead, and she had to follow him. If he should become excessively disruptive during special time, she was to simply stop playing and return later. Of course she wouldn't tolerate unacceptable behavior.

When they arrived for their next session, Hannah admitted that she hadn't found time in the previous week to do daily special times. She had been too busy. "My life is so crazy," she said. "And anyway, what are we supposed to do during special times?" She had tried once, she said, but it had turned into a huge battle. After only a few chaotic minutes, she had angrily withdrawn from the activity.

"Let's do special time here in the office," we suggested. Although we saw the reluctance in Hannah's eyes, she agreed, and a few minutes later she and Darcy were on the floor of our playroom. Hannah tried to start out on a positive note, but then Darcy took off across the floor with a Hot Wheels car. Hannah, unwilling to chase him, called him back. "You're always doing that," she accused. "I'm not going to run all over the place after you." Suddenly he turned, looked at her for an instant, and then pushed the car at her. It slid across the floor like a hockey puck and zapped her in the knee. She shot a piercing glance back at Darcy and grumbled, "You'd better cut it out—*now!*"

Darcy turned away from Hannah and played with his cars in the corner of the office. Hannah, still noticeably angry, just stared off into space. This was a stunning example of anger and distance between a stressed-out mom and her angry, defiant seven-year-old son.

It would have been easy for us to frame Darcy's problem in traditional terms: he's just a brat in need of some good, hard discipline. But we saw that Darcy's issues and his mom's issues had intersected. She is a single mom and a deserted wife, left behind by a deadbeat husband and exhausted by her two full-time jobs: work in the ER and motherhood. (Later we would learn that she also has a harsh history filled with abandonment, anger, and abuse.) Like his mother, Darcy has also been abandoned. His father has virtually disappeared from his daily life, a situation faced by millions of kids in America who live in a home apart from Dad. Many of them haven't even seen their dads in the last twelve months.

Overwhelmed by the demands of single motherhood, Hannah was barely able to muster the energy and focus necessary to get dinner on the table, let alone sit down on the floor, enter into Darcy's world, and center her attention on him. Obviously, help for Hannah and Darcy must not only include some new discipline techniques; it also must address a more central issue.

THE FUNDAMENTAL ISSUE: CONNECTING WITH PEOPLE

Although these two cases seem different, the recovery of all four people we've met hinges on the way they answer the following questions about the people they're in relationship with and about themselves:

- Are you there for me? Can I count on you?

- Do you really care about me?

- Am I worthy of your love and protection?

- What do I have to do to get your attention, your affection, your heart?

These questions point to important aspects of relationship. When we cannot answer these questions positively, our psychological, relational, and even spiritual foundations can be shaky. Furthermore, our answers to these questions significantly impact why we do the things we do in our relationships.

And, after all, relationships define the quality of our lives. If we have safe, secure marriages, we're generally happy and fulfilled. If our marriages are tortured seas of strife and mistrust, we're generally sad, confused, and in pain. If our relationships with our children are sensitive, open, and loving, they can weather the storms of teen rebellion and those awkward years that follow. But if our relationships with our children are forced and dissonant, with each side mistrusting the other, rebellion can become open warfare, and the years that follow can deteriorate into permanent estrangement.

Why You Do the Things You Do is an overarching system that explains the principles, the rules, and the emotions of life's relationships—how they work and how they don't, and what may be going on when we're with the ones we love most. To help us better understand the dynamics of relationships, we'll look throughout this book at how Mike, Sandra, Hannah, Darcy, and others view themselves and the people in their lives. And we'll see the ways that their thinking impacts how they form, maintain, and sometimes end relationships with wives, husbands, children, God, parents, and others close to them.

How About Yours?

How are the relationships in your life? Do you feel close to your loved ones? Or do you feel alone despite the connections you've made? If you're married, do you feel safe and secure, or do you find yourself frequently angry with or withdrawn from your spouse? If you have been married before, do you find the elements that tainted your first marriage creeping into your present union? Or have you been divorced several times and now realize that you've chosen the same kind of person each time, dooming the new marriage before it even began? Or do you keep finding yourself in one abusive relationship after another? Or drawn into relationships that you know will be destructive? And how are your relationships with your kids? Do you feel any distance? What about God? Do you believe He is there for you? Can you trust Him? *Do* you trust Him?

Again, there's a fascinating reason why you love, feel, and act the way you do. It's the reason why Mike and Sandra, and Hannah and Darcy feel pain in their relationships, and it's the same reason why many of us experience difficulty or joy in our relationships, even in our relationship to God.

RELATIONSHIP STYLES: HOW RELATIONSHIP RULES WORK

In this book we're going to explore the basic reason why all of us do the things we do in our relationships and, consequently, why we experience difficulty as well as joy in our relationships, even in our relationship with God. The underlying reason why we do the things we do is our *relationship style* or, to use a word we counselors often use, our *attachment* style. In this book we'll use the word *relationship*, and we'll talk mostly about connecting with people, trusting, and being intimate with them. But occasionally we may use the more clinical word *attachment*. When we do, know that we mean *attachments* in the sense of relationships and connections with people.

Right now we'll start by carefully explaining what a relationship style is and how our individual style is formed during our early years of life. Then we'll explain how our individual style helped each of us survive emotionally, even physically, during our early years and how our style continues to shape key aspects of our lives today. We'll also address the injuries that happen as we try to establish and maintain intimate relationships.

Next, we'll introduce you to the four primary relationship styles and help you identify yours. You'll also discover ways to identify the relationship styles at work in the people closest to you, and we'll share insights on how their styles interact with yours.

In the second part of the book, we'll examine the spiritual implications of the different relationship styles and explain how they affect your relationship with God. We'll also look at how each relationship style impacts some of life's important issues—dealing with loss, being married, and parenting—so that you'll be able to relate more comfortably and securely to the people closest to you. But we won't leave you there.

Throughout the book you'll see the negative impact that relationship styles can have on your life and, ideally, be motivated to make some positive changes in your own life. So we'll show you how to reshape your relationship style into a positive influence, how to rewrite the relationship rules that were formed in you early on, so that you can form healthier relationships. Remember this, though: change takes courage, and courage grows with knowledge. By following the case studies—by seeing what Mike, Sandra, Hannah, Darcy, and others have experienced and how they have improved their relationships—you'll see how you can put new life into your own relationships.

As you can see, this is important stuff! And if your current relationships are bringing you more heartache than joy, then every minute counts. So let's get started. In the next chapter, we'll introduce another case study, and if you haven't already done so, we think you'll meet yourself pretty quickly in the pages of this book.

2

SHAPING OUR VIEW OF OURSELVES AND THOSE WE HOLD DEAREST

Dynamics of Healthy Relationships

The average man does not want to be free. He simply wants to be safe.
—H. L. MENCKEN

There's not a sweeter image than a newborn baby, pink and warm, her tiny hands clenched tight in little fists, nestled in her mother's arms. A thousand threads connect mother and child heart to heart, threads of hope for what will be, threads of joy for what is, threads of dreams and desires and a love more pure than the mother has ever experienced.

Yet this precious relationship—populated as it is by two fallible human beings and led by a mother who is living out a new and unfamiliar role—is vulnerable to corruption. If this is her first child, the mother is thrust into an emotionally, relationally, and physically challenging environment—and since we're talking about the mother's effect on her child's life, it's a high-stakes environment as well. Even if the child is the latest of several, he puts one more ball in the air for Mom to juggle. The mix of personalities and jealousies is that much more intricate and unpredictable, intuition is that much less useful, and the work is that much more exhausting. A mother can only do the best she can.

And a lot is demanded of a mother because, unlike many of God's creatures, human children are born into a world utterly dependent on their mother for survival. They can't even keep themselves warm, much less fed and comforted. We are discovering more and more just how dependent children's developing brains are on their mother's sensitive and responsive care. Our earliest relationships are profoundly important. They literally shape those chemical processes in the brain that determine how we control our impulses, calm our strong emotions, and develop memories of our early family life.

In the previous chapter, we met a marriage in trouble and a single mother coping with a difficult child. Those powerful images of people locked in conflict and confusion couldn't seem further from the tranquil image of mother and child we've just drawn. Yet, in fact, they couldn't be closer. The seeds of that troubled marriage and the difficult mother-child relationship were sown in hospital maternity wards, and those seeds grew and matured over the next few years. From their own earliest relationship experiences, the mother and then the child developed their relationship models, which shape how they view themselves and those they love most.

RELATIONSHIPS ARE EVERYTHING

As you can see, we believe that mother-child relationships are vitally important to a child's development and ability to be in healthy relationships—and we're not alone in that conviction. In fact, its roots go back almost sixty years. We'll give you a little background on our basic premise that relationships are everything.[1]

It was 1948 in England, and raven-haired, green-eyed, three-year-old Annie Swan was going to a sanitarium for tuberculosis patients. She had a persistent cough and other symptoms that concerned her parents and her doctors.

In those days conventional wisdom said that raising children consisted of keeping them fed, dry, warm, and out of traffic. If parents provided these basics—the thinking went—kids would grow up just fine. This attitude was very apparent in Annie's parents as they checked her into the sanitarium. The children's ward was a long, narrow room filled with beds extending from both walls like teeth. Even though they knew that Annie would be in the sanitarium for an extended stay, her parents merely dropped her off with a nurse and left.

16

Their three-year-old daughter wouldn't see them again for about a week—and then for just a short period—yet they explained nothing about this tremendous change in Annie's life.

Annie didn't understand being left behind. The moment her mother turned to leave, Annie's little face twisted, and she began to cry. Her tiny hands reached out, and she tried to run and grab her mother's skirts. The nurse restrained her and carried her, screaming, to what would be her bed.

STAGES OF SEPARATION

Now picture English psychiatrist John Bowlby and his colleague James Robertson watching this scene. Bowlby had begun to study children in Annie Swan's situation a few weeks earlier and was beginning to notice patterns. Annie reacted just as other children had, and, as the weeks and months progressed, he saw two more stages in Annie's behavior that mirrored what he and his associate had seen in other children when they were separated from their mothers.[2]

Stage One: Protest

Like Annie, the moment the children were dropped off in this sterile, cold environment, they began to express real distress and even desperate anxiety. Then came their anger at being left. For Annie these emotions meant tears, throwing things, stomping around, even lying down and beating her fists and feet on the floor. Such rage was nearly universal. Almost every child behaved in this way regardless of the other children around or how their nurses reacted. These children wanted their mommies, and the nurses, though they were well intentioned and conscientiously met the children's physical needs, were not adequate substitutes.

Stage Two: Despair

Several days after her mother and father left, Annie slipped into what looked like a state of mourning. Dr. Bowlby watched her huddle in her bed. When other children tried to play with her, she looked at them with dull eyes and then just shook her head listlessly. When her tray of food appeared for breakfast and, later, for lunch and dinner, she paid little attention to it. At one point, she lifted her spoon as if it weighed a ton and let it drop on top of her milky cereal. Now and then, seemingly out of the blue, she would start to cry. On her face a pain-filled frown would appear, and huge tears would spill from her little eyes.

Like her initial anger, this stage of Annie's reaction to being left by her parents was like the reaction of every other child in this situation. They all eventually lapsed into melancholy, and their sense of being abandoned sunk its roots deep into their souls. Having seen this behavior a thousand times before, the nurses paid little attention to it. In fact, they welcomed it as marking an end to the emotional outbursts of the previous stage. The nurses felt that the children simply needed to understand that things will not always go their way and that they just needed to stiffen their upper lips.

Stage Three: Detachment

Over the next several months, Annie appeared to be snapping out of her melancholy state. One day a little girl with a big, floppy Raggedy Ann doll coaxed her from her bed, and they began to play. Although Annie wasn't 100 percent herself, she began to show signs of recovery. Soon she fit easily into life in the children's ward of the sanitarium. Annie, for instance, enjoyed coloring. Like any three-year-old, she rarely stayed in the lines, but each time she finished a masterpiece she'd proudly show it around. She discovered which kids liked her art as much as she did, and she reserved her displays for them. All seemed well with Annie and other children who had arrived with her; their anger and depression were gone. As this new "normalcy" eased its way through the ward, the doctors and nurses alike concluded that their method of dealing with children had once more been proven effective.

But then Annie's mother showed up for a Sunday-afternoon visit. You might think Annie would grab her favorite artwork and run happily toward her mother, merrily shrieking, "Mommy! Mommy! Look what I did." You might expect Annie to leap into her mother's arms, and after her mother smothered her with kisses, they'd excitedly pore over her colorings. You'd think so. But you'd be wrong.

Not only did Annie *not* run to her mom, but she actually did just the opposite. She hardly even looked up. And she turned over the picture that she was coloring at the moment, and she pushed others she'd done that day under her covers—hidden. When Mommy went to her bed and kissed her, Annie actually pulled away. Some might say she was just angry—and she was. But Dr. Bowlby saw more than that in Annie's response. He realized that Annie had detached from her mother. Of course she still wanted her mother's goodies—a toy and some home-baked cookies. But Annie had walled herself off from her mother at an emotional level.

Annie was not unique. Many of the children in the hospital ward detached from their parents in some way. Some avoided their parents, detached emotionally, and were indifferent to their mothers' presence. Others, who were relative newcomers, clung to their mothers and begged to be held and taken home. But they learned they weren't going home, at least not anytime soon. Each week they were left behind, feeling angry, overwhelmed, and helpless. At the end of each visit, they were pried from their mothers' necks, and then they watched powerlessly as their parents hastily scurried out of the hospital ward.

In response to this repeated abandonment, Annie and many others like her developed a calloused self. Wounded emotionally again and again, they weren't about to let themselves be hurt again. So they developed a system of replacing *things* for relationships. Annie, for instance, realized that if she allowed herself to really want her mom, she would be deeply hurt. So she switched her desire from Mom to things—to toys, knickknacks, candy, and coloring pencils. She buried her need for trust, intimacy, and closeness. Never again would she willingly reach out to anyone for emotional comfort. Instead she relied only on herself and on the material things she let herself love.

Having gotten to know Annie, do you see why we believe that addiction patterns in our lives are rooted in this kind of replacement defense? In order to cope with her circumstances, Annie replaced what she really wanted and needed (parental love) with something else (a love of things). She also learned how to wall off her emotions. She no longer expressed or acknowledged her feelings to anyone, including herself. Doing so helped her not feel so vulnerable and helpless. No longer did she feel compelled to cling to Mommy's neck. No longer did she have to worry about whether Mommy was coming to visit. No longer did she get angry when Mommy left. She eradicated her need for Mommy and, consequently, eliminated her negative feelings about being separated from her.

Now think back to the two relationships we visited briefly in chapter 1. As we will see later, replacement defenses were a part of Mike's makeup. He had become a workaholic. He focused his mind on making the next deal, not on his wife or on enjoying their vacation together. What drove him was his work, his desire for success and prestige. He was unable to attend to his wife's needs because he was cut off from his own. Sandra's pleas for closeness and intimacy utterly confused him because he had buried his own needs for those things long, long ago.

Dealing with One's Need for Relationship

Dr. Bowlby's *attachment behavioral system* summarizes his observations of children.[3] Here are its key points:

- If the significant person (mother) is sufficiently near, sensitive, and responsive, a child will feel secure, loved, and self-confident. That child will be playful, smiling, willing to explore, sociable, and showing a basic sense of trust of self and of others.

- If the significant person (mother) is not sufficiently near, sensitive, and responsive, a child will feel fearful and anxious. That fear and anxiety can result in two types of defenses: avoidance (being watchful, wary, and having a basic distrust of others) or ambivalence (being alternately angry and clingy, and showing a basic distrust of everyone).

- A fearful and anxious child will use relationship-seeking behaviors like, among other things, trying to make eye contact, signaling a need for contact, pleading, or clinging.

Now we'll elaborate.

Cries for Connection

From about the sixth month of life, children begin asking some critical questions: "Is my mom close by? Is she available to me? Can I get to her quickly if I need her? Will she be there for me if I need her? Will she comfort me?"[4] These questions reflect the *proximity principle*, and it works much like a thermostat. Think about how you set your thermostat at home to a "set point," say seventy-two degrees, and when the temperature goes too far below this point, the furnace comes on until the temperature returns to the set point. Then it shuts off.

Likewise, a certain proximity of a parent is the set point for a child's relationship thermostat. If a child believes Mom is close enough, he feels safe and secure, and he is willing to explore the world around him. If he believes Mom is not close enough, his thermostat turns on and prompts any behavior necessary for getting mother and child physically closer. Usually in infants this behavior is crying, crawling, or screaming. Once Mom has returned to a safe distance, the child feels secure again, the relationship thermostat turns off, and the child once again begins to play and explore.

Older children don't necessarily have to see their parents to feel secure. They may just need to be within earshot. Gary's dad often tells the story of how he was frequently mortified when he took Gary to Rinks, a store similar to Wal-Mart. Gary was about seven or eight years old—a child who marched to the beat of his own drum, as it were—and he would wander off, browsing through the aisles looking at things he found interesting. Whenever Gary became concerned about where Dad was, he'd just let out a high-pitched scream at the top of his lungs—"DAAAAD!?"—right in the middle of the store. Dad, of course, felt like crawling under a tire rack, but he knew if he didn't answer loudly enough for Gary to hear, he'd belt out another window-rattling scream.

And isn't it fascinating that children do not have to *learn* this behavior. It's just there. You've never seen a mother instructing her young infant, "Now listen, Junior, if Mommy isn't close by, make sure you do whatever it takes to get my attention, okay?" No! Thankfully, God programmed us to know from birth that when our caregivers are not nearby, danger lurks. This truth supports a crucial point in our discussion: *fear of abandonment is the fundamental human fear.*

It is so basic and so profound that it emerges even before we acquire the language to voice it. This fear is so powerful that it activates our body's autonomic nervous system, causing our hearts to race, our breathing to become shallow and rapid, our stomachs to quiver, and our hands to shake. We feel a sense of panic that will not go away until we are once again close to our caregivers—until we regain a feeling of security.

This relationship thermostat is not just part of *human* behavior; it's evident throughout the animal kingdom. The next time you see an *Animal Planet* documentary on bears, watch how sensitive to each other's proximity both mother and cub are. The cubs know how far they can roam from Mom. When they move beyond that point, they scurry to get closer. And when danger appears, both mother bear and cubs move to get closer together. Seeking closeness during times of stress is a survival mechanism in us human beings just as it is in animals.

Efforts of Self-Protection

If parents repeatedly fail to respond to their children's behavioral and verbal cries for connection, as in the case of young Annie's mom and dad, the child develops a pattern of defensive behavior. *Ambivalence* is one such defense. It occurs when the child desperately clings to her parents but wants to punish them for having left her. Bowlby's team observed this pattern when parents took their young children home from the hospital after a shorter stay than Annie's. These children would not let their parents out of their sight. They would throw frequent temper tantrums and were quite uncooperative and defiant. Interestingly, when doctors and nurses heard that these children behaved this way, they blamed it on poor parenting. They had no inkling that the separation from parents had anything to do with the children's anger and anxiety.

Avoidance is another defense. It is exhibited in the detachment we saw in Annie's case. These children decide, *I don't need you—and I don't want you.* They become islands unto themselves, isolated from their own feelings as well as from the feelings of others. As we've said, they replace their need for others with the desire for things. They live on the periphery of relationships and see people merely as a means to an end (material goods) rather than as worthwhile in themselves.

Relationship Styles: How We Develop Our Core Beliefs

Over time the many interactions between a mother and her infant teach her child certain relationship rules, which determine that child's *relationship style*.[5] A person's style is a mental model, a two-part set of basic assumptions, conclusions, or core beliefs about one's self and others. The first set of core beliefs, or relationship rules, forms the *self* dimension. It centers around two critical questions:

1. Am I worthy of being loved?
2. Am I able to do what I need to do to get the love I need?

The second set of beliefs forms the *other* dimension. It centers around two other important questions:

1. Are other people reliable and trustworthy?
2. Are people accessible and willing to respond to me when I need them?

Your sense of *self* as well as your sense of *other* is either positive or negative based on your answers to these four questions.

Four combinations of *self* and *other* dimensions are possible,[6] and these combined beliefs about *self* and *others* shape our expectations about future relationships. Besides working like glasses that color the way we see ourselves and other people, these beliefs guide how we behave in close relationships. In other words, these beliefs—our answers to the four questions just mentioned—determine our *relationship style.*

Various names have been given to these four primary relationship styles. In this book we refer to them as *secure, avoidant, ambivalent,* and *disorganized,*[7] and we'll examine each of them in greater detail later.

Sandra, for example, had an ambivalent relationship style. Her basic assumption about *other* people was positive: they are capable of providing love and support. But her negative conclusions about *self* made her believe that those others might choose not to help her because of her flaws. So she viewed people as unreliable, if not unpredictable, and Mike's showing up late was exactly what she had come to expect. Also, according to her relationship style, Sandra assumed that the only way to get others to respond appropriately to her needs was to punish them with her anger. So she would light into Mike with a fury and unleash her anger in the form of verbal insults.

In contrast, Mike had an avoidant relationship style. He assumed he was self-reliant and quite capable of comforting himself and handling his own needs. He also tended to think others were generally unwilling or incapable of loving him and meeting his needs. So he tended to find solace in his work and his business success rather than in Sandra. Mike's style also explains why working late and showing up late for an extracurricular snorkeling expedition was no big deal to him. Sandra's angry outburst only helped confirm his core beliefs about others as being unable to understand him or meet his emotional needs.

Measuring an Infant's Security

"So," you may be wondering, "how is this relevant to me? My parents didn't abandon me to some sterile hospital for several years when I was three years old."

The main point for you is Dr. Bowlby's realization that early childhood experiences affect the way children will relate to people in the future. The next step was to study parents and children in their home environment. A way of reliably measuring how secure a child feels in a relationship was also necessary.

Enter Dr. Mary Ainsworth. Living in the United States, Dr. Ainsworth became interested in Dr. Bowlby's ideas about relationship styles and connecting with people. But she was more interested in studying the day-to-day lives of mothers as they cared for their children. She wanted to see how mothers interacted with their newborn infants—how they responded to their children when they cried, how they looked into their children's eyes when they played, and how they comforted their children when they were upset. She wanted to see these interactions as they unfolded in the home, not in some university laboratory.

So Dr. Ainsworth trained some researchers and sent them into the homes of families with infants. These researchers meticulously coded how the mother interacted with her baby and how sensitive she was to both his cries and other bids for comfort.[8] As her work progressed, Ainsworth developed a method for measuring an infant's security. Her way of thinking about security grew out of her understanding of Bowlby's attachment behavioral system. She had noticed that when children who are secure in their relationship with their parents become upset, these children seek comfort and closeness from their parents. These children use their parents as a secure base. Once these children are calmed, they will begin to play and explore once again. Children who are not secure in their relationship with their parents will not rely on their parents. Instead they either avoid their parents or angrily cling to them.

To measure this secure-base phenomenon, Ainsworth designed a procedure called the *strange situation* and did the testing at her university lab. After all, a child's efforts to connect with a familiar person will occur when he feels anxious, and placing a child in a completely new environment—like a university laboratory—should indeed trigger some anxiety.

To raise the stakes a little higher, she added two more components. First, she had Mom and her baby sit in a room with a stranger sitting in a chair nearby. Second, she had Mom abruptly exit the room for short intervals, leaving her baby alone with the stranger.

Ainsworth focused a lot of her attention on how the infant responded to Mom when she returned to the room. The infant was very distressed about Mom's departure, and the key question was, "How did the baby use Mom to calm his feelings when she returned?"

What Ainsworth found led to the labeling of the four distinct types of relationship styles, one being a secure response and the other three—ambivalent, avoidant, and disorganized—being insecure.

The Secure Response

Secure babies were very upset when their moms departed, and when their moms returned, these babies generally made a beeline to them. Both moms and babies were happy to see each other. The babies wanted to be picked up, and once they were held in their mothers' arms, they were comforted. All their signs of distress melted away.

The behavior of these infants suggested that, in the *self* dimension, they believed they were worthy of comfort and protection. They also believed they were capable of seeking comfort effectively. Along the *other* dimension, they believed their moms were available and willing to comfort their emotional upsets. They did not hesitate to go toward their moms, implying that they believed their mothers were trustworthy and reliable.

The Ambivalent Response

Like the secure babies, the babies in this category were clearly upset when their mothers exited the room. However, the intensity of their cries was several notches higher than that of the secure babies. They were angry, and, with their full-fledged, fall-on-the-floor-and-thrash-around-violently tantrums, they let everyone know it!

When the mothers returned, their children did go straight to them, but even when their mothers held them, these babies were not comforted. They were ambivalent: their desire to get closer to Mom was mixed with anger. Wanting to be picked up and held, they reached up to their moms. But once picked up, they did not settle down. They squirmed, they kicked, they threw toys, and they even took swings at their mothers. Yet if their moms tried to set them down, these children became even more distraught.

The relationship style of these youngsters was quite different from the secure group. Apparently they had, along the *self* dimension, concluded that they were not worthy of love and that they were unable to effectively get their mothers' attention. Their thinking along the *other* dimension was that their moms were capable of giving comfort and protection, but that a simple whimper was not enough to get their attention. Loud and violent tantrums—almost punishing behavior—were the ticket to Mom's effective response.

The Avoidant Response

Unlike the first two groups, babies exhibiting an avoidant response showed very little, if any, outward distress upon their mothers' departure. Observers would be tempted to think these children were emotionally comfortable with themselves in their mothers' absence. But studies of such children's physiological responses to emotional distress have repeatedly shown that they are just as upset as the secure and the ambivalent babies are when their mothers leave. These avoidant children just suppress their feelings.

Similarly, when their moms returned, these avoidant babies did not seem to care; they did not even seek their mothers for comfort and support. Some looked away; others literally turned their backs on their mothers and moved toward a corner of the room. Their thinking along their *self* dimension was that they were self-sufficient and that, even in their distress, did not need their mothers' care.

Along their *other* dimension they had concluded that their moms were not reliable, accessible, or trustworthy, so the children considered it useless to seek them out for reassurance and fortification. This combination of *self* and *other* dimensions resulted in a baby who looked disinterested, even blasé, on the outside but on the inside was overwhelmed by anxiety and distress.

The Disorganized Response

Follow-up studies used the strange situation to learn about children from abusive families, and the disorganized response style was identified.[9] As the name of this style suggests, these children had no consistent style of relating to their mothers when they returned to the room. They showed a combination of secure, ambivalent, and avoidant responses. One child, for example, began approaching her mother as if she wanted to be picked up, but she suddenly stopped in her tracks and fell prostrate on the floor. Another child picked up a toy and approached his mother with it, but he looked away to another part of the room as he handed it to her. Some of the children classified as disorganized showed outright fear of their mothers and stood motionless for ten or more seconds as if they were terrified or disoriented. Others sought refuge in the stranger seated in the room.

The relationship styles these children demonstrated showed that they questioned their sense of both *self* and *others*. Like the ambivalent group, they did not consider themselves worthy of comfort and protection, and they were not confident in their abilities to get their mothers' attention; and, like the avoidant group, they did not regard others as trustworthy, reliable, or accessible.

MOMS MATTER

It came as no real surprise that Ainsworth could link each of these four patterns of response to a distinct style of parenting. Mothers of secure children, for instance, were very responsive to their children's needs. When their babies cried, these moms picked them up more quickly. They were also inclined to hold their babies longer, and they showed more affection and positive emotion when doing so. In short, these mothers were more sensitive to their children.

Second, mothers of the insecure infants appeared to be good parents. They were nice people who were very well intentioned. They changed their babies' diapers, fed them, and provided a warm home and adequate environment. They even enjoyed talking about their children and expressed their love in various ways. However, the difficulty arose when their babies needed to be comforted: Mothers of insecure children were less responsive, less sensitive, less attuned to their children's needs. Their babies' cries sparked conflict. Power struggles repeatedly emerged, and the mothers became more frustrated, rejecting, mean-spirited, and even hostile.

The hallmark of mothers with ambivalent children was inconsistency. At times they were very responsive and tuned in to their babies' needs, but then, for no apparent reason, would become distant and aloof. Or these moms became exceedingly intrusive and interfering. One mother we worked with, for example, had a habit of swooping her peacefully playing baby up off the floor and trying to smother him with hugs and kisses. When he responded with fussiness and a lack of cooperation, she turned up the heat, got nose to nose with him, stared deep into his eyes, and screeched in a high-pitched baby voice, "What's wrong, baby? Don't you love Mommy anymore?" When he became increasingly agitated by her intrusiveness, she complained of feeling unloved and unappreciated by her baby.

Finally, rejection was the key theme displayed by mothers of avoidant-response children. They had great difficulty responding with sensitivity to their children's cries. Frequently they would snub their children and refuse to offer physical contact when their children were upset. They tended to view crying as a form of manipulation and weakness rather than a legitimate expression of a child's neediness.

THE GREAT PARADOX

Through the years many parents and even many behavioral psychologists believed that an infant's cries are a learned behavior. But we maintain that crying is a preprogrammed behavior, designed by God as both a means of protection and a way of communicating emotional and physical needs. Likewise, a baby's efforts to seek out a stronger, wiser person for protection was regarded as a form of dependency, and it was believed that reinforcing this behavior with too much responsiveness would lead to an overly dependent, whiny crybaby, who would be unable to face the world with confidence and self-reliance.

DADS COUNT TOO!

While the emphasis of this chapter has been Mom, we believe Dad also has a profound influence on a child's ability to form and maintain healthy relationships. While many dads these days are stepping up and investing time and energy in their kids, the grave social ill of our day is—without question—the absence of Dad from the home, and our society is suffering from the effects of that absenteeism.

Dads are key to their children's growth and relational abilities, but the way a dad develops a secure relationship with his kids is different from the way a mom does. As one expert puts it, "Fathers are not male mothers."[10] Dads differ in that they have a more action-oriented way of showing love, so they need to play more with their kids. Roughhousing (pillow fights, wrestling), tag, hide-and-seek, kickball, hunting, and fishing are just a few examples of what we mean. When a dad connects with his children in these ways, bonds of love are formed. Dad becomes a safe harbor, someone who is warm and can be trusted especially in times of trouble.

But we believe that a baby's cry is hardwired. It is not a sign of weakness or overdependence. And a mother cannot be too responsive to her infant during those first twelve months of life. Babies whose mothers were most responsive and most sensitive during the first year of life were much more likely to be secure children and secure adults. Secure babies are more autonomous, and they cry less, explore more, and are much less clingy than insecure babies.

On the other hand, insecure babies are more likely to have insensitive, poorly responsive parents—parents who are well intentioned but who see their babies' cries as signs of defiance and manipulation ("She's just trying to get her own way"), not as a way of communicating their needs. Infants who have this kind of parent usually grow up to be more demanding, whinier, more defiant and even aggressive, and less likely to be appropriately dependent in relationships.

Paving the Pathway to a Loving Relationship with God

Later we will also see how sensitive, responsive parenting—besides sowing seeds of healthy autonomy and confidence—paves the way for children to seek God as a refuge during times of distress. Think about it. Before we are able to speak, we have learned whether or not the stronger, wiser others in our lives really care about how we feel. Listen to any sermon that speaks of God's love and hear it said that God understands us, He cares about how we feel, and He protects us, provides for us, and soothes our worries and fears. For those of us who enjoy secure relationships with our parents and friends (whom God provides later in life to help reprogram people who didn't enjoy secure relationships with their folks), this message comes as no surprise.

But for those of us who have been taught that our emotional needs are not legitimate—that to feel upset, to feel hurt, and to feel helpless are signs of weakness—the message of God's everlasting love is a difficult one to accept. Some people can accept that truth on a rational, cognitive level, but emotionally they feel otherwise. To make matters worse, these people too often believe that if they don't emotionally feel accepted by God, if they doubt His loving-kindness and benevolence, then they should question their salvation.

Interestingly, a study of Christian college students found that those with insecure relationship styles felt anxious, overwhelmed, and angry.[11] Those with an ambivalent relationship style tended to doubt their salvation very frequently, wondering if they had really said the right thing to God when they were saved or if they had somehow committed the unpardonable sin. Those with avoidant characteristics were more likely to have given up on God and had begun following sinful habits—idols of the heart.

The good news is that our early, unhealthy relationship styles don't have to mean lifelong difficulties with relationships. By relying on God's redemptive powers and grace, on our knowledge of why we do what we do, and on a degree of courage, we can both reinforce the positive aspects and overcome the self-defeating tendencies of our personal relationship style. Then we can begin to renew and enrich our relationships with the ones we love; we can experience stronger, more enduring relationships woven together by love and trust. Interested? Read on!

3

SOUL WOUNDS

How Injuries to the Heart Occur

A child can be the object of much affection and not feel loved.
Feeling loved and being heard are so similar,
it's difficult to distinguish between the two.
—PAUL TOURNIER

Being made fun of, teased unmercifully, laughed at, ridiculed, lied about, pushed around, put down, used—all of us have been hurt by another person. And, yes, it *does* hurt. But when you are hurt by someone who is supposed to be there for you—someone like a parent, grandparent, spouse, or caregiver—the pain and the damage are far worse. That kind of hurt causes pain that goes deeper. Pain that feels like it won't ever go away.

Why is the pain so intense? Because a lot more is at stake in these relationships. You've invested more of yourself and allowed yourself to be more vulnerable. You've also had different expectations and greater trust in the person who hurt you. Furthermore, you regarded that person as a vital source of love and comfort and perhaps even protection and care. When a relationship means so much to you, it makes sense that when that relationship goes bad, there is more to lose—and more hurt than normal.

INJURIES THAT LEAVE SOUL WOUNDS

According to the dictionary, an injury is "an act that damages or hurts a person, a wound . . . an offense against a person's feelings or dignity . . . a violation of another's rights . . . a sustained loss in value to a business or reputation."

In the context of relationships, an injury to the *self*, an emotional or relational injury, can cause a profound wound to the soul. These injuries occur when we need and expect a loved one to be there for us, and for whatever reason, he or she is not. Finding the loved one absent magnifies our pain, and if that loved one remains unavailable or is hurtful in other ways, the injury sears our soul. How ironic—and sad—that the person who says he or she loves us may be the source of our greatest pain. Our lover or caregiver may be the one who injures us the most.

Such injuries result early on when someone we love, someone whom we think should love us, fails to provide our fundamental safety and security needs. In fact, anything that keeps us from getting to that person or that threatens our sense of security—whether that threat is real or perceived—can injure our soul. And such injuries can ignite life's core pains: anger, anxiety, fear, grief, and suffering of various kinds.

Attachment injuries can result when:

- *The caregiver or loved one is simply not available, physically or emotionally, due to his or her own emotional distress or discomfort with closeness.* We had a client who was frequently depressed and became unavailable for her children.

- *The caregiver is willing but not able to be there.* Parents become ill and are either hospitalized or incapacitated, making them physically unavailable to a child.

- *The caregiver wants to be available and normally would be there, but is absent emotionally—if not physically as well—at a crucial developmental phase or during a time of crisis.* A mother may go back to school when her children become teenagers, so she has little time or energy to help them deal with the turmoil of adolescence. Or a husband may be thrust into a difficult and prolonged project at work and thus becomes unavailable to his wife when she has to deal with the death of her father.

- *The parent or loved one is there, but instead of providing a safe haven, he or she uses insensitive, off-putting, embarrassing, or sarcastic language with the needy child or adult.* A parent puts down her children when they get upset about day-to-day stressors. Or a husband ignores his wife's comments about how physically and emotionally exhausted she is after dealing with the children all day.

- *The caregiver is there but is smothering and overly concerned about safety and protection, not allowing the child or loved one the freedom to explore the world and gain confidence about mastering life's skills.* A parent who tells her children what to do without really listening to their ideas sends this message: "You can't take care of yourself, so I have to do everything for you."

The frequency and degree to which these hurtful actions occur determine the depth of the soul wound.

Ryan's Story

Children may incur attachment injuries despite the parents' best intentions—and without the parents even realizing it's happening. Consider Patti, who came to see us about her ten-year-old son, Ryan.

"I'm afraid he's been abused or something, but the school counselor can't find any significant trauma in his life. I'm not sure what's going on here. What am I going to do?" She sounded like she was gripping the end of her rope with raw fingertips.

After asking a few more questions, we learned that Ryan had become depressed and withdrawn in recent weeks. His grades were falling, and he was driving his mother nuts by constantly clinging to her. "He won't leave me alone. If I turn around too quickly, I trip over him."

We had our concerns about Patti as well as Ryan, but she told us all was well with her, and we had to take her word for it.

When Ryan came in a few days later, he perched on the edge of his seat, a hand tucked under each thigh. He looked ready to launch himself toward the door at the slightest provocation. To calm him down, we talked a little about baseball and movies. (He's definitely a *Shrek* fan!) When it was time, we eased into our concerns.

"We need to ask you something, Ryan."

"Shoot," he said, relaxing and signaling his readiness to get down to business.

"We all know you're here because your mom's worried about the things going on in your life. We also wonder if you're worried in any way about your mom." We were pursuing a hunch.

Our statement hung suspended in the room for a moment. Then Ryan's expression tightened, and a look of frightened confusion came over him. He blurted out a big "No!" but his lip quivered and he started to cry.

"Why don't you just tell us about it," we invited softly.

After another moment Ryan started talking.

A year earlier his mom had been hospitalized for a month with depression. And Ryan had recently noticed that she had been getting "sad" again. (His observation confirmed a suspicion we'd had when we first saw Patti.) Ryan had also overheard her talking about death to someone on the phone; she had mentioned how death might come as a welcome relief. Making matters worse for Ryan, his dad's job had been keeping him on the road a lot lately, which left Ryan very much alone as he faced something quite frightening.

Later, when we told Patti of Ryan's fears, she cried. Then, brushing away the tears, she told us she'd been battling depression for a few months but had been denying it and trying to hide it from her family. When Ryan and his mother talked about his fear, it was good to see them reconnecting. But there was more work to do. Although relieved, Ryan was still concerned. In fact, he was consumed with his mother's moods and fearful that she might dive into depression and leave him again. And if she left, who'd be there for him? Not Dad. And if not Dad, who?

We acted quickly, making sure Patti worked on her depression so she wouldn't have to be hospitalized again. Then we worked to get Dad back into Ryan's life, but this wasn't as easy as we'd hoped. Although he was eager to help Ryan, he believed he had no choice but to be on the road as much as he had been. "It's the only way I have of making a living," he told us. But he began praying and searching for new opportunities to be with his son—a positive step. Fortunately, Ryan's mom worked her way back quickly enough to compensate for his dad's slower pace.

We told you about Ryan because he was a normal kid in abnormal circumstances: a mom dealing with depression and a dad who was away a lot. When his mom got depressed, Ryan had no one to turn to. Feeling less secure prompted intense anxiety and sadness. Clinging to Mom made perfect sense: it kept him close to her.

The Effects of Soul Wounds

Again, as Ryan's situation shows, not all injuries to our heart and soul are dramatic, traumatic, or even easy to see. Many soul wounds are indirect, subtle in their damaging effect, and often downplayed or denied by both the injured and the caregiver. The extent of their damage depends in part on the degree of the injuries and how long the injuries were experienced (see the sidebar on page 39). Also, the effects of these injuries may lurk inside us and reveal themselves only later in our lives.[1] One more note: what constitutes an injury to the soul can change according to one's stage of life. What never changes, however, is how strongly and intensely we react to these injuries.

Why We React the Way We Do

It's not surprising that our strongest emotional expressions are tied to our closest relationships. God has programmed us this way, and feelings like anxiety, anger, sadness, and guilt are designed, in part, to help us deal with our injuries.

Remember the three phases—protest, despair, detachment—that children go through when they're separated from their mothers? Amazingly, these same reactions continue from cradle to grave. Whenever we feel that the availability of the person we care about or need is threatened, we experience anxiety or anger. Anxiety drives us to seek closeness. A baby cries to get her mother's attention or crawls closer to Mommy. A ten-year-old like Ryan may refuse to go to school and instead want to hover over his mother, not letting her out of his sight. If a baby, Ryan, you, or I don't get what we want, we protest.

But the anger of our protest is often called an anger of hope.[2] It's designed to reprimand the caregiver for abandoning us. Remember Darcy from chapter 1? His defiance and irritability were, in part, a protest against his mother's busyness. Think about the last time you were angry with someone you count on for comfort and support. Were you angry because he wasn't there for you when you needed him? Why did her being late getting home after work make you angry? In part, it's because of the meaning we attach to the other person's infraction. If we see lateness as a sign of unreliability, a sign that the person is not trustworthy and that in times of trouble we can't count on him or her, then we get angry.

But when we're angry with someone we love or someone who is our caregiver, expressing our anger is risky: if we share our true feelings, we might drive the loved one or the needed one even further away. So we may turn our anger inward, telling ourselves that we are selfish and inconsiderate. Or we may hold our anger in but express it indirectly by resorting to the cold-shoulder treatment, becoming critical, or "getting even."

When injuries are prolonged, however, our anger of hope may turn into an anger of malice.[3] In our fury at the injustice that's been inflicted upon us, we may feel hatred toward the person and, as a result, want to lash out at him or her. As one client put it, "I want to make him hurt like he hurt me." Or our anger and anxiety may turn into sadness and despair. At that point we stop caring about the events around us, and life loses its meaning and purpose. Our energy and concentration wane. Eventually we may lose hope and question whether life is worth living.

Usually, however, coping with prolonged loss means detaching from it at some point. We disguise our need for relationship with a mask of independence and self-sufficiency. We may say, "I don't need her; she means nothing to me. I'm just fine on my own." In this detached state, we may turn inward and find comfort in a fantasy life. Or we may turn to addictive behavior and replace our need for relationships with drugs, alcohol, the Internet, shopping, and/or pornography.

The bottom line is that our most intense feelings are tied to connections we make with the people we love or need the most. As we will see later in this book, we learn from our earliest connections with the people we love and need how to both handle our feelings and use them to build bridges of intimacy to the ones we love. But right now we're talking about the wounds that can occur in these relationships.

Of course, not everyone reacts to a given situation the same way. Some people are mildly irritated when their spouses show up late; others are infuriated. A child who is sexually abused by a neighbor may not experience any long-term consequences while another may be completely devastated. Some children adjust well to a parent's illness and temporary unavailability; others struggle with it. Why? Let's take a look at why we react the way we do when our soul is injured.

SOME CIRCUMSTANCES AND EVENTS THAT WOUND CHILDREN AND ADULTS

Minor Injury/Short Duration
- Parent shows up late to pick up child.
- Parent is upset, tense, and stressed.
- Parent has flu and is temporarily unavailable to the child.
- Adult often shows up late for work or appointments.
- Adult occasionally fails to keep a promise.
- Spouse goes out of town for week.

Minor Injury/Long Duration
- Caregiver is constantly unavailable.
- Parent is never there for the big things: first baseball game, school play, karate practice, dance lessons, etc.
- Parents divorce amicably without post-divorce conflict.
- Spouse works too much in order to avoid home life.
- Adult is emotionally distant.
- Adult demonstrates ongoing insensitivity.
- Spouse is uninvolved in family life.

Severe Injury/Short Duration

- Parent goes to hospital for a week.

- Child is sick, and parent is unavailable.

- Child gets lost for brief period of time.

- Spouse has an extramarital affair.

- Adults engage in intense arguments and verbal abuse.

- Physical or sexual abuse occurs more than one or two times.

- Complicated grief after loss of parent(s).

Severe Injury/Long Duration

- Parents have an abusive marriage.

- Parents divorce with ongoing conflict post-divorce—e.g., custody battles.

- Sibling gets chronic illness such as diabetes, stealing parents' time and attention.

- Marriage ends in divorce.

- Spouse gets involved in frequent extra-marital affairs.

- Domestic violence is chronic.

- Addictive behavior is chronic.

- Family is dealing with a long-term life-threatening illness.

Healthy Communication: The Great Immunizer

We all desire relationships that allow us to talk openly and honestly about our feelings, even negative ones. Such healthy communication helps immunize us from circumstances and events that could otherwise result in a wound to the soul. In Ryan's case, for example, opening the lines of communication between his mom and him eased Ryan's pain. We also encouraged conversation between his mom and dad. Patti had become depressed, in part, because her husband was gone a lot and she had no one to turn to. She understood his absence, but she still felt alone and isolated.

Unhealthy Communication: A Raging Ride in the Wrong Direction

Not being able to talk through our feelings with the ones we love and care about intensifies the pain we feel. Consider how the following four kinds of unhealthy communication keep us from resolving the pain that comes with a wound to the soul.

- *Criticism.* Complaints are generally specific: "I don't like it when you tell me you're going to take out the trash and you don't do it." Criticism, however, is much more global and is sometimes packaged as a question that implies the other person has a character flaw: "Why do you always do that? You never do what you say you're going to do. I just can't count on you for anything."

- *Defensiveness.* When we are criticized, it's easy to retaliate with more criticism: "What do you mean I never do what I say? How many times have you not come through when I needed you to help me out with the kids? You don't help. You just whine and complain that things don't happen according to your schedule!" Responding to criticism with criticism and an "I'm-a-victim-Why-does-everyone-always-pick-on-me?" attitude are two forms of defensiveness.

- *Contempt.* When criticism and defensiveness are ratcheted up several notches, derogatory remarks, put-downs, and extreme disrespect result. Failing to mow the lawn may prompt "You make me sick! You never do what you say you'll do. You're a big talker, just like your mother, but you never follow through. I've grown used to not being able to rely on you, so I'll just do everything myself—like always."

- *Stonewalling.* When the contempt gets too intense, a person can shut down and stop participating in the conversation. The person may walk out of the room or just stop talking and stare off into space. These behaviors can increase the other person's rage and spark another round of criticism.[4]

Unhealthy communication, while intended to protect oneself, may not only make the soul wound worse but also cause wounds of its own. Constant criticism, defensiveness, contempt, and stonewalling can definitely wound the soul and pierce us to the heart.

REPAIRING THE DAMAGE, PREVENTING THE SOUL WOUND

Sadly, all couples engage in some forms of unhealthy communication. We've all doled out criticism, retaliated with defensiveness, or shut down communication from time to time. We may even have crossed the line and been contemptuous or disrespectful.

Tending to the Wound

What seems to distinguish healthy from unhealthy couples is their ability to repair the damage done. Initially we might be critical or defensive in response to an injury to our soul, but we catch ourselves and recover. For example, a wife might start to say to her husband, "You never do what I ask you to do." But then she stops herself mid-sentence and adds, "I'm sorry. I was just hoping it would be done so we could spend time together this evening. I know you really do a lot of work around here. Sometimes I just don't pay enough attention." Or, after responding to her initial remark with, "All you ever do is complain," her husband adds, "I know I tick you off when I say I'm going to do something and then don't do it. It's a bad habit of mine. But please listen while I tell you why I haven't done it yet."

Healthy couples repair damage rather than letting it become permanent. Even in the midst of a heated discussion, they take responsibility for their actions or attitudes, and they accept the other party's attempt to reconcile.[5] That kind of acceptance helps protect and even strengthen their relationship. Not accepting such efforts to reconcile can continue the cycle of destructive arguing, and the relationship can fragment, deepening the soul wound and weakening the connection.

Establishing a Healthy Family Context

Your family context—the overall climate of your household—can also influence the impact of soul wounds. For example, we've worked with many children who have been sexually victimized by someone outside the family (a neighbor, a family acquaintance, or even someone at church). When the family responded with concern and comfort for the child *and* took immediate action to stop the abuser, the children seemed to recover more easily. However, when an unhealthy context (marital conflict, financial stress, family illness, one parent struggling with depression or crippling anxiety) kept parents from responding appropriately and sensitively, the abused child did not fare well.

When we look at family contexts, we consider two factors: closeness and structure.[6]

- *Closeness* refers to how involved family members are with one another. Some families are too involved with one another, and other families are too distant. Both extremes can be unhealthy for children as well as for couples. Healthy families respect one another's need for closeness at the same time that they make room for each person's individual physical and emotional space. The key is balance.

- A family's *structure* is comprised of the roles, rules, and rituals of family life. Again, structure can be too rigid, with strict, inflexible rules and roles. Or it can be chaotic, where no one knows what to expect from day to day. Both extremes are unhealthy.

Healthy closeness and a healthy structure work together to create a family context that helps protect its members against wounds to the soul. When closeness and structure are unhealthy or out of balance, wounds occur more easily—as in the case of nine-year-old Katie. A school counselor discovered that the family babysitter had been mistreating Katie, often screaming obscenities at her, putting her in hour-long time-outs, and sometimes refusing to feed her dinner.

Katie's mother was completely taken aback when she learned about this mistreatment. She had had no idea Katie was being treated this way. As we talked, however, we found that Katie's parents had indeed noticed a change in their daughter's attitude over the last month, but they hadn't asked Katie about it. They had just assumed it was the "normal" preteen attitude. They also had never asked the babysitter how the day had gone. They just assumed—again—that no news was good news. Katie, unfortunately, had understood her parents' silence as an endorsement of the babysitter's actions. As a result Katie felt betrayed and began to act out more at school.

Katie's family context lacked closeness. Family members were left to fend for themselves, and even dramatic changes in Katie's emotions were not addressed. Katie had coped with the structure, but she had concluded that her parents didn't care about her when they didn't try to figure out what was going on with her.

Relationship Styles and Our Vulnerability to Soul Wounds

In the previous chapter we introduced the four different relationship styles—secure, ambivalent, avoidant, and disorganized—and explained how they all have their roots in our earliest relationships. Our personal style creates a lens through which we view future relationships. It also determines whether we avoid injuries or feel their effects later in our lives.

Remember, people with a secure style believe that they are worthy of love and that their caregivers are able and willing to meet their emotional needs. Those people are best prepared to avoid or quickly repair the damage inflicted by injuries to their soul.

People with an insecure relationship style (ambivalent, avoidant, or disorganized) tend to question their self-worth, and they don't expect their caregivers to be there for them. Insecure styles can make people hypersensitive to soul injuries. In fact, some people with certain insecure styles almost expect to be betrayed and abandoned because, in the past, their support figures have repeatedly let them down. Case in point.

A young couple, Jim and Sheila, came to see us after only six months of marriage. Within a couple of weeks of their honeymoon, Sheila became obsessed with knowing Jim's whereabouts. Anytime he'd leave the house, even to go to the grocery store, she would call him on his cell phone a half dozen times. If she detected even the slightest irritation in his voice, she'd erupt in a rage. She was also convinced that he was having an affair. Confused and overwhelmed by her jealousy, Jim retreated further from Sheila emotionally, afraid that she and her obsession would swallow him up. They were on the brink of separation when they came to see us.

When we talked with Sheila, we weren't surprised to learn that her family context had been one of chaos and betrayal. Her father had been chronically unfaithful to her mother, but her mom could never find the strength to leave, fearing that she would never find another man to take care of her. For comfort, the mother turned to Sheila, who had no choice but to listen to her tirades about how men are "worthless and untrustworthy."

Sheila was determined not to follow in her mother's footsteps, but she realized that she was headed down the same path. She was furious with herself—but still obsessed with Jim. It was as if her past had set the stage for how her current relationship would unfold. She believed that the only way she could protect herself from abandonment and betrayal was to hover over Jim and spy on his every move. Unfortunately, her method was destroying the very relationship she wanted to preserve.

KNOWLEDGE IS POWER

Sheila and Jim's situation seemed almost hopeless, but just in time they took a crucial step toward resolving their problems and restoring love and trust to their relationship. The step they took was getting professional help. They came to us with a willingness to learn and an eagerness to acquire skills that could save their marriage and strengthen their connection with each other. First gaining knowledge about their personal relationship styles and how those styles interact, they soon learned the secrets of developing a loving and lasting relationship.

The rest of this book will show you how you, too, can acquire tools that will enrich your relationships and protect you and your loved ones from inflicting—and incurring—soul wounds.

We'll begin with a simple survey you can take to try to identify your style. Then we'll study the four styles in greater detail and help you clearly identify your own personal style. Finally, we'll give you the tools for using your relationship strengths and tempering your injurious tendencies so that your relationships with your spouse, your children, your parents, your friends, and other significant people in your life become all that you dream they could be.

DISCOVERING YOUR RELATIONSHIP STYLE

It's helpful to think about relationship styles as four distinct categories, and it's natural to ask, "What style am I?" In reality, however, only some people are clearly just one relationship style. Most folks are different shades of all four styles. You may, for instance, discover that you are predominantly one style, but that you have a few traits from each of the other three styles.

It is also important to note that your relationship style can change depending on the relationship you are in. In fact, your relationship style is not always in operation. It only appears in more intimate relationships, such as close friendships and romantic relationships. But your style with your best same-sex friends can be different from your style in your romantic relationships. Also, your style can change as a relationship changes.

Despite all that we've just said, the following survey can help you get to know yourself a little better. As you take the survey, consider how you typically feel about and relate to people you're in relationship with. We know it's tempting to answer these questions according to how you *would like* to relate to people rather than how you *actually do* relate. So you must really work at being honest with yourself as you read through the checklists.

Circle the numbers next to those statements that generally describe you. Go with your first instinct; don't overthink the statements.

The Avoidant Attachment Style

1. I don't like sharing my feelings with others.
2. I don't like it when my partner wants to talk about his/her feelings.
3. I have a hard time understanding how other people feel.
4. When I get stressed, I try to deal with the situation all by myself.

5. My partner often complains that I don't like to talk about how I feel.
6. I don't really need close relationships.
7. I highly value my independence and self-sufficiency.
8. I don't worry about being alone or abandoned.
9. I don't worry about being accepted by others.
10. I tend to value personal achievements and success over close, intimate relationships.

The Ambivalent Attachment Style

1. I really like sharing my feelings with my partner, but he/she does not seem as open as I am.
2. My feelings can get out of control very quickly.
3. I worry about being alone.
4. I worry about being abandoned in close relationships.
5. My partner complains that I am too clingy and emotional.
6. I strongly desire to be very intimate with people.
7. In my closest relationships, the other person doesn't seem as desirous of intimacy and closeness as I am.
8. I worry a great deal about being rejected by others.
9. I tend to value close, intimate relationships over personal achievement and success.
10. When I get stressed, I desperately seek others for support, but no one seems as available as I would like them to be.

The Disorganized Attachment Style

1. My feelings are very confusing to me, so I try not to feel them.
2. My feelings are very intense and overwhelming.
3. I feel torn between wanting to be close to others and wanting to pull away.
4. My partner complains that sometimes I'm really needy and clingy and other times I'm distant and aloof.

5. I have a difficult time letting others get close to me, but once I let them in, I worry about being abandoned or rejected.
6. I feel very vulnerable in close relationships.
7. Sometimes I feel very disconnected from myself and my feelings.
8. I can't decide whether or not I want to be in close relationships.
9. Other people can really hurt you if you let them get too close.
10. Close relationships are difficult to come by because people tend to be unpredictable in their actions and behaviors.

The Secure Attachment Style

1. I find it easy to share my feelings with people I'm close to.
2. I like it when my partner wants to share his/her feelings with me.
3. I am comfortable getting close to others, but I also feel comfortable being alone.
4. I expect my partner to respect who I am.
5. I expect my partner to respond to my needs in a sensitive and appropriate way.
6. Building intimacy in relationships comes relatively easy to me.
7. I let myself feel my emotions, but I'm rarely, if ever, overwhelmed by them.
8. I am able to understand and respond sensitively to my partner's feelings.
9. I do a decent job balancing my need for intimacy with my need for achievement and success.
10. When I get stressed, I feel comfortable seeking comfort from my partner and/or close friends.

Now that you've finished the survey, note the distribution of your circled numbers. What styles do you exhibit two or three traits from? Does one style emerge as dominant? What about your results, if anything, surprised you?

4
EQUIPPED TO FACE CHALLENGES AND TAKE RISKS

The Secure Relationship Style

To be loved, be lovable.
—OVID

Beliefs That Fuel the Secure Style
• I am worthy of love.
• I am capable of getting love.
• Others are willing and able to love me.

W*here is he?* Ronnie Blaire wondered as she waited for her husband, Matt, to get home from work. He was late, and she was angry—and getting angrier as she sat at the kitchen table tapping her fingers impatiently. Her nails, less the three broken by the day's events, clattered on the wood. Any second he'd turn into that driveway, walk through the side door, and the fight would be on. She could hardly wait.

It had been one of those days, and most of what had gone wrong did so because of Matt. The day had even started badly because of him. Matt had left for work at 6:30, an hour early, and the door had slammed behind him. The noise woke up Kevin, their four-year-old, who usually slept for another hour. For Ronnie, who spent her waking hours with this precocious boy who ricocheted off the walls all day, that last hour of sleep was precious. But today the tornado struck at 6:31 a.m. when it landed with an excited *whoop!* in the bed and right on top of her.

At about ten o'clock, when Kevin was in the backyard scrambling over the jungle gym Matt had built for him, the mail came, and in it was a note from the bank. Their account was overdrawn. Matt had written two emergency checks while he was out of town the week before and had forgotten to tell her about them. That meant an unplanned trip to the bank.

Oh well, Ronnie had thought, *Kevin needs new shoes. I'll take care of that now too.* But when she got into the car, she found the gas tank empty. Matt's car had been in the shop the day before, and he'd used her car to drive all over town visiting clients and hadn't filled it back up. She had to drive on fumes—and it wasn't exactly a short drive. They lived a little way out of town, and the nearest gas station was several miles away. Ronnie made it, but just barely. The car took more gas at the pump than it ever had.

The last straw fell about four that afternoon when Kevin, playing out back again, leapt from the swing, a move he'd not quite perfected. Usually he made a three-point landing on the grass and stained a knee or his cheek. This time, though, he landed on Matt's hammer, and its claw tore a gash in his thigh. A few days earlier, when Matt had found an exposed nail in the jungle gym, he had taken the hammer outside to fix it. Then he'd started playing with Kevin and forgotten the tool. Ronnie was always after him for leaving his tools around, and now Kevin was injured because of it.

And she hated when Kevin cried like he had. Silently fuming at her husband, she'd cleaned his wound and put a bandage on it. Now Kevin, his tears dried and wearing his bandage as a badge of honor, sat watching a *Winnie the Pooh* video while she waited to do battle.

Are you shocked? We expect you're probably asking, *Isn't this chapter about the* secure *relationship style? What about Ronnie and Matt sounds secure and good?*

Ah . . . our first point: there's nothing superhuman about secure people. Like Ronnie, they're real people with real feelings, common, everyday tensions, and life's unavoidable problems, some of them devastating. It's how secure people deal with those feelings and problems that sets them apart.

Beliefs of the Secure Person

When secure people run into problems, they can experience the whole spectrum of emotions from joy to depression, from confusion to peace, including anxiety, sadness, guilt, and, yes, anger. But certain characteristics—which impact how they deal with these emotions—distinguish secure individuals from others.

Confidence About Who I Am

"Play the piano for Aunt Gertrude, dear," the mother of a secure child might tell her daughter. And that secure child will climb up on the stool and bang out her latest piece. But she won't do it to prove her worth to Mom or Auntie. She's already confident that she's a valuable kid whether or not she can play the piano perfectly.

Unlike folks with other relationship styles, secure people don't feel the pressure to perform to earn their self-worth points. That pressure's off for them. They may drive themselves pretty hard, but that drive has nothing to do with proving themselves as worthy souls. That sense of value has been instilled in them since early childhood. And it continues into adult life.

This internal sense of security frees them from the hidden agendas present in other relationship styles, so they relate to others more genuinely and honestly. And that makes sense: people who feel fundamentally secure are able to express thoughts and opinions more confidently. They're not worried that they'll be harmed or emotionally bruised if others disapprove or disagree. That doesn't mean they go around saying whatever flashes into their minds. No, they practice restraint like any loving and thoughtful person would. But they're not threatened at their core by the fear that others will find fault with their opinions. When others do find fault, they try not to take the disagreement personally. In fact, depending on the subject, they might find such disagreement a welcome opening for a lively discussion.

Ronnie was furious with Matt's lack of dependability, a failing that had caused a nightmare of a day for her and Kevin—and she didn't hesitate to express her anger to Matt. Had she not had a fundamental sense of self-worth, she might have felt threatened by her anger; she might also have feared being rejected if she really expressed what she felt. Anticipating the emotional emptiness and deep sense of loss that come with rejection, Ronnie might have suppressed her anger and swept it under the nearest emotional rug—an act that sows seeds of such emotional and psychological trouble as panic attacks, debilitating guilt, deep depression, and self-contempt. Or, instead of burying her anger, Ronnie could have expressed her rage indirectly in passive-aggressive ways—giving Matt the cold-shoulder treatment or picking at him for tying his shoelaces wrong, leaving his toothbrush on the counter, or watching football instead of cleaning up the oil stains in the driveway. Her anger would be released in ways not at all related to the cause of the anger.

Instead, Ronnie's willingness to do battle for the health of her marriage said she was comfortable with her feelings. Even with her anger. She knew that anger is, essentially, a demand for change, and the changes she desired were valid and useful. She knew that anger can provide the energy and focus needed to set boundaries and express concerns. But she also knew that anger, unchecked, can be destructive. Instead of being the catalyst for positive change, it can become a tool of aggression, an emotional machete that can hack a relationship to bits.

So Ronnie regulates her emotions, including her anger. She's angry without criticizing, without resorting to "You're never there for me when I need you. You never take my needs into account. You only think about yourself." Instead she makes specific, solvable complaints: "It makes me mad when you do stuff like that. You need to be quiet in the morning so you don't wake up Kevin. It's not that hard. Just be a little more careful."

Confidence About Effectiveness

To respect someone's feelings means you believe that those feelings are valid, are based on reality, and aren't being expressed in an attempt to manipulate you. Secure people were shaped in an environment—either in the home where they were raised or along life's way—where other people respected their feelings and, as a result, they respect the feelings of others.

And that respect taught them how to negotiate conflict. After all, if both parties have valid feelings and if both parties' feelings are based on reality, then both parties can make reasonable changes to accommodate the other. Since no destructive, manipulative hidden agendas are at work, both should be willing to make the changes and accommodations that assure a vibrant, healthy relationship.

No wonder secure people effectively communicate their feelings and opinions. They're confident that they can affect other people, that they can engage their loved ones to listen to their complaints and to respond favorably—with little, if any, need for manipulation or coercion. These secure individuals are not conflict avoidant. They won't remain quiet just to keep the peace, and they can turn up the heat when necessary. But they do keep their feelings and therefore the potentially explosive situation regulated.

Also, a secure person's anger has a different "flavor." It's not born out of fear, and it's not bubbling out of some newly aroused internal volcano. In the secure person, anger generally springs from *hope*.[1] We'll explain.

Ronnie was angry about Matt's thoughtlessness, but behind her anger was the confidence that Matt would respond to her complaints and suggestions. In other words, her anger was fueled by her realistic hope for change. This hope was an integral part of her communication strategy. Granted, she probably didn't stop and deliberately choose to become angry, but her anger came from a place inside her that was saying, *He needs to understand how strongly I feel when he does this.* She knew that Matt would listen to her feelings and that she wouldn't damage the relationship if she shared them.

The anger that arises out of hope fuels adaptive conflict. Sounds like something to be sewn onto a silk pillow, doesn't it? Well, it should be as a reminder that squabbles are a necessary part of a couple's growth together. In fact, as we'll see later in this chapter and throughout this book, conflict that is carefully managed or regulated is a building block of a healthy relationship. Just as kids go through growing pains on their way to maturity, so do loving couples, and those growing pains lead to a vibrant and thriving relationship.

Trust in Others

Trusting others is not easy, and the reason is simple: trust means you're giving another person something—your money, your secrets, your future, your heart—with a degree of confidence that that thing will be handled carefully. Secure people tend to trust others.

Now, that trust isn't a naive, immature, fantasy-based trust. It's a general belief that others, those they've carefully selected after seeing them in action during the dating process or in other ways, are capable of and willing to meet their emotional needs. Secure people don't expect perfection. In fact, they're generally more tolerant of others' mistakes because they don't see mistakes as signs of dishonesty or rejection.

So Ronnie was very angry with Matt, but she didn't question his love for her. She didn't see his thoughtlessness as rejection or abandonment. Matt's behavior was not a wound to her soul; he'd just been inconsiderate. His thoughtlessness wasn't the tip of a much larger iceberg, the iceberg of untrustworthiness that jeopardizes relationships.

Instead, Ronnie expressed her anger with confident hope that Matt would respond, that he would listen to and care about her feelings, and that he would take her expression of emotion as an opportunity to empathize with her and to make some behavioral adjustments. Her expression of her anger might also give him the opportunity to understand just how difficult her day had been, which could bring them closer together.

Here's another saying for a silk pillow: *The healthy expression of anger can actually be a healing experience*[2]—especially when the other person doesn't feel overly threatened by the anger and become defensive. In fact, anger is often the catalyst that leads to forgiveness and restoration, two key aspects of healing.

PATHWAYS TO THE SECURE STYLE

Sensitive parenting lays the stepping-stones to a secure relationship style. Let's look closely at this parenting style so you can better shape your children into secure people.

Sensitive parenting is characterized by four main goals:

- *Regulating emotions*—Helping children learn to self-soothe and calm down when they're upset is foundational to healthy relationships. It also allows children to develop an ability to focus attention outside themselves and onto other people and things.

- *Knowing a warm relationship*—Parents help children experience relationships as safe, warm, and interesting. Warmth instills the notion that relationships are where one turns when upset and in need of comfort.

- *Self-awareness*—Parents help children learn how to express in words their thoughts, feelings, intentions, and physical sensations. This self-awareness helps them regulate their emotions, and it becomes the basis of empathy.

- *Developmental focus*—Children need to learn to meet the various developmental challenges of their lives: how to live within limits, how to become self-motivated, how to deal with separation from parents, how to get along with peers, how to respect authority, how to develop spirituality, how to live morally, and so on. Basically, parents teach their children how to become good people.

Pretty easy to say all that, isn't it? But of course it's not all that easy to do. Sensitive parents have a lot on their plates. And around the edge of that plate is written in bold letters: *I am trying to provide my children with a solid emotional foundation so they can experience healthy relationships for the rest of their lives.*

To make things even more complicated, each developmental stage requires a new kind of sensitivity—new skills, new levels of patience, new responses to stress. Three-month-olds and high-schoolers have very different needs! Later in this book we'll discuss those differences, but for now we'll highlight strategies and techniques parents can use in all stages of their children's development to help them become secure about relationships.

Helping Children Grow

God has set down some universal principles for how elements of His creation grow and mature, and one principle says that any growing thing matures best when it is provided with the right mixture of two critical ingredients: support and challenge.[3] We affectionately refer to the ideal mixture as "the zone."

Good coaches know the zone, and they are able to apply the right combination of support and challenge to each member of their team. When I (Gary) wrestled in college, my coach managed to always challenge me just beyond my ability. The coach never bulldozed over me by criticizing everything I did wrong. That approach would have been too much challenge, not enough support, and a discouragement to growth. Rather, the wrestling coach supported my efforts by highlighting what I did right and encouraging me to continue doing it. This combination of support and challenge caused me to improve exponentially, way beyond what I originally thought I could achieve.

Sensitive parents are good coaches. They find ways to boost their children into the zone so they can grow and develop new life skills. That's why, when we evaluate a parent-child relationship, we often have them work together on a puzzle. That way we can observe both how the child uses the parent as a source of help and how the parent balances the delivery of support and challenge. Sensitive parents help children discover the solution. They don't just solve the problem for them (too much support, not enough challenge). Nor do they just sit back and say, "You've got a brain; you figure it out," so that the child gets overly frustrated (too much challenge, not enough support).

Teaching Children to Handle Emotions

Parents also must teach their children how to handle negative emotions, among them: sadness, anger, frustration, anxiety, and jealousy. Dealing with these strong feelings doesn't come naturally to children. Just like reading, writing, arithmetic, and baseball, coping with strong emotions is a learned skill, one that requires parents and other adults to be good coaches. But how do you do that? First we'll look at three ways to *not* do that!

- *Dismissing negative feelings*—Viewing their children's feelings as unimportant or, at best, a necessary nuisance, some parents ignore those feelings or try to brush them away. Parents don't want to draw attention to and thereby reinforce the negative feelings. Everyone is expected to always be happy; sadness is not tolerated. This approach doesn't offer the right mix of challenge or support.

• *Disapproving of negative feelings*—Other parents try to stamp out the expression of negative emotions in their children by putting them down, using sarcasm, or even punishing them. These parents may think they're challenging their children to deal with their emotions, but their "help" is too negative and derogatory to be a challenge. And they typically offer far too little assistance in problem solving to be supportive.

• *Taking a laissez-faire approach*—Parents adopting this style can accept their children's negative feelings and empathize, but they have difficulty helping their children figure out what to do to solve the stress-creating problem. These parents offer lots of support but not enough challenge.

Now for a model we believe best helps children learn necessary skills to deal with negative emotion. Called "emotion coaching," it is based on the conviction that your children's negative feelings are an opportunity for you, the parent, to build a bridge of intimacy and to strengthen your connection with your kids. Emotion coaching involves the following:

1. Being aware of your children's negative feelings, even when they're at a low level of intensity.

2. Understanding and validating your children's feelings and then empathizing, letting them know that you see why they feel the way they do.

3. Guiding your children toward healthy self-awareness by helping them find words to label their feelings.

4. Working with your children to find solutions to their problems by, for instance, asking, "What can be done to make the situation better?" or "What might be a better way to look at this situation so it doesn't make you feel so bad?"

5. Setting limits on behavior. This is critical. Children must be taught that feeling intensely does not grant them a license to act out. Rather, it's an

opportunity to examine their feelings and the situation prompting them, and then to govern their feelings and command that situation, just as Scripture indicates: "Be angry and do not sin" (Ephesians 4:26 NKJV). God understands our pain and suffering, but He still requires us to live in obedience to His commands.[4]

Every day parents face opportunities for emotion coaching. We just need to seize them.

Let's say your five-year-old wants to go across the street to play with the neighbor but, for whatever reason, your answer is no. Suddenly her eyes fill with tears, her little hands clench into fists, and her small voice becomes huge with indignation: "Nobody lets me do anything I want to! It's not fair. Everybody else gets to go over to a friend's house, and I don't get to."

At this point of her emotional outburst, it would be a lot easier to send her to a corner to calm down, and that's certainly an alternative. But you could instead choose this moment for some productive emotion coaching. Pick up your daughter and set her on the kitchen counter so you two can talk eye to eye.

"Sweetie, you're really angry at Mommy and Daddy right now, aren't you?"

"You guys won't let me have any fun. There's nothing to do here." (Study her for a moment. Try to figure out whether there are any other emotions you should be aware of besides the anger. What led up to the eruption? Is she really bored? Or has an interaction with some other child gone badly?)

"I know, sweetie," you say. "There's nothing to do, and you feel bored." (You're showing empathy and support.)

"There's nothing to do, Daddy," she sobs as big tears stream down her face.

"I know. And when I get bored, I sometimes feel a little lonely." (As you label the feelings, you're offering support and a little challenge.) She nods and sinks her head into your neck, and you give her a big hug. You're connecting; she feels understood. Now you're ready for some problem solving.

"So," you begin, "let's think about what you can do about feeling bored. Your idea to visit a friend was a good one, but it just can't happen right now. So what else is there to do?" (You're presenting a challenge.)

"Nothing! There's nothing else to do!"

"I know you feel that way, honey, but let's think about some other things." (You're continuing your support while adding more challenge.)

"Like what?" she says, daring *you* to come up with something.

"Well, your brother and his friend Joel are down in the backyard playing on the jungle gym," you might say. Or, "Your sister and her friend are up in her room playing Barbies."

"Dad," she says with a bit of irritation in her voice, "the girls never let me play Barbies with them, and I don't want to play on the jungle gym."

"But you do like sneaking up on your brother, don't you?" you say with a touch of excitement in your voice.

Her eyes brighten. She's getting your drift. "Dad, what if *we* snuck up on them?"

"Oh, I think that would be fun!" you say. "Why didn't you think of that before?"

"'Cause you was busy."

"Yes, and it's very respectful of you to not bug Daddy when he's busy. But, you know, Daddy likes to make a little time for fun. You just have to ask. Sometimes I can, and sometimes I can't. But it doesn't hurt to ask."

"Okay, Dad. Now let's go!"

Now isn't that approach a lot better than sending the kid to the corner? Emotion coaching can help you and your child get through a tense situation and connect with each other at a little deeper level. It also offers the perfect combination of support and challenge: You encourage, listen, validate, and empathize even as you help your child discover ways to cope with negative feelings without acting out.

Furthermore, this parenting approach creates fertile soil for a secure self to root, grow, and mature. It helps children develop a healthy sense of connection with you and a greater trust in others. Our five-year-old friend, for instance, learned that her feelings were worth taking seriously, and that lesson strengthens her sense of self-worth. She also learned that those who love her are not threatened by her negative feelings and that she can approach them no matter how she feels—emotionally distraught, a little sad or angry, or simply bored.

Emotion coaching also has some important spiritual ramifications. When we approach our children's negative emotions as opportunities to build intimacy with them, we can see more clearly that our own emotions are steppingstones to greater intimacy with God. Do you believe that? When you get upset, do you feel God will meet you where you are—in the anger, the sadness, or the fear? Or do you think He requires you to calm down before going to Him? Scripture teaches that one reason God allows pain in our lives is so that we will seek Him and experience His goodness as He is with us in our pain. Our emotion, our pain, and our sufferings can definitely be stepping-stones to intimacy with God.

Emotion coaching teaches our children this same lesson—that God is not turned off or repulsed by our thoughts, our negative feelings, or the anguished cries of our soul. Rather, God wants us to come to Him, and, as a loving earthly father would be, He is there for us. When we respond to our children's negative emotions with love and support, we not only teach them how to better handle their feelings, but we also teach them that God is a God of comfort as they see their heavenly Father in us.

THE LEGACY OF THE SECURE SELF

When we talk about emotion coaching at conferences, we're often asked, "Doesn't this approach teach our children they can get away with having a bad attitude?" and "If you focus so much on emotion, how do kids learn discipline, how to behave and follow rules?" These are both good questions, but studies have shown that, by the time they're into middle childhood, kids who as preschoolers received emotion coaching from their parents are:

- Doing better academically: they make better grades and enjoy learning more.
- Physically healthier: they get fewer colds and make fewer trips to the doctor.
- Better equipped socially: they make and keep friends more easily.
- More emotionally stable: they display fewer negative emotions and more positive ones.
- Better behaved: they have fewer problems with authorities and fewer fights with other children.[5]

CHARACTERISTICS OF THE SECURE SELF

Sensitive parenting promotes secure relationships at home, and these secure relationships lead to emotionally healthier children. Consider the following characteristics of children whose sensitive parents raise them to become a secure self.

Emotional Strength

People with emotional strength aren't stone-faced stoics who display little or no emotion. They actually feel emotions pretty deeply. What distinguishes them is that they're not afraid of emotions—neither their own nor other people's. They don't consider negative feelings like anger, sadness, or even fear as signs of weakness or imbalance. Emotions, for them, are indicators that they're in touch with themselves and the world around them.

Because they accept their feelings, secure people—more often than not—face life head-on. They accept challenges and take necessary risks. They stand up for what they believe in with passion and fervor, and they invest in others because they're not haunted by the fear of loss.

A Willingness to Seek and Accept Comfort, Especially in Times of Trouble

God has programmed us to seek connection with and comfort from others.[6] And, when they're distressed, secure persons automatically seek people they're in relationship with just as God programmed us to seek Him. Do you seek comfort from others when you're distressed—or do you turn inward and look only to yourself for comfort? Or do you look to others for comfort, but with a level of intensity that overwhelms them? Security is both seeking and finding comfort in the ones you love.

Turning to God in prayer is a powerful sign of security-seeking behavior. In fact, prayer is turning to God for comfort even in the little situations of life.[7] Don't wait for calamity to strike. Turning to God with even minor requests—that the kids have a good day, that your spouse makes it home safely, that you get today's jobs done—is a healthy security-seeking behavior.

Courage for Love and Intimacy

Best described in 1 Corinthians 13, known as the Bible's "love chapter," love means a total commitment to another person—and it requires work! Similarly, genuine intimacy requires tremendous trust and courage. Our culture, of course, paints a different picture in the media: there love is easy, intimacy reaches fulfillment on the second date, and both are effortless. But any time you see love without work, you don't have love; you merely have infatuation.[8] And infatuation is primarily a drug-induced state of elation produced by body chemicals called endorphins. When these drugs wear off—and they always do—and if the relationship lasts, the two people involved are left with the real work of love and intimacy.

Secure people are willing not only to take the risk to love someone but also to do the work required. So it's not surprising that their past relationships have been largely successful. And, as a natural outgrowth of this track record, they freely seek wise counsel and comfort from those they love. In contrast, people with insecure relationship styles may also seek connection and comfort, but when they do, they rarely experience a sense of peace from those relationships.

In contrast, the assurance that trustworthy, supportive people are nearby and accessible provides secure folks with an internal optimism and a general sense of peace. No matter what's coming, they're not going to face it alone, so they know they can face anything. That kind of attitude prompts secure people to face their lives boldly and with confidence.

Secure people realize that there's safety in other people (Ecclesiastes 4:9), and they manifest a sense of trust and look to others for help when needed. Pessimistic people, on the other hand, expect their projects to crumble before their eyes. They're almost afraid to be happy when life goes well, because if they are, something bad is sure to happen. We call this "happy-phobia." If you are happy-phobic, you've probably never felt comfortable trusting or relying on anyone to come through for you in difficult times.

Secure people also know the truth of Ecclesiastes 7:14: "When times are good, be happy; but when times are bad, consider: God has made the one as well as the other." When parents and significant others live out this belief with us, what an incredible picture of God we get!

Optimistic people acknowledge that life is a thorny proposition and that the bumps in the road can be quite jarring. But optimism allows them to believe that no bump is so bone rattling it can't be overcome and no thorn is so sharp that it can't be dulled and dealt with. Eventually life will work out. Secure, optimistic people rest in the realities of God's perfect love for them as well as in His sovereign power over the world and their lives. These people know pain, hurt, and disappointment, and they know that pain, hurt, and disappointment will come again. But their optimistic faith allows them to bounce back from adversity. They know that God has a plan for their lives, and they trust Him that the suffering they're enduring today is merely preparation for triumph tomorrow. They believe that God will ultimately redeem every apparent misstep for their benefit and His glory.

Responsible for Themselves

Secure people feel totally responsible for who they are, for their decisions, and for their lives. Of course they can't keep bad situations from occurring—illness, the loss of loved ones, and so forth—but they *can* determine how they react to these events, and they take full responsibility for those reactions.

They generally don't feel like victims even when they are. When beset by a problem not of their making, they usually assess the situation honestly and relatively dispassionately, and then set about to change their circumstances. They engage in active problem solving, and when at first they don't succeed, they keep trying to solve the problem longer than insecure people do. If they discover they can't improve things, they decide to cope. Generally, secure people concern themselves with how they interpret their suffering: they find meaning in their pain.

Viktor Frankl was a Jewish psychiatrist held in a German concentration camp during World War II. He found that those who were able to survive, both physically and psychologically—those who did not give up hope, those who persisted and even thrived in their captivity—were those who were able to find meaning in their suffering.[9]

The New Testament Christians were like this. They were severely persecuted because they were followers of Christ. But when they were beaten and battered for their beliefs, they rejoiced for the opportunity to serve God even in their suffering and thereby further His purposes. They believed with all their hearts and they staked their lives on the fact that God is in control and heaven is sure.[10]

In contrast, people who are not secure in who they are or in their relationships with others generally feel that life just happens to them, that they have little control over it, and even that they have little control over the way they feel and how they behave when life happens. When trouble comes, these folks expend little, if any, energy in problem-solving efforts. If they do try to solve their problem and at first they don't succeed, it's time for a latte. Besides giving up more easily, these people believe that their feelings and reactions to life are outside their control, and therefore they allow themselves to take little responsibility for managing their lives. When they get themselves into trouble, they blame others, including God: "If God didn't want me to be with that person, why did He have me fall in love?"

Courage

Many people define courage as the lack of fear, but we consider lack of fear the hallmark of someone who lacks good sense. After all, fear informs us of what is dangerous or significant to us. Courage, therefore, is better defined as acting in the face of fear when we determine that action is needed. For example, a woman who has been burned in a number of relationships acts courageously when she chooses to try again. A father whose parents were very physically abusive tries to appropriately apply discipline to his children even though he fears he will misuse his power. Again, courage is daring to do right in the face of emotions that would have you do less than right or downright wrong.

THE SECURE RELATIONSHIP STYLE:
AN EMOTIONAL IMMUNE SYSTEM

People who have healthy immune systems still get sick. They get colds, the flu, sinus infections, and just about everything else, but they get sick less often, their illnesses aren't as severe as those with poor immune systems, and they get better faster.

In the same way, people with secure relationship styles get sad, angry, anxious, and just about any other emotion you can name, but they are more resilient. Not as much upsets them. In fact, it takes an awful lot to knock them off their feet. When secure people do get upset—and, yes, it happens—they're not as severely upset as insecure people, and the upset clears more rapidly. They get back to being their old selves more quickly. Furthermore, as we have already mentioned, secure people generally grow from their pain and become stronger for having endured the difficulty.[11]

Here's some great news: you can develop a secure relationship style no matter which style is currently governing your connections with people. Although powerful and influential, neither your present nor your past need to command your tomorrows. You can develop a secure base for building and rebuilding your relationships.[12] And you'll find more hope and help in the pages ahead—after we look more closely at the three insecure relationship styles.

One-Minute Review

Secure people . . .

- Aren't afraid of emotions—their own or anyone else's

- Are willing to seek and accept comfort from other people

- Know that relationships can be safe and that knowledge gives them courage for love and intimacy

- Take responsibility for themselves

- Find the courage to act when action is needed

5

THE HARDENED HEART

The Avoidant Relationship Style

The ability to trust others is at the heart of intimacy.
—CLINTON AND SIBCY

Beliefs That Fuel the Avoidant Style
- I am worthy of love based on my success and accomplishments.
- I am capable of getting love, but I depend on my own self and abilities.
- Others are either unwilling or incapable of loving me.
- Others are not trustworthy; they are unreliable when it comes to meeting my needs.

Arnold pushed out his chest, leaned back, threw his arms over the back of the sofa, and crossed his legs. He was a guy who took command: that sofa wasn't going anywhere. Then, in measured, deliberate tones, he explained to us how exhausted he was in his marriage and that his wife was entirely too demanding.

"She's everywhere I am. I can't get a break. She can't even make a decision without me. Do I care what color the new drapes are? As long as I can close them, that's all that matters. Honestly, I don't have time for stuff like that. I've got a congregation of twenty-five hundred people to lead—my sheep—and I've got to stay focused. It's what I'm called to do. God's work."

He emphasized *God* as if there were stone tablets involved somewhere.

"Time," he finally said. "It's all about time. I don't have enough of it. Everyone is so demanding, and my wife and kids just don't understand. Things are getting worse."

In fact, a few days earlier the time with his wife had become a bit hot. Tempers had ignited, and threats were made, forcing this pastor to our office. His request was simple: "You people are in ministry. You know how important the work is, how many lives we're responsible for. What do I do about her? I'm sure you've faced this at home. I need some pointers on how to communicate with her. Let her know just how important my work is. How can picking the material for those drapes compare at all to counseling a young woman about not getting an abortion? I deal with *real* issues. I'm sure if she only knew, she'd understand my schedule and the extra time I have to be away from her and the boys."

Arnold was a sea of practical contradictions. Known far and wide as a fine pastor and family man, we quickly saw how much he loved his family, but he was locked away in his world of ministry and was anything but in touch with his own family. In the pulpit he sermonized about families, even about dads spending more time with their kids. And he tried to practice what he preached. But when he was home, he was unable to connect. Good to his wife and kids? Yes. In touch with them? Nope. Emotionally, he was cut off from his family and had little idea of what his wife and children really needed from him. In fact, at times he even saw their pleas for his time and attention as part of Satan's plans to sabotage his ministry.

You'd think that a man as steeped in faith as Arnold was, a man who so often had counseled other fathers to do what he wasn't doing, would respond positively when confronted with his behavioral contradictions. You'd think he'd say, "Something *is* wrong!" But he didn't. You know why? He couldn't see it. In fact, discussing with Arnold the possibility that he was misconnecting in his relationships and using a number of substitutes for closeness with his family was like speaking to him in code—and the code was never broken. Neither was Arnold's hold on his own sense of being right. Yet until Arnold could face the real problem—his fear of intimacy—his life was going to remain very stuck.

THE FEAR OF INTIMACY

Research as well as our own experience tells us that those who connect lovingly with people are able to:

- Express sympathy,
- Understand other people's feelings,
- Remain compassionate, seeing the world through other people's eyes,
- Have an emotional connection with them,
- Disclose private thoughts and feelings, and
- Participate in nonsexual touch.

Persons with the avoidant relationship style often struggle with at least one of these three areas of intimacy:

Emotional Connection

A wife tells her husband about her difficult day with the children. Even though she's frustrated and shares her feelings in harsh tones, her husband is able to sift through the emotion, hear what's said, and sensitively respond to her immediate needs—without becoming overly defensive, retreating into his own world, or simply capitulating to the moment. Conversing and relating in this way, showing sensitivity and responsiveness to the feelings expressed by others, creates an emotional connection. Such a connection implies understanding and, even more, empathy, the ability to see the world through another's eyes. As a result, there is relational warmth and enjoyment that only comes from knowing others and being known by them.

But people with an avoidant relationship style find it difficult to listen sensitively to the thoughts and feelings of those they're closest to—their spouses and their children. Like Arnold, they're too busy, or they see this kind of listening as a distraction from their true, God-given purpose. Or they see such sensitivity as a weakness. Obviously, this is very sad for everyone involved. The avoidant person can be very desirous of a relationship, but loved ones may actually feel very unloved and abandoned.

Disclosure of Private Thoughts and Feelings

Connecting lovingly means opening ourselves up to our loved ones. We all have private parts of our lives that we want to keep to ourselves. That's normal. However, the ability to share parts of your past with the people you love creates understanding and helps you join the other person's world. Such disclosure is the cornerstone of intimacy. (We think of it as *in-to-me-see*.) We make ourselves vulnerable when we share our most intimate, personal thoughts and experiences. It's being able to tell a funny story about a difficult time in your past. It's the ability to understand how your past largely influences who you are. It's the enjoyment of knowing yourself and of being known.

In contrast, the person with an avoidant style does not enjoy being known or knowing others because it awakens repressed feelings of loss and of anger about not being known, or emotionally connected, as a child. Besides, when you grow up feeling abandoned and rejected, you learn to hide your thoughts and to distance yourself from your own feelings, even from your desire for emotional closeness. Disclosing intimate thoughts and feelings would open one up to criticism, misinterpretation, and being hurt all over again. It's easy to understand why such openness would be difficult and even scary to avoidant individuals.

Think about the millions of children who grow up in families with depressed parents or an alcoholic mom or dad. Often kids describe these homes as being very lonely. In this family context there was rarely any support and usually no one to turn to. Avoidant people may also come from homes where, as kids, they had to make it on their own. They had to "suck it up" because Mom and Dad had little room for their children's fears, hurts, and frustrations. These feelings were signs of weakness and therefore taboo. Failure was not tolerated, and success was always applauded. Finding the courage to address feelings of loss and anger that are rooted in such experiences can bring the freedom to face intimate relationships.

Nonsexual Touch

It's said that kids need physical touch, on average eleven touches per day—touches like high fives, wrestling, handholding, warm hugs, tender caresses, cuddling, and gentle kisses. It's parent-child touching, and it's also part of the warmth and tenderness of a romantic relationship in adults. Everyone needs touch.

But many avoidant people are turned off by tenderness and touch, and Arnold is one of them. He puts it this way: "I enjoy being close to my wife, but too much of that touchy-feely stuff drives me crazy."

We pushed for an example of what he meant by touchy-feely stuff. "What really gets me is when she tries to rub the back of my neck. To her it's romantic; to me—I really can't stand it! It doesn't work for me. I know I shouldn't feel this way, but my mind-set is that if it doesn't feel good, don't do it."

It's no surprise that Arnold, who felt his time is better spent on the Internet planning his next family vacation, approached his relationships functionally. He believed in doing what needs to be done. "All that intimacy stuff is window dressing. A relationship is about the two of you making it through life without killing one another."

Arnold was protecting himself. He appeared tough and even hard on the outside. Oh, he could be personable enough, and he could even be the life of the party. But all this life and energy were used to keep people at a distance. You've seen people like this. You may even see one when you look in the mirror. Breaking through the shell and actually penetrating to the point where true emotion and vulnerability live can be difficult; and the closer you might get to avoidant people's hearts, the more threatened they may feel and the more defensive they may become.

THE RELATIONSHIP RULES OF THE AVOIDANT ATTACHMENT

People with an avoidant style have two basic relationship rules:

The Rule About Others

Other people are not reliable, dependable, or trustworthy when it comes to my needs.
Individuals learned this rule when, in close relationships, they were often turned away and rebuffed whenever they made bids for comfort and safety. They

were given the message that to be needy was to be weak. So they learned that reaching out would often result in hurt, shame, and rejection. Imagine growing up in a home where a parent is struggling with a great deal of emotional distress, like depression. These parents just don't have any emotional energy to give. They can be irritable, dismissing, and rejecting because they are so absorbed with life's troubles. So these children slowly envelop their heart with a hard, impenetrable shell to protect themselves from their feelings of abandonment and rejection. The same can happen if you grew up in a home where feelings were considered a sign of weakness or of having a "bad attitude." Because your feelings are ignored, criticized, or even punished, you learn to hide them or turn them off.

The Rule About Self

I must rely on myself alone in order to meet my needs.

This assumption flows naturally from the belief that *I can't rely on others, so I must turn to myself.* The child learns to bury her feelings of weakness and vulnerability and replaces them with an inflated sense of self-confidence, an "I-don't-need-you, I'll-do-it-myself" mentality. She hides her sense of vulnerability and can be impatient with the neediness of others, including, later in life, her children.

With these relationship rules, it only makes sense that the avoidant person becomes hardened. If those nearest him can't be trusted, why should he let anyone in? Oh, he's not paranoid. Arnold, for instance, knows that his wife, Sheila, isn't out to hurt him, but he just can't bring himself to trust her *not* to hurt him inadvertently. She's not perfect. She might make the wrong decision or say the wrong thing at the wrong time. In fact, she has. And Arnold took this "failure" as just another confirmation of his relationship rule: *others* always *let you down, just when you need them the most.*

Because avoidant persons don't find anyone qualified to be let in, they have no one to confide in—no one to share the hurt with, no one who'll understand *why* they're hurt, and no one who knows them well enough to help them deal with it. So they rely on themselves to provide comfort.

What's amazing to us is how much inner strength some of these armored adults and children have. Many are very reliable, capable, and competent. They can make good leaders because of their avid self-reliance and their ability to not be weighed down with emotion. Beneath the tough veneer, however, they are empty. Because they give so much emphasis to success, their world can quickly come crashing in when they stumble. And though they often deny painful emotions, they are prone to depression and even anxiety.

More frequently, these empty people turn to an alternate substance—anything that replaces the other person, anything that creates the illusion of intimacy, warmth, or love. We believe, and research suggests, that the genesis of addictions lies within this pattern of relationships. The reason addictions are so hard to break is that they mean so much. They've been used to replace, literally, what can't be replaced—relationships. The man addicted to pornography (i.e., the woman who is always available to him through books, magazines, or the Internet) creates a false intimacy. Even positive addictions and rituals—like studies, sports, and religious activities—can create a false sense of closeness in which habits and things replace our need for relationship. These addictions medicate and temporarily numb the emptiness that only God can fill.

Arnold's Wife, Sheila, Speaks Up

Arnold, still sure that all he had to do to stop his wife's "nagging" was convince her that his time was too valuable to waste on trivial issues, invited Sheila to attend a counseling session with him.

The instant she stepped into our office, we could see that she was angry. An attractive woman with shoulder-length auburn hair, she seemed capable of an easy, winning smile—but she wasn't smiling. Her lips and brows were drawn into tight lines, and her eyes, narrowed. Yet there seemed to be more than anger at work. She walked with a telltale weariness, like someone who was deeply frustrated and rapidly losing hope.

"He's gone all the time," she said, speaking to us as if Arnold were waiting in the car instead of sitting at the other end of the sofa. "He's either at the church, away at this conference or that, or off at some *important* meeting." *Important* came out sarcastically. "I'd probably see him more often if I put a podium in the living room. But then he'd complain that it blocked the TV. And when he *is* home, he's worn out. He comes in, flops into the recliner, grabs the remote, and hides in the news channel—or reads the paper. I *guess* he reads it. I can't tell what he's doing behind there. He could be sleeping, for all I know. Unless the phone rings. Then he perks up—like a dog on the scent again. And he'll talk for a half hour to people he doesn't even know—complete strangers, for crying out loud. I can't get a word out of him, and with them he won't shut up."

"They're my job," Arnold protested, leaning forward. "I'm a pastor. My job is to win people to Christ. Even complete strangers."

"Well, that's only part of your job," she groaned back. "There are two vast wastelands in our house." She turned back to us. "When he does talk to me, it's not about anything important. It's never about love or the kids or about feelings—his or mine. I don't think he *has* feelings." Managing to add even more sarcasm, she said, "He's successfully weaned himself from having to carry the dead weight of all those emotions around. I just want someone to love me—that's all. I know he works hard. He is a good man . . . a good pastor. But as for me . . . I'm just alone, me and the boys. And he doesn't even know it."

Arnold offers an example of classic avoidant behavior. When he is around people he doesn't have to be intimate with, he's social and outgoing, but he keeps his loved ones at a distance. He dodges intimacy. After all, intimacy is foreign and uncharted territory for him. Most of us fear what we don't know, and Arnold is *afraid* of intimacy.

THE ADULT ATTACHMENT INTERVIEW

Research has shown that what is significant is not so much *what* people say about their childhoods but *how* they talk about it.[1] Avoidant people, for example, tend to idealize their parents. They'll use words like *wonderful*, *great*, *warm*, *loving*, and *kind*, but they are unable to recall specific times when their parents actually behaved this way. These people want to believe everything about their childhood was great, but they have no specific experiences to back up their assertion that Mom and Dad were wonderful.

Arnold's Attachment Interview

From the start, Arnold saw no need to discuss his childhood, but he finally shrugged his shoulders and said, "Okay, I guess there won't be any harm done. But don't take too much time. I have things to do."

We began by asking him for a general impression of his childhood. As we expected, he painted a rosy picture. He told us his dad worked a lot at the family business—a little grocery store on the edge of town—while his mom stayed at home with the five kids, Arnold being the oldest. "Everything was neat, clean, and orderly," he said. "Mother kept us fed, Father kept a roof over our heads, and everything was good. We were all close and very happy."

Attachment to mother. We asked Arnold to describe his relationship with his mom using a number of adjectives, and he chose grand concepts like *loving*, *kind*, *warm*, and *caring*. We asked him to give us specific, concrete examples of each behavior. What specifically did she do that was loving? Did she give him his favorite snack in his lunch bag? Or did she dry his PJs in the evening so they were warm when he put them on? Did she do things like that?

As Arnold thought for a second, he looked to his right, an indication that he was retrieving memories from the brain's left side—the more logical, factual side. He finally gave up. "I can't really recall any specifics, but Mother was just that way." He couldn't support his general description with specific memories.

We also asked Arnold about times when he had been upset during his childhood. He remembered that, whenever he was sick enough to stay in bed, his mom would exile him to the back bedroom and only appear when she brought him meals.

"Did she do anything else?" we asked.

"No," he said, vindicating her by his upright posture. "She was a very busy woman. She didn't have time to sit and cuddle. She just made sure I had what I needed." And, we noted, she didn't seize this opportunity to foster intimacy with her firstborn.

Arnold also remembered fracturing a bone in his foot. Afraid she'd get mad at him for goofing off and getting hurt as a result, he had managed to hide the injury from his mom for nearly a week. He wasn't sure what she had said or done to him once she discovered the injury, but he did remember it required a cast. Once again Arnold's story showed his mother being busy and critical, offering no safe haven for Arnold in times of trouble. She certainly didn't seem the caring and loving mother Arnold had described.

Attachment to father. Arnold described his dad using only two adjectives: *hardworking* and *loving*. He had plenty of good examples to show his dad as being industrious, but he had nothing specific to illustrate how he had been loving.

"Do you ever remember being hugged by your dad?" we asked.

Arnold shifted his eyes away, almost as if ashamed, and shook his head. "No," he whispered.

This interview was hard for Arnold but very important. Part of him desperately wanted to believe that his parents had been ideally warm and loving, but his memories revealed a different story. But there was a promising sign: the moisture in his eyes when he acknowledged that his parents had never even hugged him.

Like all of us, Arnold longs for intimacy, but he doesn't know he does. Those tears might help him see the truth of what he has hidden inside. With work, he might begin to understand how much his wife and children yearn to connect with him—and how much he yearns to connect with *them*. It's a yearning Arnold had long ago sealed off. But it was there; he just needed to rediscover it.

Jerry's Connection with Longing

Another client, Jerry, came to us in his late thirties in an attempt to deal with marital problems—and, we discovered a little later, a pornography addiction. Although we suspected his issues stemmed from a longing for intimacy, the proof of it came unexpectedly. He was telling us about a recent phone conversation he'd had with his sister, who was complaining that he didn't visit the family often enough. Ten years earlier he had moved several states away for a new job. Since then he'd been home to visit only a handful of times. One of those visits had been for his mom's funeral. "She died a few months after I moved," he said. "I rushed home for it but had to come back for work right away."

"How'd you feel about your mom's death?"

"We weren't all that close. I don't remember being very sad," he admitted. He went on to tell us that his mom and dad had remained married out of convenience and that, as a result, both parents always seemed depressed. "I was alone most of the time. I'd come home from school, and the place would be empty. Mom and Dad both worked second shift, and my older brother and sister were always out with their friends. I put myself to bed most nights." Then one of Jerry's buddies introduced him to pornography. "Talk about being hooked," he admitted. "I couldn't get enough of the stuff."

He'd finally found the drug to feed his intense emotional hunger. But as Jerry recounted the phone call with his sister, we heard a hint of anger. "She got after me about not coming home. She said that I really didn't care about her or the rest of the family, that I never really loved Mom or Dad. She said I'd left and become absorbed in my own world and shut everyone else out."

"What did you say to that?"

He paused. Then large tears began to sear his cheeks. After a moment he took a deep breath. "I asked some questions of my own: 'Where were you guys when I needed you as a kid? Where was the whole sick family when I came home from school? I cooked my own meals, kept myself company, put myself to bed. Where were you and Mark? [Mark was his brother.] Where was Mom? And Dad?' Everyone was gone. I was alone. Now I take care of myself because I've always taken care of myself. I envied other kids in the neighborhood when they whined that they had to go home to eat dinner and do homework. At least someone was waiting for them at home, someone who cared. No one waited for me. So if I don't come home and visit the family now, it's because no one cared if I came home then."

A rage boiled inside Jerry, one equal to the desire within him that had gone unmet in him as a child—a yearning to be held, cared for, and warmly kissed good night. He had armored his breaking heart. Only these many years later, when confronted by his sister, did his heart soften up enough to let out a small bit of the rage and resentment. This was an important event in Jerry's life journey. It allowed him to identify what he really desired. It was the first step on Jerry's road to healing.

Three Forms of Insensitive Parenting:
The Pathway to Avoidant Behavior

Research has identified insensitive parenting as the one behavior that most consistently leads to insecurity and an avoidant relationship style. And in a moment we'll look at three forms of insensitive parenting: dismissive parenting, rejection, and intrusive parenting.

What Does It Mean to Be Sensitive?

To better understand *insensitive* parenting, let's first consider what it means to be *sensitive* to a child. First, for instance, sensitive parents, especially parents of infants, adjust their behavior to help the little ones remain calm, and when the babies do get upset, sensitive parents help them become calm as quickly as possible. They understand that infants communicate by crying. If they're hungry, they cry; if cold, they cry; if lonely, they cry; if wet—you guessed it—they cry. Sensitive caregivers respond to these cries by satisfying the need—and they don't do it angrily or resentfully. If the baby is hungry, the parents feed her; if wet, they change her. These parents know the little one's not trying to manipulate them or drive them nuts with the crying. He or she is just a helpless human being who, in order to survive, needs to be taken care of responsively.

When infants are cared for responsively and tenderly, they develop relationship rules like *My emotional needs are important, and I can count on others to help me in times of trouble.* These relationship rules are recorded in the deepest parts of our brain and become emotionally charged, gut-felt beliefs.[2] Paradoxically, instead of leading to self-centeredness, as one might expect, this foundation seems to equip a maturing child with empathy, the ability to more fully see and respond to the needs of others, and confidence in his own ability to act. This is the opposite of what many insensitive parents believe will happen. They generally believe responding sensitively to their children's crying leads to spoiled children who can do nothing for themselves.

Having seen the value of sensitive parenting verified in our practice, we find ourselves quite concerned about those parenting programs that emphasize structure over sensitivity. These programs falsely teach that sensitivity is a form of spoiling a child. They underscore the need for a plan—a sort of cookie-cutter mentality that places infants on rigid feeding and sleeping schedules that ignore the child's basic temperament and physical hardwiring.

We are pro structure, but we are more sensitivity based, especially in the first two years of childhood. The fact is that sensitive parenting creates a solid foundation; it also literally shapes the brain structure[3] that leads to better-behaved kids who can care more deeply about others.

Insensitive parents, however, tend to dismiss their children's crying.[4] They work their own schedules, believing that to respond sensitively to their children's distress would be coddling or spoiling. Also, when holding their babies, insensitive parents are less affectionate and tend to be brusque. They find it hard to respond appropriately to their children's relationship needs.

Dismissive Parenting

Dismissive parenting is a form of insensitivity that primarily involves dismissing the child's emotions, especially any negative ones. For example, when a nine-year-old girl comes home from school in a grumpy mood, she's gruff with her younger brother and complains to their mom about having to empty the dishwasher, her usual job. A sensitive mom might ask, "What's wrong? You seem awfully grouchy today." She invites the child to figure out why she's so irritable.

A dismissive parent, however, ignores the emotion or labels it a bad attitude. She might say to the grumpy child, "I don't know what your problem is, but you'd better change that attitude right now." The dismissive parent acts as if the child's feelings are unimportant.

Rejection

A much stronger type of insensitivity, rejection involves almost complete disengagement from the child. Rejecting parents aren't merely cold; they are emotionally disengaged from their children, sometimes mocking or even ridiculing them. When their babies cry, these parents can become noticeably angry and troubled, and they tend to criticize the infants. Such parents avoid emotional closeness, and they dislike close physical contact as well. Their hugs for their children are rarely tender, warm, or gentle.

Intrusive Parenting

In contrast to rejecting parenting, intrusive parenting provides too much of a good thing. Infants and children do need to be held, hugged, and talked to in comforting tones, but intrusive parents overdo it. They fail to read the child's subtle, nonverbal cues that say, *Okay, Mom, I feel better now. I want to go play.* The intrusive parent may dismiss or "guilt-trip" a child's requests to be left alone and say, for example, "You really don't want to push Mommy away, do you, dear?"

Again, these parents fail to read the child's cues probably because they don't care to read them; they just run over the child with their own wants.

THE THREE SHADES OF AVOIDANCE

Avoidant people like Arnold have usually experienced one or more of these insensitive parenting environments. But avoidant people can also have other characteristics in common. Usually those with an avoidant relationship style come in one of three shades: narcissistic, exiled, or compulsive perfectionist. Let's take a brief look at these.

The Narcissist or Inflated False Self

Narcissism is a state of excessive, inflated self-love. This sense of self-love is considered a *false self*[5] because below the layer of superiority festers a deeply rooted sense of worthlessness. Nonetheless, several characteristics about a narcissistic character style can make life difficult for others. Typically this person:

- Seeks excessive praise from others

- Tends to be arrogant and condescending

- Displays an inflated sense of self-worth

- Fantasizes about fame, fortune, and power

- Is very sensitive to criticism and can respond with intense anger

- Takes an "I'm-first-and-everyone-else-comes-later" attitude

- Manipulates others to achieve his or her own ends

- Envies other people's success

- Associates with "special" people and engages in lots of name-dropping

- Shows little empathy for others

- Is externally focused, living with a "you-are-what-you-have" attitude

For the more successful narcissists, especially those who engage in entertainment, politics, public speaking, and even Christian ministry, manipulation and exploitation are common themes. These individuals often gather around themselves a handpicked staff of extremely devoted followers who provide their charismatic boss with uninterrupted adulation.

To complicate things, narcissists become even more self-absorbed under stress. When they receive negative feedback, for instance, they become angry and contemptuous. Their defense systems shift into overdrive, and they inevitably alienate those around them as they strongly, even indignantly, defend their actions, no matter how indefensible they may seem. They may even counterattack, challenging their critic for his or her failings or for having the gall to confront them. As a result, their problems go unaddressed and may worsen. After the negative feedback, narcissists will probably simply avoid their critics and continue on in their same harmful behavior.

The Exiled, or Disconnected, Self

Unlike the narcissist whose ego feeds off the praise of others, the exiled, or disconnected, person[6] is robed in self-sufficiency. These persons do not feel the need for acceptance or approval from others. In fact, they have very little desire to connect at all. Like narcissists, they believe they must count on themselves to provide emotional and psychological support, and here are some of the results:

Extreme introversion. Typically, the exiled self has cut himself off from people. He looks inward to a world of fantasy to find pleasure and comfort. To those around him, the exiled self may look cold, distant, and aloof.

Self-sufficiency. When caregivers failed to be reliably available and trustworthy, the exiled self learned to fend for herself. Having to depend on others for emotional support provokes anxiety, which leads to profound feelings of vulnerability.

A sense of superiority. The exiled self believes that only he can provide adequate comfort and safety for himself. He also prefers inwardness and fantasy over genuine emotional connection. He has very little drive for external pleasures and derives little, if any, enjoyment from interacting with people.

Emotional desert. To wall off the self from people, this person barricades herself from her emotions and experiences few intense feelings about anything. Life appears bland and colorless. But she likes it that way: calm, cool, and without much intensity. Unlike the narcissist, the exiled self remains tranquil when criticized because she doesn't seek acceptance. Like the narcissist, however, the exiled self has little empathy for others. She cannot identify and label her own emotional experiences, let alone understand why and how other people feel the way they do.

Loneliness. Just below the exiled self's sense of superiority lies an inner longing for connectedness. But his fear of being controlled and overwhelmed by others blunts it, so much so that he may never admit to himself or to others that the longing exists.[7]

The Compulsive Perfectionist

"I can't talk to her about anything," Frank told us, referring to Kathy, his wife. "She complains endlessly. Nothing is ever right, and nobody can please her. The kids won't take their problems to her. She starts preaching at them the moment they do, about how they should do this and shouldn't do that. She drives them nuts because she's such a control freak. And I'm caught in the middle."

Frank is talking about a perfectionist. As children, perfectionists achieved attention only for significant successes; they were ignored or sternly criticized for anything less. They were discouraged from showing intense feelings, and they were severely chastened for expressing anger or frustration. Their parents, emotionally cold and distant, were very uncomfortable with physical expressions of affection or intimacy. Perfectionists value logic and order. For them, feelings and relationships are sort of like ants at a picnic.

Here are some other characteristics of the compulsive perfectionist:

- Pays excessive attention to details, order, and organization

- Controls others, frequently using guilt

- Demands that self and others submit to rigid, moralistic rules with lots of do's and don'ts

- Has difficulty sharing; viewed by others as stingy of time, money, and resources

- Is uncomfortable with emotions; very constricted

- Is uncomfortable with physical touch

- Has difficulty displaying affection toward others

- Tends to procrastinate because of such high standards for performance

- Is reluctant to delegate tasks because others are viewed as incompetent[8]

Perfectionists are prone to depression, especially after losing control of some element of their lives. They are also vulnerable to anxiety problems and worry. And when they are worried about something, their compulsive perfectionism intensifies, and they become quite irritable and cantankerous.

DISTURBING TENDENCIES

Because of the way avoidant people see themselves and their relationships to others, they tend to develop addictive behavior and/or an angry resentment of God.

Addictive Behavior

As we noted earlier, addictive behavior stems from turning away from others, especially God, and looking to the self, and only to the self, for comfort. This state of inwardness sets the stage for addiction as the avoidant person looks for substitutes for intimacy. The focus of this self-feeding process can include such behaviors as an excessive fantasy life, pornography, Internet addictions, eating disorders, compulsive masturbation, substance abuse, shopping sprees, and compulsive thrill seeking (driving fast and other types of high-risk behaviors).

Angry Resentment Toward God

The avoidant person's belief that *Others are either unwilling or incapable of loving me* is all too easily transferred to God.[9] They turn away from God because they believe that *God is not really there for me; I've prayed and prayed, yet He never comes through. I don't need Him; I just need me.*[10]

Not surprisingly, many of the atheists we have met are notably avoidant in their relationship style. They rely on no one, including God. Similarly, many avoidant people stop seeking God, stop praying, and give up on the church community. Having regarded God's purpose as making sure nothing goes wrong in their lives, they now blame God for a life with problems: *See? God doesn't care about me. This just proves He is not involved in my life. I'm definitely not turning toward Him. He lets you down, just like everyone else in this world.*

This mind-set assumes that God's purpose is to make sure we don't run into trouble, and it downplays God's role in providing comfort during times of trouble. Both these thoughts perpetuate the avoidant person's isolation. And often his or her life is so pressed and stressed that it's easy just to keep on keeping on without ever coming to a place of honesty.

RELIEF FROM RELATIONAL POVERTY

As you read this chapter, did you recognize yourself or someone you love? If you cringed at the descriptions—if you recognized forces that are at work in your own or your loved one's life and that are tearing apart your relationships—don't despair. Help and hope are waiting for you in the second part of this book. We'll show you how you can break free from destructive tendencies, overcome the forces in the past that shaped your relationship style, and begin to restore and revitalize your relationships with those people you hold dearest.

One-Minute Review

Avoidant people . . .

- Turn away from God and other people and look to themselves for comfort

- Are often angry and resentful toward God

- Can be narcissistic, self-sufficient, or compulsively perfectionistic

6

DON'T ABANDON ME!

The Ambivalent Relationship Style

The biggest disease today is not leprosy or tuberculosis,
but rather the feeling of being unwanted, uncared for,
and deserted by everybody. The greatest evil is the lack of love.
—MOTHER TERESA

Beliefs That Fuel the Ambivalent Style
- I am not worthy of love.
- I am not capable of getting the love I need
without being angry, clingy, or desperate.
- Others are capable of meeting my needs but
might not do so because of my flaws.
- Others can be trustworthy and reliable,
but they might abandon me because of my worthlessness.

Remember when you first had feelings for that special boy or girl and you played the daisy game? *She loves me, she loves me not.* Sadly, some children grow up continually playing this "game" as they wonder how their parents feel: *Do they love me or not?*

There is a tentativeness in their minds. They're not always sure of where they stand. Why? Because from early in their lives they have struggled with the notion that their parents might leave them. One client recently said, "It's like

87

Mom can love and hate me in the same breath. It's her way of control, really."
As a result, these children become perpetual people pleasers and mold themselves to their parents' expectations and, later, to the expectations of others they love. They become dancers who are always onstage.

The problem is obvious: no one can always please everyone all the time. But these children try hard, walking on eggshells throughout their childhoods. They fear that the slightest misstep will destine them for anger, disappointment, and rejection. Only a fragile sense of self develops, but it is filled with strong yet ambivalent emotions. Sometimes these people feel intense love, sometimes intense hate. The comments of four clients illustrate this ambivalent relationship style.

Todd: "I guess you could say Dad loved the game. He loved to watch me play baseball. Get a hit, and he was right there beside me. But if I struck out or made an error, he would lose it. Then he ignored me, wouldn't even look at me. There were times after I'd messed up in some way when he would leave the game and not even come back to take me home. Before long, I quit playing baseball."

Rebecca: "Nothing was ever good enough for my mother. She scrutinized everything I did. Oh, she never called me names or put me down, but she would launch question after question: Why this? Why that? She was always controlling and basically questioning everything I did. All those whys stung with their implication that what I was doing was never quite right. So I just left. What scares me is that I'm now seeing a lot of my mother in me."

Joyce: "It's like Mom and I are best friends. She tells me everything about her life—her job, her friends (or lack of them), her fears, even her sorrow. Now it seems like I spend most of my time worrying about her, wondering if she is okay. It was the same way when I was a child. I felt like I had to take care of her or she would fall apart."

And now, in greater detail, Amy, a nineteen-year-old college student living three thousand miles from home. Her story shows how the ambivalent style can make a person vulnerable to soul wounds. Tears seared her cheeks when she came to our office, and she wiped them tentatively, almost fearfully, with a Kleenex wadded in her hand.

During the past few months, Amy had suffered at least a dozen sudden episodes of having the overwhelming feeling that she was going to die or that she was losing her mind. After several trips to the ER, where she underwent a number of extensive medical tests, her family doctor finally diagnosed her as having panic disorder. He wrote her a prescription for Paxil, an antidepressant commonly used to treat the disorder, and sent her in for counseling.

For Amy, these panic attacks seemed to have come from nowhere. Her life growing up in a Christian home had been relatively free of fear. Then *bang!* One day her heart began pounding, her insides seemed to knot up into a tight tangle, and she was gripped by what she could only describe as acute terror. Now, having been diagnosed with the disorder and told that the attacks wouldn't actually kill her, as she had feared, she wanted to know more.

"Okay, I'm having panic attacks," she said to us. "What causes them? And how do I get rid of them?" Neither Amy nor her doctor had considered the possibility that these attacks had *relational* roots. But after talking with Amy for a little while, we thought they might.

As it turned out, Amy's six-month relationship with her boyfriend had heated to a point where Amy found herself in a moral bind. Her boyfriend was pressuring her to go much further sexually than she felt comfortable with.

"I want to put the brakes on, but I'm afraid he'll get mad," she told us. "I constantly worry he's going to lose interest in me and find somebody else. I don't know what to do. I couldn't handle it if he left."

Amy's greatest fear was to be abandoned—by her parents, by her boyfriend, eventually by everyone close to her. And this *fear of abandonment* goes to the very core of how she sees herself and how she expects others to see and react to her. Amy believed she had no inherent value in herself. So she thought she had nothing to offer her boyfriend except sex and that if she didn't give in to his demands, he would abandon her. Now that she was living away from home, she was even more vulnerable to that fear of being alone. And this fear of abandonment is the core of the ambivalent relationship style, and it fuels a very sobering internal war.

THE FEAR OF ABANDONMENT

The person with an ambivalent style grows up in an emotionally confusing climate: At one moment the people we love, those we turn to for emotional and physical support, give us the distinct impression that we're in their lives on borrowed time and that at any minute we'll be left on our own. Often they tell us just that, and we might even see them abandoning others in their lives—friends and maybe even the spouse, our other parent. Then, moments later, they're in a good mood and all is well. We're smothered in hugs and good feelings, and we know we've never lived in a better, more caring environment. Momentarily we're reassured, believing, *No one who loves me this much could ever leave me.* Then, a little while later, the angry finger is shaking in our face again, and the fiery eyes are threatening to throw us out.

This kind of yin-and-yang atmosphere corrodes our sense of self and clouds our belief that we have the ability to be loved, to get the love we want and need. This unpredictability is crazy-making behavior. As such, two core beliefs develop: *I'm poor at getting the love and comfort I need* and *I have to please my loved ones, or I will be worthless and unlovable.* Amy's story shows us how these beliefs play out in negative behavior patterns in our adult relationships.

Blinded by Romance, Frozen by Fear

Amy met David a couple of days after arriving on campus. Less than a month later, she felt he might be "the one." As she spoke about David, it was clear she was smitten. Even when she told us less-than-flattering things about him, she couched them in terms that relieved him of all responsibility. Her prince's shining armor glistened, and she certainly wasn't open to questions that might tarnish him. Which is a problem in counseling.

Such obsessive romance is diametrically opposed to the kind of help we offer. Romantic images conjure up idealized images of the boyfriend or girlfriend and place that person on an unassailable pedestal. In sharp contrast, we who counsel search for truth and balance.[1] Therapy is about bringing people like Amy to a safe place where they see and accept the unvarnished fact that their hero is less than perfect. Talk about a chore!

This goal becomes doubly difficult to attain when the client is looking for a hero, someone to rescue him or her from a persistent, nagging sense of aloneness or emptiness. Persons who are preoccupied with idealized, romantic images take a don't-bother-me-with-the-facts attitude when it comes to their sweethearts. Sound familiar? If so, you probably know the pain this kind of relationship style can cause.

Amy, however, believed that her panic attacks were merely a product of bad biology—which *can* be true. We did find out that Amy's mom was also quite anxious and prone to occasional panic attacks. So biology might have aggravated Amy's situation, but we didn't think it was the total answer. We quickly taught Amy some skills (breathing exercises, how to relax, and ways to change her negative thinking) that would allow her to cope more readily with the attacks when they occurred. We felt this would, first, help Amy deal with the attacks and, second, help foster her trust in counseling. Then, ever so delicately, we began to explore Amy's relationships with her parents and with her previous beaux.

Her relationship with her mom had always been turbulent, so she had mixed feelings about leaving home. On the one hand she was ready to dance in the streets. How great to finally be out from under Mom's demanding, controlling ways. On the other hand, Amy was sad, even anxious about leaving, worried about her mom's relationship with her dad. He had cheated on her mother in the past, and Amy was convinced that she, the beloved daughter, was the glue that had kept them together—or at least had kept Mom sane. At times Amy even felt guilty for leaving her mom alone. And now she worried that, with the "glue" three thousand miles away, her parents might separate.

But the situation was even more complicated. Her mother struggled with anxiety and depression, and Amy had become her confidante, the person Mom looked to for support and comfort. This not uncommon parent-child role reversal stifled Amy's emotional and spiritual growth. In a lot of ways, she began to parent her mom—which meant that Amy herself never really had a parent she could turn to. It also meant she desperately wanted someone she *could* turn to, someone she *could* count on.

David, her boyfriend, looked a little like Brad Pitt, had a great sense of humor, treated her like a princess, and was always there when she needed him.

So it only made sense that he quickly became Amy's safe harbor. She came to rely on him for just about everything, especially emotional support, and he came through. For the first time ever, she felt she'd found someone she could trust. But then things began to change. As their relationship progressed, their time together became more passionate. "He wanted to do more than kiss and hold hands," Amy said, staring at her wringing hands. "We both know its wrong, but his values get shoved aside when he pushes me to get more physical."

"Or his hormones shove his values to the side," we suggested. Then we asked, "What keeps you from putting on the brakes?"

"I don't know," Amy said pensively.

"What do you think he'll do if you *do* say something?" we asked.

"I don't know," Amy repeated, a little irritated that she was being pressed.

"Take a guess."

"He might leave me."

"And that scares you?"

"Of course it does!" Amy fired back, surprised at her sudden anger. "Where will I be when he leaves? And what if I'm pregnant when he does?" Fear burned at us from behind her blue eyes.

Asking the Right Questions

Have you ever been afraid to let someone know who you are or how you feel because you're worried you might be rejected? That was exactly where Amy found herself. We asked, "What would happen if you talked to David, straight up, and told him what you're thinking, what you're afraid of?"

"I don't know," she said, avoiding the answer that would terrify her.

"Stick with this one, Amy. Just close your eyes and imagine telling David that you want to talk with him about something important. Now imagine telling him that you really care about him and that you hope your relationship lasts forever. Then imagine telling him that you really want to save yourself for marriage and that you want to stop getting into situations where you two are so close to giving that up. What would he say?"

"I don't know!" she said as she began to cry.

"What would happen, Amy? What pictures do you have in your head?"

"I see him getting up and walking away from me."

"And if that happened, then what? What would become of you?"

"I don't know!" Her crying turned to sobs; her breathing became labored. "I'm starting to feel panicky right now."

"Just focus on your breathing; slow it down. This is abandonment anxiety. It hurts, but it can't damage you. Let it be there. It's telling us a lot about what triggers your panic attacks. You feel that if you set a boundary with David about your sexual behavior, he will . . ." We left the sentence incomplete, hoping she would fill in the blank.

Which she did: "He'll walk away from me; he'll lose interest in me."

"He'll abandon you?" we said, expressing the root issue.

"Yes! Abandon me."

"And if he did," we asked, "what would happen?"

"I don't know!"

One of the biggest lessons in life is learning to face our fears. When we do, the truth about our life begins to surface.

Amy's panic attacks were triggered primarily by her fear of abandonment. Over the years, she'd developed a relationship style to ensure that loved ones would not leave. Her strategy was simple: Perform. Dance. And then just hope everything works out. The difficulty, of course, is that everything might not work out.

Think about it. When you always have to dance to be loved, you are constantly onstage. You're only as good as your last A, your last sale, your last hit. And when your loved ones' view of you changes—and it can in an instant—that change cuts to the core of your being, tears at your soul. Yet you plod on. Why? Because we were made for love. We need it from the cradle to the grave, so we struggle to dance better and more often. Ultimately this way of life keeps us focused on what others think, feel, say, and do. As a result, a dependency develops, a sense that we are nothing or of little value apart from someone else. Talk about power! Talk about control! In Amy's relationship with her mom, who had the power? And now, with her boyfriend, who had the power?

Dependency:
The Heart of the Ambivalent Relationship Style

Those with an ambivalent style are wonderful people to be around. They have a powerful way of making you feel good about yourself, and they can experience life with intense emotion, love, and laughter. But inside they are needy people who have some very strong core beliefs:[2]

- I am/feel incompetent.

- I struggle to handle things on my own.

- I need a strong protector to care and do things for me.

- This is a cold and dangerous world where people will hurt me and disaster will strike at any time, so I need to play it safe and stay close to those who are stronger and wiser.

People who hold these beliefs will unavoidably develop some pretty negative feelings. If they feel incompetent, when they're presented with even a normal challenge, they'll be visited by stifling anxieties and nearly debilitating self-doubts.

Imagine what it's like for people who feel they need a strong protector to care for them. They can't even think of going on a trip alone, dealing with hotel and plane reservations, or figuring out what to do when things go wrong. The mere thought of doing such activities alone is terrifying. These dependent people see the world crawling with danger: cars run out of gas, airline tickets get lost, and jobs evaporate. And because they view themselves as needy, they diligently search for someone to rescue them from all these possibilities.[3]

When you believe you can't survive without the protection of someone you perceive as stronger and more competent, you're willing to go to great lengths to keep that other person around. You have to please that person. So the template for living your life is *Make no waves*. If you're hurt, say nothing. If you're afraid, say nothing. If you need the salt, get up and get it yourself. In all things, serve with unwavering devotion. Whatever you do, don't let your beliefs, your moral values, or your sense of self get in the way of pleasing that other person. Tuck them away.

Persons with an ambivalent style are terrified that, if they assert their own beliefs, desires, limits, and opinions, they will anger the persons they need most, and those figures will run screaming from the relationship. Now, that's a tough way to live. And it's more common than you might think.

The fear of rejection can breed some pretty destructive behaviors and feelings in people who have an ambivalent relationship style:

- Very low self-confidence

- Fear of making decisions; looking to others to make major life decisions

- Rarely expressing disagreement with others

- Frequently seeking assurance, nurturance, and support

- Feeling obsessed with the fear of being left alone (for example, the fear that their spouse will die suddenly)

- Feeling helpless when alone

- Desperately seeking new relationships when others end

- Frequently subordinating themselves to others

- Perpetually seeking advice

- Often working below their ability level

- Accepting unpleasant tasks to please others

- Having a tendency to express distress through medically unexplainable physical symptoms rather than emotional pain (for example, they may develop headaches while doing unpleasant activities rather than saying, "No, I can't do this. It's too stressful.")[4]

DEPENDENCY DEVELOPMENT:
THE PATHWAYS TO AMBIVALENT ATTACHMENT

You might wonder how this type of dependency develops. Let's take a look at four common scenarios that can produce a dependent personality most likely to develop an ambivalent relationship style.

Now keep in mind that the primary goal of good parenting is to help children become autonomous adults who are able to function independently of their parents. But some parents do just the opposite. Their goal is to foster compliant, always-there-for-the-parents kids—dependent children who are discouraged from being independent.[5]

The Cold-Shoulder Treatment

The dependent personality can begin when the child behaves in a way the parent disapproves of and the parent refuses to talk to the child or turns an emotionally cold shoulder toward the child. These parents, often uncomfortable with strong emotion, especially adapt their frigid-shoulder demeanor when the children assert their sense of self, their own opinions, and the differences between their parents and themselves. Ice also forms on these parents' shoulders when their children express strong emotions, like anger or frustration.

Don't get us wrong here. We are not suggesting that parents allow their children to be rude or obnoxious when they disagree with their parents. Children *should* be allowed to disagree, and that disagreement should *not* be automatically interpreted as "bad attitude" and followed consistently with the cold shoulder to correct their nonconformity.

Overprotection

When parents keep children from participating in ordinary, age-appropriate activities for fear that the children would be in too much physical or emotional danger, the children never learn to deal with the normal bumps and bruises the world hands out. As a result, they remain dependent.

Safety and overprotection are two very different things.

Withholding Affection and Approval

Dependency develops as parents withhold their affection and approval when children get excited or experience joy independently of the parents.[6] This parental response dampens the children's sense of autonomy and makes it too dangerous for them to explore outside the parents' world.

Invisible Fences

Maybe you've heard of those invisible electronic "fences" buried around the perimeter of the yard that can teach Rover, who is wearing a special collar, to stay in the yard. Just as the dog comes to associate the high-pitched sound the collar triggers with a painful electric shock, so the child comes to associate painful disapproval with the experience of autonomy and independence, with any expression of their own opinions or their feelings of anger or frustration. The dependent person becomes fearful whenever faced with independence and anxiously seeks refuge in the caregiver.

THREE SHADES OF DEPENDENCY
THAT LEAD TO AN AMBIVALENT RELATIONSHIP STYLE

Anxiety, uncertainty, and self-doubt rumble just beneath the surface of dependent people. Their goal is to manage their anxiety, but how and how well they manage it differs.

The Anxious Dependent

Anxious dependents are like turtles without their shells. They feel vulnerable to everything and everyone all the time. All they ever want is security and protection, but they never get it, or at least they never feel that they do. Instead, a foreboding sense of danger follows them like a little black cloud. Their strong dependency is combined with the dismal sense that others will inevitably reject them. Their greatest fear is that people will get to know them for who they really are—inadequate and defective. And they are sure this awareness will lead to instant and outright rejection.

Consequently, anxious dependent persons hesitate to start a relationship unless they are certain they won't be rejected—and how many relationships like that do you know? Some characteristics common to anxious dependents include:

- A tendency to avoid close relationships because of fear of rejection

- An unwillingness to get involved in activities that require social interaction

- A pattern of restraint and reservation within social situations

- Excessive fear of criticism

- An aversion to embarrassment, one of the most feared emotions

- Low self-esteem, a feeling that the person is fundamentally flawed or defective

- A tendency to exaggerate risks, especially the risk of being embarrassed socially

- A tendency to be easily sidetracked and overwhelmed by otherwise minor failures or disappointments

These behaviors are viciously reinforced by a number of negative thought patterns:

- I feel flawed; no one could possibly like me.

- Every failure verifies that I am flawed.

- If someone rejects me, it proves I'm flawed.

- People who like me must not really know who I am, or else they're poor judges of character.

- If I feel embarrassed, it will be overwhelming and unbearable.

Furthermore, these people who are fearful of abandonment actually tend to behave in ways that invite rejection from others. Like Gina, for example, they fall into a self-defeating cycle of social behavior. Case in point: Gina felt flawed, and she feared that if others knew her true self, they'd reject her. So she withdrew socially to keep people from knowing her. But they interpreted her standoffishness as a sign of disinterest and conceit. They reacted angrily and withdrew from Gina, which she interpreted as confirmation that she was flawed and worthless.

The Melodramatic Dependent

While anxious dependents deal with the fear of rejection by withdrawing, melodramatic dependents, often women, are far more active about avoiding rejection. Instead, they seek attention with great enthusiasm and tenacity.[7] Unfortunately, when trying to achieve their goals of acceptance and social applause, they tend to rely too heavily on their looks and theatrical displays of emotion. As a result others tend to see them as shallow and immature.[8] Their ambivalent relationship style is characterized by dependency and attention seeking, especially attention from men. More specifically, many melodramatics:

- Are "onstage" all the time as they seek to be the center of attention

- Tend to perceive relationships as closer than they really are

- Are strongly impacted by the opinions of others

- Pay excessive attention to their physical appearance

- Always want to stay looking young

- Dress in sexually provocative ways but get little pleasure from sex, even in marriage

- Shift emotions rapidly, often quite dramatically

- Speak in a very impressionistic way, paying very little attention to details

- Generally try to downplay stronger emotions (even though emotional displays may be quite dramatic) and present themselves in a very favorable light[9]

In addition to struggling with basic dependency issues, melodramatic dependent people wrestle with three fundamental beliefs:

- I must be the center of attention or I'm not worthy/lovable.

- I need someone, especially a strong man, to constantly offer me reassurance and praise, or I will feel awful about myself.

- In order for others to want to be around me, I must always be fun and exciting.[10]

It's no wonder that those nearest them consider them shallow—because they just might be! After all, they spend so much time and energy on the externals and pay little attention to the internal. Self-knowledge is often avoided. It feels strange to look too deeply into their own thoughts and feelings. Because self-reflection was somehow threatening to their parents, it was shunned and ignored as they were growing up—and it still is today.

When she got involved in a small group, forty-year-old Lizzi exhibited many of the characteristics of the melodramatic dependent. At one meeting a member confronted Lizzi on her lack of substance, her tendency to focus on wealth and prestige rather than on character, feelings, and thoughts. He was tired of hearing about her money, her clothes, and her church activities. The rest of the group chimed in with similar questions, but Lizzi shut them off as she collapsed into a histrionic display of tears.

To Lizzi's credit, she stuck it out with the group. And over time she gathered some important information about herself and her marriage. She also came to understand that if she wanted deeper, more intimate relationships and she wanted to dampen her nagging sense of loneliness, she had to get *real*—both with herself and with others. This was rocky, uncharted territory for Lizzi, but she slogged her way through it.

Next, through a series of heart-to-heart conversations with others in the group, she learned that her looks were not synonymous with her self-worth and lovability. She discovered that others enjoyed hearing about her opinions, her insights, her thoughts, and her feelings. When she shared those aspects of who she was, they felt closer to her. And, to her surprise, she felt closer to them—and far less lonely, less clingy, and less dependent.

Lizzi's relationship with God also grew stronger. She began to realize that no man could meet the deepest longings of her heart—only He can. We witnessed how she started turning to Him for a sense of safety and security and began to rely less on the things she had.

The Angry Dependent

Although anger seems out of character for a dependent person, it's a common trait—if we define it right.[11] One kind of anger arises when we recognize that we've been wronged or mistreated. Also called righteous indignation, it's the sense that *This just isn't fair. I don't deserve what you've done to hurt me.* A second and unhealthy kind of anger frequently ignores the event that provoked the anger and suppresses the emotion. This repressed anger is tamped down, stuffed, and overly controlled because the person is afraid to be direct about it.

But anger can't ever be totally repressed for very long. In time it will surface—maybe physically, in problems like ulcers or high blood pressure, or perhaps emotionally, through irritability and nagging. A husband arrives home late without calling to let his wife know his schedule, and dinner is ruined. She might say, "I'm mad. When you do that, you don't seem to care at all about the work I do around here. Next time this happens you're sleeping on the couch with the dog." That kind of confrontation is healthy—and far healthier than if she said nothing when he got home but later began criticizing him about how he strews his clothes all over the bedroom or how he never completes a project. The husband fights back, and as the battle between them heats up, she may escalate from criticism to contempt,[12] assaulting his character or his prowess as a father, a husband, or a follower of Christ, and so on.

Dependent people tend to exercise the unhealthy kind of anger, causing those exasperating and unsatisfying emotional wars of the type we just described. But, even worse, that anger can cause the partner to emotionally disengage from the dependent person and go silent. The walls thicken and become impenetrable. The dependent person's anger can easily degenerate into rage, and inevitably the relationship deteriorates. When this happens—fulfilling the dependent's worst nightmare—a morbid depression or devastating anxiety may consume the soul.

BREAKING THE CYCLE

To be honest, we feel a little uncomfortable sharing these disturbing descriptions of the ambivalent relationship style with its clinging dependence and its self-feeding tendencies toward anxiety, anger, and despair. If you've recognized yourself or a loved one in the pages of this chapter, you've probably been hurt by the stinging descriptions and bothered by the disturbing depictions. You might even have been embarrassed—and we know how fearful you are of that unwelcome emotion. But we encourage you to keep reading. You *can* break free of this destructive cycle of dependence. And the information we share in the second half of this book can help you break free to a new life of close, rewarding relationships.

One-Minute Review

Ambivalent people . . .

- Are afraid that they'll be rejected and abandoned

- Go to great lengths to please people

- Depend on others rather than themselves

7

THE GRASS IS ALWAYS DEAD ON BOTH SIDES OF THE FENCE

The Disorganized Relationship Style

*Being abandoned, treated with inconsistent love and abuse,
and being subjected to contradictory communication
all contribute to a child's sense of helplessness.*
—LOUIS BREGER

> **Beliefs That Fuel the Disorganized Style**
> - I am not worthy of love.
> - I am not capable of getting the love I need
>   without being angry and clingy.
> - Others are unable to meet my needs.
> - Others are not trustworthy or reliable.
> - Others are abusive, and I deserve it.

Persons with a disorganized relationship style find darkness everywhere they turn. As they look out at the world of relationships, the grass is always dead on both sides of the fence. Why? Because they hold a negative view of others *and* a negative view of themselves, and the resulting behavior causes a variety of relationship problems. They can behave like those who have an avoidant style and look inside themselves for satisfaction as they emotionally wall off those close to them. Then they can change strategy without warning and become desperately clingy and dependent, hoping like those with the ambivalent relationship style that someone stronger and wiser will come to their rescue. Surprisingly, at other times, they may appear quite secure as they relate to others in warm, trusting ways.

These sudden shifts from one relationship strategy to another often leave those closest to them confused and frustrated while the "disorganized" persons themselves feel trapped in a chaotic world, one of rapidly shifting emotions, impulsive behaviors, and muddled relationships.

Do you know people like this? We do, and we'd like to introduce one of them to you.

Traumatized Twice

"I don't know what's wrong with me," Linda said. Her raspy voice, heavy with a New York / Latin accent, was electric with confusion, worry, and desperation. "My family doesn't even think it's safe to be around me no more." As she said that, her face became tight with panic. She was heavyset and middle-aged, and it was obvious that years of bad choices had taken their toll on her.

"I feel like I'm going to explode!" she went on. "All these stupid doctors I've been seeing—they don't know what's going on with me." Linda now became angry. Not only was she struggling emotionally, but her body was plagued by unexplainable physical symptoms: neck pain, lower-back pain, occasional chest pain, tingling in her hands, cramps in her stomach, extreme fatigue. And the doctors' medical tests had found nothing.

"So what brings you to see us?" we asked, almost rhetorically.

"Well," she began, rather sheepishly, pausing for a second or two, "I told my doctor I'd bust his head if he didn't figure out what was wrong with me. He didn't like that too much. So he sent me here. He said if I didn't get counseling he wasn't going to treat me no more. So here I am."

Not exactly the circumstances under which we see most people, but . . . whatever works. We asked Linda to tell us her story.

Two years ago, while working the late shift in a convenience store, a young man came in to buy some beer. When she asked for ID, he reached into his coat, pulled out a shortened broom handle, and whacked her across the face with it. She fell to the floor, and instead of just running off with the beer, her attacker jumped the counter and began savagely kicking her in the ribs.

The incident traumatized her—and stayed stuck in her mind. She'd be thinking about something completely unrelated, and suddenly her mind would flash onto the event. Sometimes it was just a momentary flashback, but sometimes her mind would transport her behind that counter again and she'd again feel the toes of his shoes digging into her side. Or in the middle of the night, she'd awaken after reliving the terrible event in a dream so real she could taste her own blood.

"And suddenly, when I'm driving somewhere, or when I'm sitting alone at night watching television, I look at my life, at me, and I feel hopeless. Really hopeless. And when that happens, I feel emotionally numb. Like I'm hollow inside. Empty. But I don't always feel like that. Sometimes I feel so mad—so angry. It just comes on me, especially if I see something that reminds me of—well, the event. If I see a young man who looks like the attacker, I break into cold sweats, and I'm sure my life's going to end right there and then."

She was describing a full-blown panic attack. But there was more to the story from that terrible night she was attacked. When Linda went to the ER, the doctors found something quite unexpected in the X-rays. The films showed a lot of old bone fractures in Linda's hands, her wrists, and her ribs; there were even bone fragments in her face and on her skull. Their first guess was that, as a child, Linda had been in a car accident. But she had no memory of an accident. Plus, an accident severe enough to cause the kind of trauma the doctors were seeing would have almost certainly involved another visit to the ER—and surely she would have remembered that. So what had caused these injuries, and why hadn't they been attended to?

Dissociation: A Normal Response to Abnormal Circumstances

Eventually we learned that Linda's devastating experience in that convenience store was just one of the unfortunate experiences that had been visited upon her as a young teen. But, although Linda grew up in the projects of New York City, the perpetrator wasn't some tough-looking member of a neighborhood gang. The offender was her mother. Linda's father had died when she was only seven.

Two years later her older brothers moved out of state to work the coal mines of Appalachia. Soon after that, her mother remarried a man named Ed.

Ed found Linda attractive, and within months of marrying her mother, he began slipping into Linda's room at night after her mother had fallen asleep. Before long her mother knew about Ed's evil intrigues. But instead of protecting her daughter, she turned on Linda—often with a broomstick in hand. In fact, she hit Linda with it every chance she got. She also bent Linda's fingers back until they popped. "There were mornings when Mom threatened to kill me if I told anyone that it was her hitting me and not me just falling down. I don't think my teachers believed me, but they never said anything. No one ever showed up on my doorstep or anything like that." So no one ever knew that Linda was the target of a tragic triangle—her stepfather's sexual abuse and her mother's physical and psychological torture.

The Loss of a Safe Haven

As we discussed in chapter 2, we form relationships because we, as needy children, seek someone stronger and wiser to protect us from a dangerous world. One of parents' fundamental roles is providing a safe haven for their children. As the children mature, they internalize this safe haven as a sense of *felt* security. The support and comfort they receive in their safe haven makes them confident that they can get the support and comfort they need from other people—from a spouse and close friends. They trust that these people will be available when they're needed.

In contrast, children like Linda who have been traumatized by their own parents are in an awfully tough spot. Their parents are both the "source of and the solution to"[1] their fear and anxiety. Which simply means there is no solution, there is no safe haven, there is no place to go that's calm and reassuring. Yet, in their hearts, the children know that their parents ought to be the safe haven. God programmed children to believe, *They ought to love me. And I should love them, not dread them.* But no matter what *ought* to be, they still have no solution when anxiety rises. Consequently, these children become emotionally disorganized and fragmented during stressful times.

Dissociation as a Solution

Linda's only way to manage the volcanic emotions and animal pain triggered by her stepfather's sexual abuse and her mother's physical abuse was to go emotionally and psychologically limp. "I just let go," she said, her eyes still full of questions. "I let go of who I was, of who I wanted to be, of—me. And I went into another world. Off to never-never land. I could still see what was going on. But it wasn't me anymore getting pounded, getting hurt by him, by them. It was someone else."

This *dissociation* is the ability to turn off thoughts, feelings, and even physical pain and move those experiences to some other part of the consciousness. Young children tend to use dissociation to cope with life's normal anxieties, and as children are repeatedly abused, they rely increasingly on dissociation as a way of coping. Infants and toddlers exhibit dissociation in odd, sometimes contradictory, and often disorganized behaviors, especially when they're anxious or frightened. For example, when the mother reentered the room following a brief separation, some of these children would be clearly upset. They wanted their mommies, searched for them, but in the middle of their quest, they'd stop and just stare off into space. Still others put their hands over their mouths and then hunched their shoulders in fear. These were outward indications that these children viewed their parents as both the "source of and solution to their fear." These signs of dissociation were also omens foretelling a broken self in the future. These children generally grow up to be adults who have difficulty controlling their emotions.

THE ABUSIVE FAMILY:
THE PATHWAY TO THE DISORGANIZED RELATIONSHIP STYLE

In 1962, the *Journal of the American Medical Association* published an article entitled "The Battered-Child Syndrome."[2] Before this, most Americans, including the medical profession and the church, turned a blind eye to childhood abuse and its devastating impact on a child's emotional development. But during the 1970s and '80s, with the Vietnam War and the increasing awareness of childhood sexual abuse and domestic violence, experts began to notice an interesting pattern: survivors of trauma, no matter the source—war, domestic violence, sexual assault, incest—all had a very similar pattern of symptoms, very much like Linda's. According to one expert in the field, "Home is the most violent place in America."[3]

In this chapter, as we discuss the different types of abuse that occur in homes—from subtle forms of psychological abuse to incest—our goal is simple: to help you understand just how devastating its impact is on a child's developing psyche and how it can lead to the most damaging of relationship styles. You'll see just how pervasive child abuse is and how it impacts not only our children but our society. We strongly believe that the church needs to get involved in preventing child abuse. First, the abuse of children—which isn't confined to nonbelievers—is a sin, and the church needs to help members confront and mortify their sins. Second, the church needs to help prevent child abuse because those exposed to its toxic effects are often so fearful and confused about relationships, particularly about their relationship to God, that they're either hardened to the gospel message or unable to grow in three important elements of the Christian life—faith, hope, and love. Usually this happens because of fear—especially a fear of trusting those who are expected to be stronger and wiser. We believe this problem of child abuse, like no other psychological issue, deeply affects the church and its members.

What Is Child Abuse?

Our definition of abuse may seem radical to some, so we'll begin with a quick preamble. As complex as being a good parent is, there are essentially just two goals: parents help children grow up to follow rules and live within limits, and they prepare children to love and be loved.

As parents, we want our children to feel secure about themselves and about their ability to offer warmth and support to others. We want to lay the foundation for them to accept love from others and to trust others to be reliable, available, and supportive. When others fail them, we want our children to offer them grace and forgiveness, understanding and mercy. And when they hear the message of the gospel, we want them to gravitate toward God's love and transfer their ultimate hope and security to Him. That said, we believe abuse is anything we do that keeps our children from developing these capacities.[4]

Now some people might think that by concentrating on issues like those just outlined, the child might end up spoiled. Not so! In fact, overindulging children is really another form of abuse. A child who has not learned how to deal with limits and who cannot tolerate normal day-to-day frustration isn't in a position to love or be loved.

Still others think that teaching a child to love and be loved will mean not teaching children limits. But research verifies that children who are treated sensitively and who are prepared for the business of love are more likely to live within the limits God has prescribed. There's a saying: rules without relationship lead to rebellion. And it's love that makes living within the rules, or limits, tolerable and desirable. Remember, the two greatest commandments are to love the Lord with all your heart—and to love others as you love yourself. All other commandments are merely extensions of these two (see Matthew 22:36–40). When we prepare our children to love and to be loved, we lay the foundation for them to live contently within limits. Love and limits go hand in hand.

Six Types of Child Abuse

In this section we're going to present six forms of abuse, starting with the most subtle and moving to the most obvious. Even though each stands on its own as a separate behavior, a common thread runs through the six types of abuse: in every instance the child is treated merely as an object or a piece of property, devoid of thoughts, feelings, and intentions.

Psychological Abuse

Hard-handed rejection, sarcastic put-downs, callous harshness, confused inconsistency, and unreliable care are but a few forms of psychological abuse. Many parents who are psychologically abusive are in denial about how rude and insensitive they are to their kids. They literally ignore how often they yell at or psychologically intimidate their children.

If you wonder if you're being psychologically abusive to your child, here is a litmus test: do you treat your children with greater kindness, patience, and understanding and with a softer tone of voice when you're around acquaintances and friends?

Emotional Neglect

As one wise observer put it, "Children need more than food, shelter, and clothing. They need at least one person who is crazy about them."[5] Some parents focus only on the physical needs of their children. They make sure their kids have food, clothing, a bed, probably a Nintendo, a computer, a Game Boy, and so forth. When asked if they're good parents, these moms and dads might tell you, "The kids won't starve." But there is no warmth, no physical touch, no emotional connection. The child's emotional needs go unmet.

Physical Abuse

We realize there's a fine line between a spanking and physical abuse. We're not talking about spanking. We *are* talking about clear-cut forms of physical abuse, like those Linda experienced: "any nonaccidental physical injury, such as beating, punching, kicking, biting, burning, and poisoning."[6] This type of parental behavior devastates kids and makes it nearly impossible for a child to form healthy attachments.

Sexual Abuse and Incest

Sexual abuse is defined as sexual contact between any child from infant to midadolescence and another person who is at least *five* years old. If the victim is an adolescent, the definition includes engaging in sexual activity.[7] This contact may range from fondling to full intercourse.[8] We also add lewd looks and suggestive sexual talk to the list.

Individuals outside the nuclear family instigate the majority of sexual abuse incidents. However, when sexual abuse occurs within the family, it's called *incest*. It involves a parent or an older family member taking sexual liberties with a child—whether it is exhibitionism, fondling, mutual masturbation, or intercourse.

Exposure to Severe Marital Conflict

All couples argue from time to time. In fact, children learn how to manage conflict by observing their parents disagree and then work things out. But when the squabbles turn into screaming matches, physical struggles, or violence, a child's sense of security is threatened. The child worries, *What if the home breaks apart? What if one hurts the other?* Then, even though he worries about both parents, he may be compelled to side with one and hate the other. That alone produces anxiety. No child likes to hate a parent.

Addictive Behavior

Many types of abuse overlap. For example, psychological abuse and emotional neglect are frequently mixed together. Addictive behaviors, such as alcohol abuse, substance abuse, or Internet addictions, set the stage for other types of abuse.[9] One expert described the addicted family as one of "chaos, inconsistency, unpredictability, unclear roles, arbitrariness, changing limits, arguments, repetitiousness and illogical thinking, and perhaps violence and incest. The family is dominated by the presence of the addiction and its denial."[10]

THE SINS OF THE FATHER

Scripture makes it clear—and psychological research confirms—that people are not islands unto themselves. The effects of sin, for instance, actually do pass from generation to generation because we take in, or internalize, the way we've been treated. If we've been loved, we feel lovable. If we've been hated, we feel self-contempt. If we have been both loved and hated, we feel ambivalent about ourselves. Put simply, "A child's sense of self is shaped by the way others treat him or her."[11]

Recently during a radio talk show on childhood and relationship issues, a young father called to ask us how he could stop screaming at his children.

Cutting to the chase, I (Tim) asked, "Jeff, were you screamed at as a kid?"

The answer? Of course it was yes.

The talk-radio format didn't allow us enough time to go into Jeff's entire experience, but we encouraged him to remember what life had been like for him as a child and then to empathize with his own children. If he could put himself into their shoes as he yelled at them, if he could remember the pain and fear he'd felt when his parents had yelled at him, then perhaps he could stop himself from yelling at his kids.

Victims of Untold Stories: The Legacy of an Unresolved Past

When people are traumatized or when they suffer significant losses, the emotional pain can be excruciating. Due to its intensity, most people bury the pain beneath a ton of forgetfulness. Then, in the same coffin, they bury everything that reminds them of it. Burying painful memories is the same thing as dissociation, and we call these dissociated memories *untold stories.*

When memories of traumatic events are buried, they are stored in different parts of the brain. Researchers using brain-imaging techniques have shown that when victims are reminded of the trauma they experienced, the parts of the brain associated with intense emotions and visual images become active, but the part of the brain associated with speech turns off.[12] The result has been aptly called "speechless terror,"[13] the inability to tell the story of the horrific event.

Many traumatized individuals bury their stories quite well, and doing so lets these people function pretty effectively in their daily lives—at least on the surface. We've seen quite a few of them as successful professionals who completed college, took on tremendous responsibilities at work, manage their time effectively, and make important decisions for their companies. But the toxic effects of their tragic past surface in situations usually involving intimacy, aggression,[14] abandonment, and fear.

The Power of Reflection

God made us in His image and blessed us with the amazing ability to verbally describe the world around us as well as the world within us. And the more we understand that world inside—our feelings, our thoughts, even our physical sensations—the better we understand the world at work inside others. We are more able to empathize with them and see the world through their eyes.

This ability to describe our internal experiences, a process called the power of reflection, and to empathize with others adds some important elements to our lives:

- Knowing and understanding feelings helps us manage them. We know what our emotions are, and we understand that they're only emotions and that, even when they're intense, they don't have to take over our lives.

- Knowing and understanding feelings helps us manage our impulses and recognize when we're acting on something unusual and unexpected. For example, you may want to tell your boss to pound sand, but the power of reflection keeps the thought locked up and harmless.

- The same intellectual and emotional process that allows empathy also allows us to feel close and connected to the ones we love. It is the basis for caring and compassion.

- Finally, reflection lets us believe we can influence others with our words, not just our actions. This is the foundation and reason for prayer. We believe that God can understand our needs and that He is affected by our words.

Trauma Destroys the Power of Reflection

Let's go back to the concept of dissociation. When children are traumatized or constantly threatened with trauma, their power of reflection goes undeveloped.

Trauma forces children to step outside the self and leave the trauma behind. This disconnection from their self-awareness is the very essence of dissociation. Abused children adapt this way, or they would be overwhelmed by fear and anxiety.

Dissociation and reflection are incompatible. The more the brain dissociates, the more difficult it is to develop the power of reflection. It's no surprise, then, that abused children struggle to use words to describe what's going on inside them. When they lack the power of reflection, their untold stories fester within their inner world.[15]

Revisiting Hannah and Darcy

Remember Hannah and Darcy from chapter 1? Hannah brought in Darcy, her rebellious seven-year-old, for counseling. He had an explosive temper and exhibited some pretty defiant behavior. Hannah's husband had left them awhile back, and she tried to juggle being an ER nurse as well as both mom and dad to Darcy. Whenever she played with her son, even in our office's safe, structured environment, an abrasive power struggle erupted. When their unhappy playtime finally ended, Hannah felt powerless; she would frequently just go limp and stare off into space.

We worked with Hannah, offering her support and suggesting ways to better handle Darcy's difficult behavior. But we suspected there was more to her story than what we'd been told. We suspected Hannah had had some severe trauma in her past. Her long, cold stares seemed a subtle sign that Darcy's behavior triggered something inside her that she didn't completely understand. When we got her to open up about her past, we discovered we were right.

Reluctantly Hannah talked about her past and how her dad had left her when she was young just as Darcy's dad had left him when Darcy was young. Hannah's mother was devastated and tumbled into a deep depression. Hannah described her mother slumped at the kitchen table, smoking one cigarette after another and drinking cup after cup of coffee. "The look in her eyes was almost frightening. Looking into them was like peering into empty caves. Yet there was something in them—like she wished she'd never been born. When she did talk to me, I was an interruption, a nuisance. And when she got mad . . ."

Hannah paused for maybe twenty seconds. Her narrowed eyes looked past us. We were suddenly nowhere in the room. Then she came back, as did we. "She gets really, really mad. I'm so scared . . ." We noticed that the tense of her story switched from past to present. Hannah was experiencing emotions she had buried long ago, emotions she had desperately tried to keep buried. But as she remembered them, she slipped back into her childhood and relived them.

"I don't know what to do . . . I can't do anything."

"What would happen, Hannah? What made you so scared?"

"I . . . I . . . I'd just run away. I have to . . . I have to hide from her." Her voice constricted to a whisper.

"Where'd you go?"

"Under my bed," she said as she drifted into another long pause, her eyes darkly hollow again as they stared at the floor on the left side of the room, which suggested to us she was accessing memories from the right side of her brain, the side responsible for intense emotional reactions.

Hannah struggled mightily to tell us her untold story. When it finally came out, broken and fragmented, it was a tale of her mother's rage and physical abuse. What she didn't realize was that those shadowy scenes from her life interfered with her relationship with Darcy. When she was with Darcy, his demands on her brought her face-to-face with her own childhood.

The Compulsion to Repeat the Past

Some people with horrific pasts learn from them and later lead calm and ordered lives, but others tend to experience more catastrophes. They might be convinced that tragedies stalk them, seeking to corrupt their lives like unholy phantoms. Of course, those unholy phantoms are usually the people themselves, and their misfortunes are a result of either their own poor choices or their I-don't-care attitudes—but they don't see it.

Outsiders, however, can see the wounded self re-create the trauma it knew all too well: "War veterans may enlist as mercenaries, victims of incest may become prostitutes, and victims of childhood physical abuse seemingly provoke subsequent abuse in foster families or become self-mutilators. Still others identify with the aggressor and do to others what was done to them."[16]

Traumatized victims may even become addicted to trauma. Whenever we are under extreme stress, the brain releases chemicals called *endogenous opioids,* God-given painkillers that are the brain's equivalent to heroin. One study, for example, showed that after viewing a fifteen-minute violent movie, the brain released the equivalent of eight milligrams of morphine.[17] Imagine those fifteen minutes repeated over and over again in a stressful, even violent, situation. The brain could easily become addicted to the drug, and withdrawing from that drug can be as difficult as breaking a drug addiction. Increasing the difficulty is the fact that the withdrawal symptoms mirror the nightmare of the traumatized person: emptiness, tension, irritability, and an internal sense of unrest. To relieve these symptoms, the person may return to the trauma and its "morphine."

Fear of the unfamiliar is another way addiction to trauma can develop. Researchers see this when they place a rat in a "shock" box and shock it, making the rat painfully uncomfortable. But over time Mr. Rat becomes familiar with the situation, and pain is its way of life. When the researchers opened the box so the rat can escape, you'd expect that critter to put as much distance as possible between itself and the box. But it didn't happen that way at all. The rat did leave the box, but whenever it faced something unfamiliar, it returned to the pain-inflicting box. Why? The box was familiar, so that's where the animal retreated whenever it was anxious.

A Need for Chaos and Turmoil

Research tells us—and our experience confirms—that children from abusive and/or chaotic homes come to regard such abuse and chaos as familiar. Furthermore, their brains are addicted to the constant release of endogenous opioids because of those homes. So when they experience the unfamiliar, even the *positive* unfamiliar like intimacy or deep friendships, they feel an overpowering urge to return to the familiar, which is chaos. That's one reason why adults fleeing an abusive relationship, even after they seem to have escaped it completely, will one day return to, or create for themselves, another turbulent setting in which to live. Often that setting will come complete with an abusive relationship.

Repeatedly we've seen clients start to make positive changes in themselves, like exercising, eating right, and committing to Bible study, prayer, and small-group work. Moving through this process, they face low levels of anxiety, an unfamiliar domain that offers no internal morphine. So they sabotage their progress and retreat to their old, well-worn, chaotic behavioral routines.

Passing on a New Story

Hannah tried to wall off her childhood and sever all her connections with it. But connection came anyway when she repeated her past—when she married an angry, abusive man and when she became an ER nurse surrounded by continuous trauma.

Connection also came as Hannah replayed her own mother's anger in her relationship with Darcy. And why wouldn't she? Her untold story remained very much alive, and it seeped back into her life in the form of irritability, impatience, and anger. Influenced largely by her past, Hannah was passing on the legacy of her unresolved trauma to the next generation.

Our goal was to help her understand her whole story: what happened; how she felt; what she did to protect herself; how she handled her feelings; how she survived; how what happened to her influenced her selection of a husband; and how her feelings about her childhood affected her picture of her son. Was she seeing Darcy in the same way her mother had seen her? Was she afraid to get close to Darcy? Was she afraid to acknowledge his feelings of anger, abandonment, and fear because they reminded her of her own buried feelings? Did she identify with her mother's aggression, her mother's despair and hopelessness? We thought she might be reenacting her own childhood with a role reversal in which she played the role of the aggressor and Darcy the victim. But Darcy was not willing to lie down and take the abuse as easily as Hannah had. He was fighting back. His temper tantrums reflected the same rage Hannah had felt as a child but had never expressed.

Only as Hannah came to trust us did she take the incredibly courageous step of telling us the devastating story of her upbringing. But as she did so, and as she acknowledged her fear, her anger, and her sense of betrayal, she was able to better understand what Darcy was experiencing. She wept bitterly when she came to see the situation through his eyes. She held him in her arms and cried.

Now she was no longer afraid to meet Darcy at his level. She came home from work looking forward to seeing him, hearing about his day, and watching him play with his GI Joes before bedtime. She no longer avoided him emotionally.

She learned to set limits without becoming enraged. She learned, when he challenged her, how to stay calm and not be overwhelmed with memories and sensations from her past. Yes, Darcy was still a challenging little guy, but he was better able to deal with the loss of his father without worrying about whether his mom would slide away into a sea of despair or go off into a screaming fit of rage if he asserted his budding self.

Hannah's courage freed her and Darcy to write a new story and pass it on to the next generation.

The Key to Breaking the Cycle

Research into the disorganized style of relationships has produced some pretty straightforward data. Parents who have had significant trauma, emotional and/or physical abuse, or even the loss at an early age of one or both parents are likely to pass the toxic effects of that trauma on to their children. Often, the result will be as if the children have experienced a parent's trauma firsthand. The key to breaking this cycle is the victim's ability to get in touch with his or her particular story, the whole story. That means recalling incidents and patterns, all the facts and all the feelings related to the story, most of which have been stored away, deep in the parent's brain, since the incidents occurred. When adults are able to piece together the story's components into a coherent narrative, it buffers them from the toxic effects of their traumatic past.

On the other hand, when the story goes untold, the very act of keeping it bottled up forces it to gain pressure. It's like when you shake a Coke: the carbonation increases the pressure on the cap. Either it blows or, if it's in a porous container, it thrusts itself into the weaker surroundings. Hannah's untold story thrust itself into her relationship with her son. The untold stories of Linda, a victim of incest and the grocery store break-in, also seemed to catapult her into the next devastating event. We've already shared the evil perpetrated on her by her stepfather and the subsequent violence visited upon her by her mother. Linda has also known multiple rapes and several abusive marriages, and five years earlier she had been the victim of another store robbery. Ironically, the robberies seemed like the least traumatic events of her life, yet the last robbery brought her emotions to a head.[18]

How about you? Did you come from a tumultuous environment that you find yourself constantly going back to—maybe not walking the same exact steps to the same exact front door, but ending up at places that might just as well be where those steps and that door took you before? If you do, you may have an addiction to turmoil. Later in the book, we'll take a thorough look at what you can do next to break this tragic addiction. For now, just be aware that there is hope. Hannah and Linda managed to escape this vicious cycle. So can you or the ones you love.

THE EFFECTS OF THE DISORGANIZED RELATIONSHIP STYLE (THE SHATTERED SELF)

As Hannah's and Linda's experiences show, trauma can shatter the self, and you may not even be aware of the extent of the damage. You may be thinking, *I have some emotional problems, but who doesn't? Is it worth making a big deal out of this? Is it worth turning my world upside down just to get a little peace of mind?*

The answer is yes. Working to tell your untold story is definitely worth both your time and your emotional energy. If you're not yet convinced, the next few paragraphs will show you some of the core effects of the disorganized relationship style. You just may see some of them in yourself or your loved ones.

Identity Problems

A sense of identity and the personal strength that accompanies it allow us to form strong values and to commit ourselves to goals. Our sense of identity is the internal glue that helps us decide what we like and what we don't like. It also helps the "who I am now" to remain stable over time and across various situations. With a strong sense of identity, we can make and stick to our commitments, our relationships, our jobs, our goals, and even the precepts of our faith.

But when the self is shattered by trauma and turmoil, so is the sense of identity. As a result, shattered selves—people with a disorganized relationship style—act on the emotions of the moment but have great difficulty staying on task when their emotions change . . . and they tend to shift rapidly. These people may commit to some goal during an emotional high, but when the high fades, they have no internal sense of self-value to keep the commitment alive. Thus the commitment dies. These persons can also fall out of love as quickly as they engage it, so relationships are threatened, and chaos rules, reinforcing their relationship style.

Two more identity-related problems are common. First, people with a disorganized style have trouble learning from past experience. For example, they may have financial problems stemming from unchecked shopping sprees, but they don't stop shopping. Because of their identity problems and their lack of self-reflection, they are unable to recall the pain associated with past overspending and apply it to the present.

A second problem is the inability to see how current behavior will affect the future. For example, when dealing with a difficult boss, a disorganized person may smart off to the boss without even considering that inappropriate remarks could lead to unemployment. These two problems are direct results of the identity difficulties of the disorganized style.

Emotional Storms

People with a disorganized relationship style also struggle to regulate emotions, calm themselves down, or gear their emotional response to the situation. What might trigger mere frustration or worry in healthier folks might instead result in inappropriate fits of rage or full-blown panic attacks in these disorganized persons. Chronic feelings of depression are common. These folks feel glum and emotionally hollow for no apparent reason. They find little pleasure in their day-to-day life and little joy in thinking about the future.

The disorganized style also makes an individual prone to slip into deep depression. Because this person has been borderline depressed and anxious throughout life, when certain events occur—job loss, conflict with a friend, financial struggles—he or she can be rapidly plunged into serious depression.

And then there are the flashbacks, those emotional experiences that are similar to how the person felt in the past during the actual event. And flashbacks of being unreasonably beaten by an enraged parent can create quite the emotional storm. What can be particularly disconcerting about once again feeling those past extreme emotions is that the emotions now being felt are totally out of proportion to the triggering event in the present.

One of our female clients had been sexually abused by her stepfather when she was nine. She avoided the gynecologist for many years without ever making the conscious connection between her being abused and her reluctance to be examined. When she finally decided to go for a checkup, she experienced a full-blown panic attack while she sat in the doctor's waiting room. When she talked with us about it, she realized that her time in the waiting room was like waiting at night for her stepdad to slip into her bedroom after her mother dozed off. She had experienced a flashback.

Physical Arousal

Hyperarousal is a state of physical alertness in which the body is ready to either fight or flee. The heart races, the pupils enlarge, hot or cold flashes occur, and the body is in a state of tension. Hyperarousal is a central feature of the response to trauma, no matter what the source of the trauma, and it leads the person with a disorganized attachment style to respond to new stressors with panic, anxiety, and a sense of extreme helplessness rather than focusing on problem solving.

Identification with the Aggressor

Could there be anything more difficult for a child than dealing with the reality that the person he or she looks to for safe harbor is the very person who seems to be trying to sink the child's boat? Can there be a greater dilemma for a child than having no one to turn to for help, than having nowhere to go for protection and comfort? For the child, these are basic needs, akin to food and air. The child can't exist for long without them. So he or she manufactures a new image of the parents. Instead of seeing them as bad and faulty, the child directs the blame for the situation inward, on the self. And when, as a child, you can't turn against your sources of pain, it is much too easy to become like them.

Faulty Assumptions

By identifying with the aggressor, the abused child can continue to view the parent as a person with whom relationship is possible and even desirable. The unfortunate outcome, however, is that the child is riddled with self-blame and guilt: *The reason I'm being hurt is that there is something fundamentally wrong with me. I am a really bad person; nothing I do is right.*

A sense of learned helplessness also develops. Abused children often believe nothing can be done to change their situation. Even when beset by relatively small stressors, they can feel completely at the mercy of forces beyond their control. They think, *Events just happen to me, and I can do little, if anything, to change them.*

At the other end of the scale, victims can overcontrol.[19] They become obsessed with every little detail of their lives and may spend hours scrubbing floors, dusting furniture, making beds, doing dishes, and straightening whatnots. They may approach relationships the same way. Trying to take complete control of others is a reaction against their persistent sense of powerlessness. They invariably alienate their loved ones by trying to control them, which adds to the intense feelings of betrayal, abandonment, and hopelessness they're already dealing with.

Distressed Relationships

Relationship distress is the hallmark of those with the disorganized style. Their shattered self means difficulties with trust, a fear of abandonment, a fear of intimacy, and an altered concept of sexuality, all of which doom relationships.

Disorganized people can respond by being a control freak on the one hand and being a doormat on the other, and both extremes create problems. The control freak ends up driving loved ones away, and the doormats are angry that people they love walk all over them but fearful that their anger might push those important people away. Also, as we've seen, disorganized people are often compelled to repeat the trauma and turmoil they know all too well. People become familiar with abuse, chaos, and even threats of abandonment. And their psychological systems are set up to repeat the past,[20] and they do so in several ways.

Faulty Selection. It's common for traumatized persons to select partners who treat them as their original abusers did; they often select partners who are prone to aggression, manipulation, and rejection. But the disorganized person won't even see, much less acknowledge, these faulty personality traits in the other person and will proceed with the relationship, even though everyone else can see the abuse coming.

Distortion. Even when their partners aren't behaving in abusive or rejecting ways, the shattered selves may read rejection or abandonment into their partners' behavior. Eddie, one of our clients, came from a chaotic, rage-filled home where both parents were unfaithful and they eventually divorced. So we weren't all that surprised when Eddie said, "I know my wife is having an affair; I can just tell by the way she looks at me."

"How can you tell that just by how she looks at you?"

"I can just tell. There is something different about her."

"Well," we said, "there may be something different about her, but why does that have to mean she's having an affair? Maybe something at work is bothering her, or maybe she is worried about something."

But Eddie was not really open to an alternative explanation. He was convinced that she was having an affair, and he treated her that way. He couldn't see that he was distorting the situation to match his past.

Provocation. In extreme cases people with a disorganized relationship style may engage in behaviors that actually provoke others to abandon them or behave aggressively toward them. A disorganized person's life becomes a self-fulfilling prophecy. In Eddie's case, his angry distrust and constant accusations eventually pushed his wife away, causing her to seek a temporary separation. Of course this fueled his feelings of betrayal and strengthened his belief that she was being unfaithful. He was seeing the past in the present, and he was sure that the past was repeating itself. Tragically, he just couldn't see how his behavior triggered the scenario unfolding before him.

TIME TO RECAP

Before we move on, let's quickly recap the unhealthy relationship styles we've looked at.

- Individuals with an *avoidant* relationship style have negative views of others that turn them away from loved ones, especially during times of stress.

- Those with an *ambivalent* relationship style have a positive view of others but hold themselves in rather low esteem. When under stress, they become determined to extract comfort and reassurance from people close to them. But they pursue this refuge with an intensity that generally drives their loved ones away. The ambivalent person is left dealing with deep feelings of betrayal and abandonment.

- The *disorganized* relationship style, the shattered self with its untold stories, can mean—among other problems—dissociation; the inability to know, understand, and manage emotions; a compulsion to repeat the past; an addiction to chaos; and a weak sense of identity.

Now here's the great news: you can develop a secure relationship style no matter which style is currently governing your relationships. Although powerful and influential, your life—your past—doesn't have to command your tomorrows. You can develop a new and healthy base for building and rebuilding your relationships. You can overcome the damage that's been done to you in the past; you can learn to connect with those you love most in a secure and wonderful way. There is hope and help in the pages ahead.

II

Unlocking the Secrets to Loving and Lasting Relationships

8

GOD AND YOU

Embracing the Relationship That Transcends All Others
WITH GEORGE OHLSCHLAGER

Relationship or bonding . . . is at the foundation of God's nature.
Since we are created in his likeness, relationship is our most
fundamental need, the very foundation of who we are. Without
relationship, without attachment to God and others,
we can't be ourselves.
—DR. HENRY CLOUD

It took a long time for Rita, a thirty-nine-year-old mother of three, to realize that no man could fill the void that runs deep in a woman's soul—and that she couldn't completely satisfy the longings of a man's heart.

One evening her husband, Frank, dropped the children off at the babysitter's and returned home to prepare a special meal for just the two of them. Rita, warming up to the evening, stepped out of the kitchen to light the fireplace's gas logs. Mission accomplished, she took a quick step back toward the kitchen and, over the warm crackle of the flames, she heard a thud in the kitchen. Knowing instinctively that something was wrong and feeling her heart in her throat, she darted into the kitchen. Her worst fears were realized. Frank lay facedown on the kitchen floor. She managed a horrified gasp as she lay a tender, hesitant hand on his throat. Frank was dead. At age forty-three, he was killed by a massive heart attack.

Not long afterward, Rita came to us for help. It hurt us physically to listen to her story. Frank had been her high-school sweetheart, they'd been married twenty-two years, and now he was gone—without so much as a good-bye.

Among other challenges, she now faced the turmoil and joy of raising their three children alone.

We sat wishing we could help her make sense of what happened. But we had no answers. At that moment, the knowledge that God has a purpose in all things seemed irrelevant. Rita's pain was too raw.

Making Relationship with God the Top Priority

In times of trouble, God can seem far away, but He never is. God is always near, and He wants us to know that. He wants us to feel His embrace and to feel secure in Him. But when trouble strikes, we either move closer to Him or further away. And, as you might expect, our choice is often determined by our relationship style.

Imagine a mother sitting on a park bench as she watches her eighteen-month-old son, Junior, explore the nearby world. As he does so, both he and Mom are very aware of the distance between them, a distance that is usually eight to ten feet max. Junior keeps a wary eye on his mother, and if he encounters something he's unsure about, he looks back to Mom to see if it's okay to keep going. If Mom gives a little smile or has a neutral expression, he will proceed. If she frowns or looks fearful, he will hesitate.

Now imagine that a train roars down the tracks adjacent to the park, and the explosion of sound frightens the little boy. He instantly makes a beeline to his mother. She scoops him up and holds him close. She buries his head in her neck as she presses her hands over his ears. Shielded from the noise, Junior calms down. Then, after the train disappears, Junior's eyes meet his mom's. She smiles down at him. "Boy, that was really loud and scary," she says, validating his fear. Then she gives him a reassuring kiss and snuggles him even closer, loving the fact that he's come to her for comfort. A few moments pass before Junior squirms to get down. His curiosity slowly returns, and he begins to explore the sandbox near Mom's bench.

This scene illustrates several core components of a healthy, secure relationship (see the boxed list on the following page). Junior keeps an eye on Mom to be sure that she's accessible and available. When threatened, he seeks *proximity* to his mother. His mother provides a *safe haven*, which comforts Junior when he's distressed. Once he is comforted, his mother is the *secure base* from which he begins further exploration. If Junior were suddenly separated from his mother, though, he would undoubtedly become anxious and upset. And if he lost her, he would grieve and experience deep sorrow.

Now think about our journey in this life. Our relationship with God satisfies all the conditions of a healthy, secure relationship—if we allow it to happen. We seek closeness to Him in times of trouble. He is our refuge, our place of safety, and we seek *proximity* to Him. We look to Him to provide us with a felt sense of security; He is our *safe haven*. He's also our rock, our *secure base*, our foundation from which we can face the world with boldness, strength, and confidence. The thought of separation from Him produces significant anxiety—we find it scary. For us to give up on God or for us to feel that God has withdrawn from us produces grief and sorrow. Confusion can come, however, if we feel that God has let us down, that He somehow authored an evil fate for us, or that He could have prevented pain in our lives and didn't.

FIVE CHARACTERISTICS OF A HEALTHY, SECURE RELATIONSHIP

1. We seek proximity (closeness) to the caregiver, especially in times of trouble.
2. The caregiver provides a safe haven, a felt sense of security.
3. The caregiver offers us a secure base from which to explore the world.
4. Any threat of separation induces fear and anxiety.
5. Loss of the caregiver prompts grief and sorrow.

Knowing with Our Heart, Not Just Our Head

Before Frank's death, Rita walked closely with the Lord. She went to church, she prayed, she was involved in women's ministry, and she talked to her children about the Lord. Her faith was real, but she explained that she saw God as the One who kept bad things from happening to her, while she looked to Frank for comfort.

We don't know why Frank died. We never will on this side of heaven. But Rita, in her state of brokenness, was forced by her circumstances to learn that her relationship with God is to be her first priority. After all, He will always be there. He applauds our uniqueness, He cheers our joy, and He weeps with us in our sorrows. He will never die. His presence is eternal and His love is everlasting. He works in every aspect of our lives—our brokenness, our rebellion, our plainness, our beauty.

Rita knew all this before her husband died, but she'd be the first to tell you she didn't know it in her heart. But Frank's death stripped away everything she thought she knew about herself and God. She was forced to reconstruct her worldview so that God became the center of her emotional universe. Before she had thought she loved God, but now she hungered and thirsted for Him. That doesn't mean she wasn't angry with God or that she didn't grieve the loss of Frank. Her material world, her things and relationships, were undoubtedly God's blessings, and they were good things in themselves. But they were unable to help her in this time of crisis. Her utter vulnerability to the fickleness of this world was exposed, and she knew at a deep, bare-bones level that God was all that separated her from the abyss.

Feeling so hurt, so alone, so vulnerable, she was poignantly aware of her need for God. Again, she had known that she needed God prior to Frank's death, but not in the same way as now. Before, Frank had been her primary caregiver. Whenever she was in trouble, she always turned to him first. Now she had no choice but to turn to God first—to look to Him for guidance, for direction, for security, for safety.

Now we're *not* saying that God took Frank's life to teach Rita a lesson. What we are saying is that, as she dealt with the pain God had allowed into her life, Rita learned in her heart something she had previously known only in her head.

A Refuge for the Wounded Soul

God knows how hard our lives can be, not only because He's God but also because He experienced life on earth Himself. After all, God and His Son,

Jesus, and the Holy Spirit are all one Being, the Holy Trinity. So when God sent His Son, Jesus, to live on earth as a human being, He was actually sending Himself. While Jesus was here, Jesus and therefore God Himself experienced the same joys and the same hardships we know in our lives today. For example, just as we mourn the loss of loved ones, Jesus wept outside the tomb of His friend Lazarus. But throughout His earthly lifetime, Jesus made His relationship with God His priority. And He expects the same of us today (Matthew 10:37). He wants us to turn first to Him, not to our parents or our spouses or anyone else. When we do look to Him first, our lives become properly ordered. In the words of C. S. Lewis, "Whenever we try to put second things into the first place position, we lose the joy of both God and whatever we are trying to replace Him with." Rita's loss was what Lewis called a "severe mercy." It became God's megaphone by which He called her nearer to Him.

Making our relationship with God our first priority doesn't mean we need God and no one else. Rita has lost Frank, and God doesn't come in and take over the place in her heart where Frank lived. Her improved relationship with God doesn't mean that she'll never long to see Frank again or that the break in her heart will immediately heal. Rita's heart will continue to ache; she will continue to groan inwardly and to experience pain and sadness as she grieves. But God will meet her and be with her in the midst of her pain. He will comfort her as she suffers. He will see her through the pain but not remove what hurts. Like a loving parent, God comforts His hurting child without healing the malady itself. He becomes a safe haven, a refuge for the wounded soul.

Your Relationship Style and God: Responding to Tragedy

Rita's response to her dreadful loss was to seek increased security. She moved toward God, expecting Him to provide not only security but comfort as well. Which He did. And because He did, her affliction and anguish resulted in a stronger relationship with Him. But not everyone would respond the way Rita did. Your relationship style strongly influences how you react to those crises that call for a new worldview. Let's look at some of the different responses.

Avoidant Relationship Style

During times of distress avoidant people move away from God and cling to possessions, success, or their addictions. They may angrily say, "Just as I expected, God can't be trusted. He gives you someone you can love and then just tears that person away. Who needs a God like that?"

Other avoidants express their anger at God and self-medicate their pain by pursuing sinful habits. One husband whose wife was dying from ovarian cancer was consumed by guilt as he confessed to us that at night he would lie next to his ailing wife and fantasize about how, after her death, he would go to Las Vegas and sleep with a prostitute. And he thought about doing this because he felt God deserved to be "repaid" for taking his wife. Unlike Rita's circumstances, his crisis prompted him to move away from God.

Ambivalent Relationship Style

Ambivalent people are prone to vacillate. They feel rage toward God at the same time that they are consumed by self-incrimination and excessive self-blame for their loss. Like avoidant individuals, ambivalent persons don't turn to God for comfort. But instead of turning to things like success and addictive behavior, they may search frantically for someone else to be in relationship with. Obsessed with their desire to have someone close, they may bounce from relationship to relationship. If no relationship materializes, their anger, sadness, and grief may eventually become a deep, morbid depression.

Disorganized Relationship Style

Disorganized people view life's crises as a continuation of their life story of loss. From their perspective, God is malicious just like their early caregivers were. Consequently, these people respond with a mixed set of behaviors: addictions, self-protection, clinginess, anger, and even fiery rage. Even if they see God as seething with wrath and their personal tragedy as something they deserve, they may actually bury their feelings of resentment, anger, and even rage. They are, of course, terrified to express these feelings for fear that, in savage response to them, God may unleash even greater punishment. But these buried feelings probably won't stay covered for long. They may resurface as general anxiety, worry, and even panic attacks. Whatever happens, the results are the same: fear, anxiety, and pain.

Secure Relationship Style

Rita shows us the secure relationship style. Of course she was devastated by her husband's death, and she vacillated between anger and sadness. She also struggled with survivor's guilt, wondering, *Why him? Why not me?* She spent hours praying for God to show her the answer to all the *whys*. She felt lonely and afraid. She felt vulnerable. But ultimately she turned toward God and changed her *Why?* to *How?—How do I go on?*

She cried out to God and found Him waiting with open arms. And from that secure base of His love, she was able to view her tragedy differently. Mindful of her all-powerful yet loving God and a waiting heaven, she faced her pain and grew with it. She could see God's hand working things for good—though she would always and forever miss Frank. God may never completely remove her pain, but when it presses in on her, she knows to press in closer to God.

RELATIONSHIP AND SPIRITUALITY

Remember Junior and his mother and the scene in the park we described earlier? Interactions like that one occur many times a day and thousands of times during a child's first several years of life, and these stress-induced interactions lay the groundwork for how children respond to God in the future. These interactions with Mom answer questions like *Is God present? Is He accessible? Will He welcome us into His lap for comfort, or will He trivialize the pain and send us with a bony, accusing finger from His throne room? Is God trustworthy and dependable?*

First, an Awareness

We believe a core aspect of spirituality is an awareness of our vulnerability. As we become increasingly aware of our need and how truly vulnerable we are, we find ourselves more open to relationship with God, and we're motivated to seek His presence.

Think about the events of September 11, 2001, a horrific day by any standard. Terrorists intended to throw America into chaos and fear, but it had the opposite effect. The attack peeled away our veil of impenetrability and stripped away the robe of safety so many Americans wore with pride. As we acknowledged our susceptibility, our helplessness, and our apparent fragility, we sought refuge in God and ultimately found comfort in Him.

Relationship and the Fear of Death

Ask children what scares them, and they'll say monsters under the bed or in the closet—and losing their parents. This thought literally terrifies children. From the moment their lips touch the breast, their parents are a part of them, the part that comforts and satisfies them.

Megan and Zach (Tim's kids) both went through phases of obsessing about dying. Zach, at age six, said, "Dad, you're going to die, aren't you, and I'm the youngest. One day I'll be all alone." At age six! To children, the thought of losing a parent becomes tantamount to being totally annihilated themselves—and that's enough to scare anyone. Children's sudden awareness of this separation anxiety prompts them to seek closeness and search for comfort.

As children develop, separation anxiety turns into a fear of death—death anxiety. What are they afraid of? It has to be more than the sense that we're all going to die. Anxiety about it means we're afraid of something on the other side of the divide. For example, we know a wonderful Christian woman who at age eighty-three is afraid of death. She wars against it. Why? Because she senses that she has lost her ability to control her life. She is coming to the end of self—her safety. And now she faces an unfamiliar future.

Christian philosopher Peter Kreeft put it this way: "Life is always fatal, no one gets out alive." He goes on to quote Saint Augustine: "As doctors, when they examine the state of a patient and recognize that death is at hand, pronounce, 'He is dying, he will not recover,' so we must say from the moment a man is born: 'He will not recover.'"[1]

Many people try to defend against death anxiety by denying its existence. They rarely or never attend a funeral; they never talk about loss and death. They press on in their Reeboks, looking for the fountain of youth. But the crises of life (among them, illness, accidents, rejection, and tragedy) can cause death anxiety to rise to the surface. When it does, the various relationship styles serve as a defense against it:

- *The avoidant style* avoids intimacy and dampens emotions in personal relationships. For these folks, closeness brings fear of rejection. So they remain on the periphery of intimacy and instead attach themselves to things and success. This defense ultimately destroys the true bond of love that can exist between two people.

- *The ambivalent style* does the opposite. These people seek intimacy but cling to it too tightly, perhaps believing that by doing so, they can avoid separations and ultimately even death. Unfortunately, this defense can lead to the same outcome as the avoidant experiences: feelings of alienation and aloneness.

- *The disorganized style* may use an avoidant or ambivalent response or even a mixture of both. These people also tend to go numb, feeling as if the world around them is not real.

- *The secure style* can consciously and courageously invest in close relationships, but holds them loosely because they know that while relationships provide comfort and safety, they can, and ultimately will, end.

If you have any of the insecure relationship styles, your fear of separation and your unwillingness to face it can keep you from living life to its fullest. You shrink away from fully investing yourself in meaningful, intimate relationships, and you fail to be motivated to carry out God's purposes.

On the other hand, if you have a secure relationship style, you know that Jesus came to conquer our fear of separation. His death and resurrection promise us everlasting life *with Him*, and He promises we'll *never* be separated from Him. As the writer to the Hebrews said, Jesus came to "free those who all their lives were held in slavery by their fear of death" (Hebrews 2:15).

The apostle Paul echoed this truth when he wrote, "'Where, O death, is your victory? Where, O death, is your sting?' . . . Thanks be to God! He gives us the victory through our Lord Jesus Christ" (1 Corinthians 15:55–57). And because the fear of death has been doused, we can boldly and fully invest in life, in ministry, in relationships and know it is all meaningful: "Always give yourselves fully to the work of the Lord, because you know that your labor in the Lord is not in vain" (v. 58). Secure people know that they'll be separated from earthly relationships, but that death unites them with fellow believers as well as with the supreme heavenly Father for eternity.

OUR SOURCE OF SECURITY: OUR RELATIONSHIP WITH GOD

Our relationship with God is to be our primary focus, but we still need other relationships. In fact, we know that God brings people into our lives to provide, in an earthly setting, what He wants us to have. But when we're in trouble, we are to turn to God first, for He is the One "who sticks closer than a brother" (Proverbs 18:24), the One who will never leave nor forsake us (see Hebrews 13:5).

We also know that we're most motivated to find God when we become aware of our earthly helplessness and vulnerability. We understand from our earliest childhood experiences that our greatest fear is separation—being left alone, left at the mercy of the surrounding, hostile elements. As we mature and become more self-reliant, that ever-present fear of being left alone morphs into the fear of death. One of Jesus' chief resurrection goals was to free us from the fear of death and provide us with a place of refuge. So He hands us the keys to heaven where we will serve Him forever in the halls of His love. And that's ultimate security.

As we embrace our rock-solid relationship with God in Christ, we find ourselves more freely seeking intimacy with others, knowing that in the end we will ultimately be with both God and the ones we love who know and love Him. As Peter Kreeft so aptly states, God's "love is stronger than death."

How to Experience God's Presence and Peace

The heavenly kingdom provides refuge for our souls in times of trouble, and we are able to experience that because—in Jesus' words—"the kingdom of God is *within* you" (Luke 17:21, italics added; see also Acts 1:8; John 14:16–18.) So the burning issue becomes *How do we embrace all that God offers us? What can we do to experience God's presence and peace in our everyday lives? Do we have to go through the kind of suffering that Rita endured? Do we have to lose someone we love to realize God's place in our lives?*

First of all, God is eternally present; there's no question about that. But we're certainly not as aware of His presence as we should be, even in times of severe crisis. So how do we become aware? Experiencing God's presence is a skill like carpentry or sewing that must be developed and then sharpened, but it's a skill we can use anytime, anywhere. We don't have to wait for tragedy before finding God. In fact, in the midst of such exceeding pain, we may not find Him as quickly as we'd like because at those times we're often quite confused. The time to hone our awareness of God is in our day-to-day journeys, those times when we're confronted by small challenges—difficulties at work, troubles with our parents or children, the results of our own sins. If we haven't learned to find God in these small events of our lives, it may be painfully difficult to find Him when we're thrown into deep troubles.

So how do you develop the skill of being aware of God's presence? We're glad you asked! We have outlined some steps you can take to heighten your awareness of God in your daily life. As a side benefit, this path will lead you to become more secure in your relationship with both God and your loved ones.

The Pathway to Spiritual Growth and Awareness

We know that probably the last thing you expect to hear about right now is Little League, but that's a great place to learn a basic fact about spiritual awareness.

If you wander out to your local field, you'll see two kinds of coaches. One assumes kids just inherently know how to play baseball, so he sees his job as coaxing that ability out from beneath their skin and into their shoes, their gloves, and their bats. He sees himself as a motivator. If a child makes a mistake, then the kid's obviously not motivated enough. He might say, "Johnny, what are you doing? You know better than that! Now, get your act together and catch that ball. Do you really want to win on Saturday or not? You know we can't win if you don't catch those easy balls. Now come on. Make it happen."

A second type of coach assumes kids don't know a baseball from their elbow and need to be taught. Mistakes mean a lack of skill. And correcting mistakes means teaching new skills. This type of coach might say something like, "Okay, Johnny, you went after the ball, but you didn't stay down on it. Remember to get in front of the ball like this." Then he slaps a knee to the grass as though a grounder is coming full speed. If Johnny makes the same mistake again, the coach pulls the kid aside again and, in a tone that has nothing to do with motivation, focuses more specifically on the skill needed to make the play. If the boy blunders anew, he might even create a drill for the kid to practice at home. Of course, whether the child practices at home or not is largely based on motivation.

The first coach doesn't understand the fundamental nature of growth. When his players don't perform, he chides them for "not wanting it bad enough." In contrast I (Gary) remember my high school wrestling coach: If we lost a match, he'd pore over the films with us. He'd identify our weaknesses then help us find a drill that would cultivate the skill we needed. He even held match-specific drills to target specific deficits in our techniques. The results were astonishing.

In *The Spirit of the Disciplines: Understanding How God Changes Lives*, Dallas Willard shows that spiritual growth is governed by the same principles that regulate growth in other areas of our lives, like those experienced by the Little League players. Willard zeros in on Paul's first letter to Timothy: "Have nothing to do with godless myths and old wives' tales; rather, train yourself to be godly. For physical training is of some value, but godliness has value for all things, holding promise for both the present life and the life to come" (1 Timothy 4:7–8).

Willard tells us, as Paul told Timothy, that to lead God's people effectively, we have to train in the "spiritual gymnasium." The comparison to physical exercise continues: "There is a specific round of activities we must do to establish, maintain, and enhance our spiritual powers. One must train as well as try. An athlete may have all the enthusiasm in the world; he may 'talk a good game.' But talk will not win the race. Zeal without knowledge or without appropriate practice is never enough. Plus, one must train wisely as well as intensely for spiritual attainment."[2]

Simply put, spiritual growth is strengthened by exercise. Yet many Christian leaders still talk about spiritual growth like that first coach talked about baseball, implying that growth is all about having the willpower or motivation to live in a Christlike manner. Or, in lieu of motivation, they talk as if God will strike us with a bolt of the Holy Spirit and instantly make us into godly men and women. So we sit back and wait to hear that perfect motivational sermon or to get hit by that perfect bolt of lightning, believing either one is fine, because either one will enable us to walk as Jesus walked.

But What Would Jesus Do?

A few years ago jewelry, license plates, and bumper stickers started asking us WWJD—what would Jesus do? Based on Charles Sheldon's novel *In His Steps*, this popular movement has inspired and challenged millions of people around the world. But it assumes that motivation alone brings about the change described above, that if we want to be like Jesus, we'll simply take the action He would take in the situation at hand. When we figure out what Jesus would do, we'll "just do it." (This is the Nike approach to change.) However, as Dallas Willard points out, the premise of Sheldon's book and its approach to spiritual growth spring from an inadequate view of how humans change:

> The book is entirely focused upon trying to do what Jesus supposedly would do in response to specific choices. . . . There is no suggestion that he ever did anything but make right choices from moment to moment. And . . . there is no suggestion that his power to choose rightly was rooted

in the kind of overall life he had adopted in order to maintain his inner balance and his connection with his Father. The book does not state that to follow in his steps is to adopt the total manner of life he did. So the idea conveyed is an absolutely fatal one—that to follow him simply means to try to behave as he did "on the spot." . . . There is no realization that what he did in such cases was, in large and essential measure, the natural outflow of the life he lived when not "on the spot."[3]

Practicing the Spiritual Disciplines to Strengthen Your Attachment

Just as we learn that effortlessly fielding an eighty-mile-an-hour ground ball doesn't come naturally, so we learn that walking closely with God doesn't just arise out of the mere desire to make Him first. Both require training, and training starts with discipline. As Dallas Willard puts it, "A discipline is . . . nothing but an activity undertaken to bring us into more effective cooperation with Christ and His Kingdom."[4] A discipline helps us learn to rely on Him so that in times of crisis we've already developed the habit and we can find Him much more easily. A little later, we'll offer some specific examples of disciplines you might practice to develop a keener spiritual awareness. But for now, let us give you an overview of the impact they can have on your life.

Besides cultivating a more secure relationship with God, these disciplines can help us break free from addictions. (In this case, we use the word *addiction* broadly to refer to anything that repeatedly replaces our need for an intimate relationship with God.) Second, the disciplines also help us know God as our *safe haven* and learn to rely on Him as our *secure base*.

God is indeed our comfort in times of trouble, and we can rest in the knowledge that He is always there and that He is more than able to meet all our needs. Armed with this sense of security, we can approach life boldly and with confidence, and obeying Him comes more easily and naturally. After all, rules without relationship lead to rebellion. Rules with strong relationship lead to willing obedience.

But we too easily allow material possessions, other relationships, business, success, or even ministry to replace God, don't we? Too often we find our "rest" in them, not in Him. We feel self-sufficient, perhaps like Adam and Eve felt in the Garden. When they ate the forbidden fruit, they were in essence telling God, "We don't really need You." Which, of course, is what we're saying when we turn to possessions, positions, or other people for the comfort and security that only God can provide.

No Pain, No Gain

Besides being hard work, the disciplines may produce uncomfortable feelings like anxiety, depression, irritability, and intrusive memories about bad past events, particularly for those who have a history of abuse and other trauma. (If that could be you, consider practicing the disciplines at first under the watchful eye of a trained pastor or counselor.) But don't avoid the disciplines just because they may cause some discomfort. The turmoil they trigger is often necessary, like the muscular discomfort experienced when lifting weights or the labor pains of childbirth.

But because pain may be involved, practicing the disciplines requires courage, the willingness to endure the necessary cost to achieve something far better. When we avoid necessary pain, we only invite unnecessary anguish later. As Carl Jung noted, all neurotic suffering, or unnecessary pain, is caused by the avoidance of legitimate pain.

So what disciplines are we talking about? Well, for starters there is corporate worship, Bible reading, prayer, and fasting. You probably know about and hopefully practice some of these disciplines already (whether or not you have *thought* of them as spiritual disciplines). Here we'd like to discuss a few others you might not have considered.

Searching the Scriptures

People who approach God must first believe that He rewards those who diligently seek Him (see Hebrews 11:6). So how do we go about seeking Him? Where can we learn about God? Where can we find truth? The answer is . . . the

Bible, the sixty-six books of the Old and New Testaments. It is God's special revelation to us about Himself, about how we should live and, most importantly, how we can know Him. In the Bible God reveals Himself more fully than He does through nature, reasoning, or science. And He does so because He wants us to know Him—not just know *about* Him, but to know Him personally, as a dear and intimate friend, as Savior and Lord, as Redeemer, as Spirit, as Father to His children.

Second Timothy 3:16 tells us that "all scripture is given by inspiration of God and is profitable for doctrine, for reproof, for correction, for instruction in righteousness" (KJV). Steeping ourselves in God's Word prepares us for everything life can throw at us. It speaks volumes about children, health, safety, and security in this life, and it teaches us what to do when faced with temptation and challenges. No wonder the psalmist wrote, "Thy word is a lamp unto my feet, and a light unto my path" (Psalm 119:105 KJV).

Now Joshua needed exactly that kind of light when he faced the difficult task of taking over for Moses and leading the Israelites to the Promised Land. Where would his courage and strength come from? You guessed it. God told Joshua, "This book of the law shall not depart out of thy mouth; but thou shalt meditate therein day and night, . . . thou shalt make thy way prosperous, and then thou shalt have good success" (Joshua 1:8 KJV). When the Word of God intersects with human need, guidance as well as security, healing, peace, and hope come. The Holy Spirit uses the written Truth to teach and guide us in all things. The bottom line is this: God's Word is true. And His truth frees us to learn and to live. Furthermore, searching the Scriptures prepares us for other disciplines.

Solitude

Solitude is a missing ingredient in our everyday lives. Everyone needs at least ten to fifteen quiet minutes every day. But as a spiritual discipline, solitude is far more than just a few moments we set aside for ourselves each day. Spiritual solitude usually involves a retreat. Wherever you go for solitude, put some distance between yourself and other bipeds. Take just a Bible, a pen, and a journal—and remember that radios, televisions, cell phones, and pagers are forbidden!

When we seek solitude, our goal is to disconnect from life's distracting and normal routines, from those activities and elements that interrupt and interfere with our relationship with God. In solitude that relationship is strengthened as we hear His quiet, still voice and let it direct and shape our vision of reality.

Solitude helps us strip away the almost unconscious defenses we use to soften our experience of aloneness and our fear of death. When we get away from others and from our typical daily routine, we more easily recognize our total dependence on God for our very existence. This realization can provoke some pretty stiff anxiety. But remember, it's this anxiety, this helplessness, and this vulnerability that expose our need and heighten our thirst for God; they compel us to seek refuge in His peaceful sanctuary. In contrast, people who constantly have the gas pedal to the floor are doomed to be godless.

Solitude can be especially powerful for those with ambivalent and disorganized relationship styles. *Ambivalent persons*, for instance, separate themselves from those they look to for guidance and direction. They become anxious and fearful: *I can't do this; I'm too anxious. I can't stand to be alone. I have to have somebody with me.* They may also struggle with feelings of guilt: *This just proves what a bad Christian I am. I try being alone with God and look how upset I get.* If you experience thoughts like these, endure them. They come from your past, not from today's reality. Know that, as you practice the discipline of solitude, the power of God will take over. Eventually the Word of God and the leading of the Holy Spirit will give you a true sense of security and safety. God will also show you just how ably He can bring you peace.

Now our clients have responded in a variety of ways when we've suggested that they practice the discipline of solitude. Edward's eyes popped open in terror. He was a very dependent person, and he experienced several partial panic attacks in our office as we tried to convince him of the discipline's merit. Gradually we convinced him that he would never develop a true dependency on God if he continued to replace God with other people and his business, if he didn't get alone with God. Reluctantly, Edward agreed to try it.

We asked him to keep a journal of his thoughts and experiences during his retreat. After the first three hours, he wrote comments like these: "I feel so inadequate. I really don't think I can do this for four whole days. . . . I've never felt so lonely in all my life. . . . It feels like I'm going to die. I can't stand it. . . . I want to go home."

However, Edward stuck it out, and as the time melted away, so did his anxiety and his feelings of aloneness. His journal entries became: "The Lord is good. . . . He has seen me through my fear, my aloneness. I know the Lord is near. He will meet me in my darkest hour, if only I will let Him into my heart."

When he returned from his retreat, Edward was ecstatic about his encounter with God. We encouraged him to practice this discipline on a routine basis for six months. We also added other disciplines, such as fasting, Bible study, and simple prayer. And, interestingly, the more Ed practiced solitude, the more secure he became in his connections with others, especially his girlfriend. She'd found him too clingy and controlling and had even considered breaking up with him. But as he became more dependent on God, he was able to relate to her on a more mature and secure level. The same paradox can work for you. The more dependent you become on God, the more independent you become in life.

Ed also became less dependent on his parents, which, predictably, caused *them* some anxiety. Ed was approaching the point where he could honestly and boldly set appropriate boundaries with his parents—not an easy move for him. Previously he would have worried that they'd be angry with him or that he wouldn't survive without their constant guidance and support. But now he was ready and able.

So what about you? How long has it been since you were alone with the Father?

In persons with *disorganized relationship styles*, solitude can produce many of the same results, so it should be entered into carefully. If you have a significant history of trauma, we recommend that you practice the discipline of solitude only under the guidance of someone experienced and trained in working with trauma victims. The reason is that solitude literally dismantles defenses, which can allow flashbacks and other intrusive recollections to come rushing back. Under the right person's care, however, solitude can be quite appropriate and even healing.

Silence

Silence is the essential ingredient of solitude; without silence the impact of solitude is greatly minimized. Obviously, it's nearly impossible to completely isolate yourself from sound, but by drastically reducing it, you will become aware of just how often sound drowns out the Lord's voice.

Dallas Willard notes that silence is frightening because it strips us as nothing else does. It reminds us of death, which will cut us off from this world and leave only us and God. And what if, in that total quietness, there turns out to be very little to just "us and God"? Furthermore, think what it says about the inner emptiness of our lives if we must always turn on the CD player or radio to make sure something is happening around us.[8]

Silence, when combined with solitude, dissolves our normal defenses that keep the feelings of aloneness and vulnerability at bay. When we're silent and alone, we may actually feel naked before a very large universe. But there, without all of life's distractions, we can seek God's face and respond to His invitation: "Come to Me, all you who labor and are heavy laden, and I will give you rest" (Matthew 11:28 NKJV).

Like solitude, silence touches—and can bring freedom from—the fear of abandonment in both the ambivalent and the disorganized relationship styles. It can also be an effective discipline for those with the avoidant relationship style, especially narcissists with an inflated sense of self-love (see chapter 5) who seek the company of people who offer frequent praise and adoration. These folks also love to listen to music, watch television, and hear people prattling around them. The discipline of silence can help neutralize all these defense mechanisms when you lay them at the foot of the cross.

On a practical note, we can suggest two other versions of solitude and silence. The first is a scaled-down version of solitude in which you wake up in the middle of the night to meet God alone in the silence of your home. This form of solitude is most suitable for those with the disorganized style because it provides the safety net of the home in case emotions begin running too strongly.

A second version of the discipline of silence involves silencing the tongue. This discipline can be practiced within our everyday lives at home, work, or church. It doesn't involve being rudely silent to people, but it changes your focus from talking to listening—to being deeply, intently aware of subtleties you may normally overlook.

Such silence can help the various relationship types make some important changes. It helps an avoidant person like Arnold (whom we introduced in chapter 5) engage others on a different level. Arnold did a lot of talking, and if he wasn't talking, he was ignoring people. Practicing the silence of the tongue forced him to tune in to his wife and children and to ease into their worlds. Not only did this practice improve his relationships with his family members, but as he learned to bridle his tongue, he also became more sensitive to God's gentle urgings.

This silence of the tongue helps disorganized people by slowing them down and letting them listen to and label their own thoughts and feelings, rather than just blurting them out. This discipline helps increase the power of self-reflection (see chapter 7).

Simplicity

When you practice the spiritual discipline of simplicity, you stop complicating your life with your pace and your possessions.

Keep life simple for a while: Kill the TV for a couple of weeks, put the credit cards away, stay out of the mall, and buy only essential food, toiletries, and other basics. Slow down, declutter your calendar of activities, and, in short, stop doing anything that complicates your life. Then see what happens.

Simplicity's goal, much like that of the other disciplines, is to help us seek God first. It's so easy to be blind to how strongly our material possessions control us and how much we actually look to our possessions for emotional comfort. It's an incredibly strong bond, but you may not even be able to see it.

Simplicity also involves slowing down. After all, it has been said that if the devil can't make you sin, he'll make you busy instead. Much to his delight, we live at a frantic pace. We drive our kids to ball practice, ballet, school plays, movies, and concerts. We attend church meetings, church socials, extracurricular activities related to work and school, and so much more. And where's our time for God? During coffee breaks, if we take them? Or do we snatch a moment to listen to Chuck Swindoll or Charles Stanley in the car on our way home from work?

Slowing down means reducing the number of activities we get involved in. Maybe not permanently, but at least for a season. The idea is to give yourself time to rebuild your relationship with God. Chaos and a frenzied pace create the illusion of a full and productive life when they are actually distracting us from our need to be in relationship with the Creator. God doesn't want what you do—He wants you! Remember, if we never slow down, sooner or later we'll *be* slowed. And then it will be difficult to move closer to God. Simplicity helps us identify and break our addictions before they break us.

You might be like our client Jennifer. Before we suggested simplicity, she would never have dreamed that she was addicted to money and possessions or that she relied on them for comfort and a sense of safety. But once she began practicing simplicity, she quickly realized just how attached she was to her belongings. You may find the same or a similar addiction within yourself.

The discipline of simplicity focuses you inward, and consequently it may force radical changes in how you spend your time and your money as well as how you use your talents. As you change inwardly, your perspective on external things will be transformed. Jesus challenged us to make this change, saying, " 'If you want to be perfect, go, sell your possessions and give to the poor, and you will have treasure in heaven. Then come, follow me' " (Matthew 19:21).

Secrecy

You may not be addicted to material goods, but you may be addicted to your reputation, your success, or your prestige. Those aren't bad things. In fact, Scripture encourages us to have good reputations in order to advance the cause of Christ.

In the discipline of secrecy, however, we keep our successes, our accomplishments, and our good qualities secret. We not only abstain from self-aggrandizement, but we actively work to prevent news of our achievements from getting out, as Jesus advised in Matthew 6:3–4: "But when you do a charitable deed, do not let your left hand know what your right hand is doing, that your charitable deed may be in secret; and your Father who sees in secret will Himself reward you openly" (NKJV).

The rationale for this discipline is to help us "lose or tame the hunger for fame, justification, or just the mere attention of others."[6] As we practice this discipline, we learn to focus on what's above, not the adoration of man, and even to accept misunderstanding without the loss of the true peace, joy, and purpose we get solely from God, through Jesus.

Simple Prayer

Paul told the Thessalonians, "Pray continually" (1 Thessalonians 5:17). The idea is not to live on your knees beside your bed or flat on your face before a chapel altar. The admonition refers to a state of mind where we constantly talk with God about our ideas, thoughts, feelings, and concerns. And if we're not talking to Him, we're consciously including Him in every element of our daily walk.[7] We filter everything through His perspective—maintaining fidelity to the Word of God, remaining sensitive to the leading of the Holy Spirit, and seeking wise counsel from godly friends.

Another dimension to the discipline of simple prayer is that we look for God's presence, His comfort, and His security in the nooks and crannies of our lives. And as we talk to Him and include Him constantly in our consciousness, we come to Him as we are, not as we think we should be, believing that He can, and will, meet us where we are. Richard Foster states, "To believe that God can reach us and bless us in the ordinary junctures of daily life is the stuff of prayer. But we want to throw this away [because it is] so hard . . . for us to believe that God would enter our space. . . . We must never believe the lie that says that the details of our lives are not the proper content of prayer. Share your hurts, share your sorrows, share your joys—freely and openly. God listens in compassion and love, just like we do when our children come to us. He delights in our presence."[8]

Just as Junior constantly looked to Mom to feel more secure, reassuring himself that Mom was nearby and accessible, we use simple prayer to cultivate our sense of God's presence, His availability, and His accessibility. Just as Junior became willing to explore the park after reassuring himself that Mom was there for him, so our readiness to boldly face this world and endure its hardships, to love others deeply and intimately, and to live with a sense of purpose and meaning is grounded in our unshakable belief that "the Lord is near" (Philippians 4:5).

As Paul exhorted his Philippian brothers and sisters, "Do not be anxious about anything, but in everything, by prayer and petition, with thanksgiving, present your requests to God. And the peace of God, which transcends all understanding, will guard your hearts and your minds in Christ Jesus" (Philippians 4:6–7).

Now we'll briefly look at things another way: prayer connects us with God the same way crying connects babies and mothers. Even though tiny babies can't express their needs in words—they can't say, "Hey, Mom, I'm famished!" or "Mom, I'm sitting in a lake here. It's definitely time for a change"—sensitive moms know and do whatever is required to bring their infants comfort and security. Likewise, God understands our prayers, our inward groaning, and He responds to our needs. The Bible says, "The Spirit helps us in our weakness. We do not know what we ought to pray for, but the Spirit himself intercedes for us with groans that words cannot express" (Romans 8:26).

Meditation

In the same way that talking and listening are two sides of the same conversational coin, prayer and meditation are two inseparable dimensions of our relationship with God. When we pray, we present our requests, our concerns, our worries, our frustrations, our hopes, and our dreams to God with thanksgiving for all He's done for us.

But there's more to prayer than that. As Søren Kierkegaard observed, "A man prayed, and at first he thought that prayer was talking. But he became more and more quiet until in the end he realized that prayer is listening."[9] When we meditate we learn to listen to God, to discern that still, small voice that directs us and comforts our souls. As Richard Foster points out, "Christian meditation, very simply, is the ability to hear God's voice and obey his word. It's that simple." Paul guides us on this journey of meditation in Philippians 4:8: "Finally, brethren, whatever things are true, whatever things are noble, whatever things are just, whatever things are pure, whatever things are lovely, whatever things are of good report, if there is any virtue and if there is anything praiseworthy—meditate on these things" (NKJV).

We encourage you to practice prayer and meditation together. They're equally important elements of our ongoing conversation with God. As we practice them, they amplify our awareness that He's present and active in our lives. If we ignore these disciplines, it'll be tough to trust that He's close. We'll eventually lose sight of Him. In contrast, when we are anchored in His truth and fill our hearts and our minds constantly with Him, we will know the peace of God that passes all understanding (see Philippians 4:7).

FIRST THINGS FIRST

As Saint Augustine once noted, "Man was made for God, and he'll never find rest until he finds it in the One who made him." God created us to be in relationship first with Him—and then with those who share our lives. When our relationship with God is secure, our other relationships become richer, easier, and more rewarding. Thus, our first priority is enhancing our relationship with God through worship and the spiritual disciplines—including those we've discussed here as well as fasting, confession, Bible reading, submission, and celebration. Each one of these plays an important role in transforming our relationship with God.

And, as we've seen again and again in our practice, when individuals work on strengthening and, as needed, healing their relationship with their Creator, they soon see noticeable changes in their relationships with others. The result is akin to a whole new start on life and the joys it offers. Do you want a new start on life? Then strengthen your relationship with the One who created you—and start today!

9

TAMING EMOTIONAL STORMS

Conquering Depression, Anxiety, Anger, and Grief

---

*Love can be angry . . . with a kind of anger in which there
is no gall; like the dove's and not the raven's.*
—SAINT AUGUSTINE

Joe was at the pinnacle of his career as CEO of a prestigious insurance company. His children were grown and married, and he and his wife had five beautiful grandchildren. His wife was a lovely, gracious woman who loved him and supported his every effort. They owned a stately colonial home near his work and also had a glorious lake house in the mountains. Joe had always walked closely with the Lord and was very active in a local Presbyterian church. But recently Joe sat in a miserable, nervous heap on our sofa. He was barely able to make eye contact with either of us.

It was about a year after landing his new job, and Joe had become riddled with panic attacks. He had tried a number of medications but was overly sensitive to the side effects. His wife had urged and then insisted that he see a therapist.

Joe's story was a tragic one. He had grown up on a dairy farm in Indiana. He remembers his dad as a hardworking man, devoted to his family and the farm, always putting in no less than fifteen-hour days every day of the week, even Sundays. But he always made some time for his kids too. When Joe was nine years old, his dad was stacking hay in the barn when he died of a heart attack right in front of his son. He was fifty-five years old.

Joe was left feeling helpless and was never able to grieve because he inherited much of the responsibility of the farm. He spent the rest of his life trying to forget what had happened. But he lived out his father's spirit: hard work, devotion to a cause, and love of the family.

Five years ago, Joe's mother died in the hospital of a heart attack. While the nurses were trying to revive her, Joe had his first panic attack. "I was standing there in that little waiting room. My head was spinning. My heart felt like it was going to leap right out of my chest, and I was having a hard time breathing. I was breaking into a cold sweat. Then I started getting that weird feeling like I wasn't there, like I was standing outside myself looking in . . . I thought I had died and was looking at myself from the other side."

Joe pulled himself out of subsequent panic attacks when they occurred, but he did so by completely numbing himself to all his feelings. He remembers that he couldn't cry at his mother's funeral. He also became very focused on his work, and his family supported his efforts to succeed.

So now Joe had accomplished in his career what he had always dreamed of, but he felt numb and empty. And within a few months of starting his new position, he became intolerably grumpy and irritable at home and at work.

His anger continued to escalate. Soon Joe was going off on everyone: his wife, his children, and his coworkers. It got so out of hand that about six months earlier, his company's board of directors recommended that he get some help to deal with his anger. His wife, Sarah, also told him that he needed to get some help or she was going to leave with the kids until he did. Joe didn't seek help; that would be out of character for him. Instead, he stuffed his anger—just as he had learned to do when he was a kid. In his family, anger had not been allowed, especially after his father died.

It wasn't long after Joe got the ultimatums from his wife and at the office that he started having the paralyzing panic attacks.

RELATIONSHIP STYLES AND REGULATING EMOTION

Simply put, how you approach relationships reflects how you "do" emotion. As we've seen, people with insecure relationship styles handle relationships differently from people with a secure relationship style. Not surprisingly, they handle their feelings differently as well.

- Those with a *secure* style aren't afraid to feel even powerful feelings like fear and anger. They use their feelings judiciously to help them make decisions and to motivate behavior, but they aren't ruled by their feelings.

- Persons with an *avoidant* style tend to keep people at a distance, avoid true intimacy, and value success and power over relationships. They also tend to keep feelings at a distance and work to deny or repress any negative ones. They are more prone to feeling empty and hollow on the inside (the consequence of avoiding intimacy), and they use addictive behaviors (like pornography, substances, or workaholism) as a substitute for intimacy and to help them feel alive.

- Those with an *ambivalent* style become entangled in relationships and experience lots of ups and downs as well as excessive concerns about rejection and abandonment. They are often consumed with a whirlwind of emotions. Whereas the avoidant person overregulates feelings, an ambivalent person underregulates them, allowing normal, healthy emotions to mutate into more intense, destructive, and self-defeating outbursts.

- Those with *disorganized* style bounce back and forth among the insecure styles. At times they might be like the avoidant person, keeping people at a distance and overregulating emotion. On other occasions, they might shift into an ambivalent style, becoming more clingy and entangled in relationships and underregulating emotions. Also, those with a disorganized relationship style might be overwhelmed with feelings from the past. Especially when trauma is part of that past, this person might be consumed with flashbacks and intrusive recollections about past losses and terrifying experiences, and not just remembering those times but reliving every detail of the terrifying events like they were happening all over again—now.

Have you ever considered how you feel about your feelings? Some people feel that emotions, especially anger, sadness, and fear, are dangerous and should be avoided. Others believe that feelings are inconvenient and troublesome, and these folks take a more logical approach to life and tend to put their feelings on the periphery. When they experience feelings, they either stuff them, like Joe did, or they become very critical of themselves for having such feelings. Still others consider their feelings to be valid expressions of their internal world, and they allow them to come and go without becoming overly consumed with them.

Primary and Secondary Emotions

When God created us, He gave us emotions. Our emotions shade the world and add color to our experiences. But more importantly, emotions motivate and prepare us to take action in an organized, goal-directed way.

Each emotion provides energy for us to act. For example, if someone were trying to harm one of your children, anger would move you to take action. You wouldn't have to think about it. There would be no mulling over in your mind, *Gee, I wonder why that person is trying to take (or hurt) my child. Would it be good to say something to him? What would be the possible outcome? What are my alternatives?* None of that would be going on inside your head. Instead, you would probably act and act quickly. You might control yourself and try not to hurt the person, but he or she would get the picture, loudly and clearly: *Keep your hands off my child.*

Emotions also help us make important life decisions. Those who totally restrict their emotions can't just choose from the gut; they get caught up in endless cycles of pondering the pros and cons: *Should I do this? Should I do that?* They never really feel like they *know* what is the best course of action. So they get stuck, often obsessing endlessly about what they should do. Many people with avoidant relationship styles struggle like this. Having cut themselves off from their emotions, which do offer valid input to the decision-making process, they now have difficulty making decisions. Those with an ambivalent style might also have difficulty making decisions, but for the opposite reason. Their emotions are constantly changing. One moment they might feel an action is right, and the next moment they change their minds.

As we mentioned earlier, our emotions are built-in responses that help us achieve a sense of closeness in our relationships. So a child who is frightened will seek closeness to his or her parents or caregiver. If that person fails the child in some way, the emotion of anger is designed to send a specific message: *You'd better not do that again.* It's an anger of hope because the intention is to bring the person back into a state where he or she is again available and accessible.

If that significant person is permanently lost, the emotion of sadness informs you of just how important he or she was to you. If experienced fully, and if you don't become flooded with a sense of hopelessness (e.g., *I can never heal from this wound; nothing will ever work out for me),* the sadness will run its course,[1] and you will ultimately return to normal functioning. But a return to "normal" doesn't mean the lost person is ever forgotten or could ever be replaced by someone else. A sense of sadness remains, but it doesn't keep you from living with a sense of purpose, meaning, and direction. It doesn't stop you from loving again.

Reacting emotionally to a situation in real time is a primary emotional experience. In those situations, our emotions give us the energy and focus to accomplish important goals. These God-given emotions are not "wrong" or "bad." In fact, they drive adaptive, productive behavior. Think of Jesus' anger when He went into the temple and found merchants buying and selling their goods—a literal Wal-Mart set up right there in God's house (see John 2:14–16). Jesus set a clear boundary, grabbed a whip, and drove away the merchants and their animals. His anger fueled and organized His behavior so He could accomplish a specific goal: protecting His Father's house. We call this a primary emotional reaction.

Secondary emotional reactions, however, usually involve trying to deny or repress emotions. For example, Ashley recently complained of feeling very anxious and nervous. When she couldn't figure out why, she began to feel self-critical and guilty about not being able to control her emotions. But because we knew Ashley, we could see what was happening. Her new boss was placing entirely too much pressure on her. He wanted her to stay after hours and frequently asked her to take work home. It was really interfering with her family life; her husband and kids were becoming perturbed.

Ashley was angry with her boss, but her underlying assumption that anger was always bad kept her from experiencing her anger. She had learned to fear anger, especially toward authority figures, and she thought if she let herself feel it, she would "lose control." So she stuffed her primary emotion, which led to a secondary emotional reaction: fear and anxiety. Because she also believed that fear, and now worry, were signs of weakness, she started to feel guilty and depressed. Ashley's secondary emotional reactions were covering up her anger, the primary feeling that could have helped her deal with the situation at work.

You might be thinking that Ashley just needed to set a boundary with her boss and tell him that she was only able to work normal hours. We agree. But before she would be able to have that conversation and stick with her decision, she would have to get in touch with her anger. She soon learned how to access these feelings without being overwhelmed by them. She also learned that anger, if used correctly, is not a bad thing and could even work to her advantage. Now she was motivated to take action. Of course she was nervous about having to set the boundary, and she feared that she would get fired, but she was willing to take the risk: "I was not going to let a job come between me and my family."

Ashley's boss actually responded quite favorably to her assertiveness and backed off. He said he had no idea that she was being stressed out by his demands. He had perceived her eagerness to please as a sign that she did not mind doing more than "normal," so he had piled on the work. There are still times when he starts to press over the line, but Ashley is more willing to quickly speak up before it gets out of hand.

A Tale of Frozen Grief

Another primary emotional reaction that people often stuff is grief. Sadness and grief are common emotions when we lose someone very special. We may also feel these emotions when we lose an important dream or when we realize that we never got to experience something very important—like the warm, tender love of a mother or the precious time and attention of a father.

Joe was in that position. He lost his father, and his hardworking farm family took no time to grieve. Instead, they stuffed their emotions and reorganized their lives. Joe became the new man of the house. His mother tried to keep the family in good spirits by telling them, "We have to move on; your father would want us to do it that way."

Joe was able to get by. The frozen grief and the anger he felt toward his dad for "abandoning" them was turned into productive energy. He had become a successful businessman, but his mother's unexpected death five years earlier and his recent promotion had caused the buried emotions to resurface. When they did, Joe was overwhelmed.

Instead of getting in touch and working through the feelings, however, Joe stuffed them. To him, these feelings were a sign of weakness. The result was irritability, depression, and explosive episodes of anger. When his work and marriage were jeopardized by this anger, he tried to stuff that too. The end result was panic anxiety and more depression. Joe was simply miserable. If we were to help him, though, he needed to get in touch with, validate, and heal these primary feelings. Ultimately we wanted him to grow closer to his loved ones and to experience God in a new and very different way.

We believe that, when primary emotions are experienced and processed, they lead to a transformation of our souls and our behavior. Up to this point, Joe's sorrow had not been completely processed. He had been frozen in time, trapped in the past for too long. He realized he had everything he ever wanted (wife, family, friends, success), but there was a deep wound in his heart that had never been healed. Now he was ready to let God heal that wound. God wouldn't completely take away the grief, the heaviness in Joe's heart, because to do so would diminish the importance of his father and mother. But God would help Joe live with it in a different, more courageous way.

FIVE TRIGGERS OF EMOTIONAL STORMS

Now that we've explained the difference between primary and secondary emotional reactions, we'll identify five triggers that can lead to emotional upheaval.[2]

Any one trigger is sufficiently powerful to stir up emotional distress, but people often experience a combination of some of the five.

Trigger One: Relationship Disputes

A relationship dispute involves you and at least one significant person in your life (spouse, parent, family member, close friend, boss, coworker, etc.) in an unresolved conflict. Such disputes can occur on different levels: renegotiation, impasse, or dissolution.

At *Level one (renegotiation)* you can be very angry at one another and actively argue and bicker about your differences. Poor communication skills—like excessive criticism, defensiveness, contempt and put-downs, and stonewalling (refusing to talk about the problem any longer)—may keep you locked in chronic conflict.[3] The emotions felt are often a mixture of fear and anger—fear that the relationship is in danger and anger either about being wronged (whether in reality or perceived) or about the other person's not being accessible, trustworthy, or reliable. But at this stage the anger is fueled at least in part by hope, by the desire that things be resolved.

Level two (impasse) begins when you are "argued out" and begin to emotionally disengage from one another. At this stage, you may still talk with one another, but not about the problem. Your relationship has changed: you no longer confide in or trust one another. The anger here steps up a degree to resentment and even bitterness.

Level three (dissolution) involves complete emotional cutoff. There is little, if any, communication, and you may treat one another as complete strangers. The resentment builds, and you may attempt to live in denial of your anger and the grief that comes with losing an important relationship.

If level one disputes are resolved within a few days, the emotions usually evaporate fairly quickly. However, if they persist, the conflict usually advances to levels two and three. Then the primary emotions of fear and anger are buried, leading to a host of secondary emotions. When Ashley denied her anger, for example, she quickly began to experience worry (negative thinking), panic anxiety, and eventually depression and hopelessness.

Trigger Two: Transitions

Scott, a nineteen-year-old college freshman, had become mildly depressed about two months after arriving at school. A farm boy from Wisconsin, he had really loved high school, where everything came easily. He'd been a celebrated sports hero, and he'd had a girlfriend, lots of friends, a close family, and loving parents. He had been heavily recruited by several large colleges, but he chose a smaller Christian school's athletic scholarship offer instead.

For Scott, leaving home was like leaving his whole identity behind and starting over. In college no one knew him, he was getting "rocked" a little on the baseball field, his sense of being special was gone, and his identity was shaken. The pillars on which he had built his sense of self-worth were weakened; his self-esteem was floundering.

Even positive transitions in life—leaving home, going to college, playing baseball at a higher level—can rattle our sense of self. The things we come to trust for safety and security are often taken away. That was definitely Scott's experience, but he proved easy to work with. This was in part due to his underlying sense of security. He knew he was loved, and his parents were extremely supportive, even though they stayed back home in Wisconsin. Scott drew on his internal resources to shake the depression, and we helped him challenge the negative, self-critical thinking that so frequently accompanies depression. He started to do what he already knew how to do well. He made new friends, buckled down on his studies, and got back into the groove in baseball practice. He was also challenged to reexamine his relationship with the Lord. Scott had known how to talk about God's goodness, but now he turned to God for comfort, a step that strengthened his relationship with the Lord.

Clearly, Scott's transition presented a new developmental challenge: leaving the quiet, comfortable, safe nest of his home and moving into adulthood, where he had to take more responsibility for his life. A similar transition occurs for the so-called "tweenagers," those kids moving between childhood and the teenage years. In school, they graduate from having one primary teacher to having five or six. Physical changes begin, and their bodies begin to change into adult bodies. Relationships, especially with the opposite sex, become more complex, especially as hormones add new feelings and bodily sensations to the mix. Tweenagers are also introduced to the challenge of developing a sense of individual identity apart from their parents. A secure relationship style helps make this transition easier, but it challenges both children and parents to reorganize their relationships.

During such developmental transitions, the insecure relationship styles add jet fuel to already heated situations. Without an inner sense of security and a fairly healthy sense of self-esteem, children are extremely susceptible to a host of negative emotions.

For women, another important developmental transition occurs when they enter their early forties. Not only are they encountering the sea of hormonal changes that come with premenopause, but they and their families are facing a number of serious role transitions. Their children are preparing to leave the nest and launch out on their own. Some women are becoming mothers-in-law and grandmothers; others may be dealing with the pregnancy of an unmarried daughter. With the children leaving home, mothers may have to reorganize their relationships with their husbands, whom they may have lost contact with while the children were growing up. To complicate matters, these women may also be taking care of their own parents or in-laws, whose health may be deteriorating now that they are into their senior years. They may also be considering career changes or even entering the work force for the first time, or they may be advancing into more senior-level positions. All these changes can be positive, but they can also challenge a woman's inner sense of security. Such shifts can trigger changes in biology and in mood as well.

Men face their own set of transitions, which also begin in their early to mid-forties. By this time they have usually reached the apex of their careers and often find the top to be a very lonely place. They have sacrificed time with their wives and children to get to this point, and now they are ready to plug in to family life. But their family members may be angry and resentful, unwilling to reconnect with Dad.

Other men may find that, while they are successful in their careers, they derive very little meaning and satisfaction from their occupations. Other men may start having health problems like high blood pressure and cholesterol during these years. These diseases, combined with the deterioration of their own parents' health, can be something of a wake-up call. Many men walk around believing a personal fable: *I am invincible. Death only happens to other people; it will never happen to me.* Coming face-to-face with the reality of their own mortality, men may enter into what is classically called the midlife crisis, which begins with basic emotions like anxiety about death and sadness and grief about a past that may have been lost.

One forty-two-year-old truck driver who came to see us had been mildly depressed for several years. His mood had begun to change after he was diagnosed with severe rheumatoid arthritis. He had lost his physical abilities, something he had prided himself on his whole life. He was a hard worker. When he wasn't at work, he loved to tinker around the house, work on cars, mow the lawn, plant the garden, or chop firewood. But he couldn't work like that anymore. This transition forced him to rethink his definition of self. He also had to reexamine his view of God. Up to this point, he had believed that God would always protect him from getting sick. Yet God doesn't always protect us or deliver us from infirmities, but He does help us draw closer to Him in the midst of our suffering.

If you reflect back on the transitions in your own life, you might see that they triggered sadness, anxiety, or even a full-fledged depression. However, you might also see how God's hand was involved and how you were able to grow from the challenge. While unpleasant transitions are not in themselves good, they can lead to incredible spiritual, emotional, and relational growth.

Trigger Three: Unresolved Grief

When we looked at Joe, whom you met earlier, we saw a man frozen in grief. When Joe lost his father as a boy, he had little time to come to terms with the incredible sense of loss and sadness that accompanies such a tragedy. Instead he learned to stiffen his upper lip, and he stepped into his new role as the man of the house. For a while this seemed to work. He learned to replace grief and anger with a drive for success.

Likewise, when his mother died five years prior to his promotion to CEO, Joe responded in a similar way. He sucked up the grief and became even more focused and driven. But role transitions, even positive ones, can strip away the layers of denial and repression used to block out grief and other painful feelings of loss.

Then when Joe reached the pinnacle of his career, he expected to feel differently. He expected to feel alive and complete. Instead he only felt a gnawing emptiness, a feeling far too close to the grief and sadness he had locked away many years before. So he replaced his sadness with anger, an emotion that often accompanies grief; but when it is directed toward others and oneself, it only creates more problems. Joe's anger almost cost him his career and his marriage. For the first time, he was faced with feeling helpless, and it triggered the immobilizing panic attacks.

Surprisingly, many people who have developed a case of clinical depression do not see the relationship between their mood problems and their unresolved grief. In some cases, the loss occurs within six months to a year before the onset of depressive symptoms. In other cases, like Joe's, the onset is more subtle, and the unresolved grief is not so easily identified. Important transitions, whether positive or negative (for example, graduating from college, getting married, birth of a first child, retirement, demotions, unexpected moves, layoffs, etc.), cause us to reflect on the ones we love, those who have stood behind us, those who have hurt us, or those who have betrayed us. They also cause us to confront the past. When the past has been checkered with loss, especially unresolved loss, we can find ourselves spiraling into a depression. Or we may try to avoid these feelings by intensifying addictive behavior.

Trigger Four: Loneliness

We all need people we can count on to be there for us. In some cases, though, we may have friends and loved ones in our life but still feel lonely on the inside. This loneliness may be a chronic sense of being disconnected, or it may have a relatively recent onset. When loneliness is chronic, it can be linked to different forms of insecure relationship styles. When loneliness has a recent onset, it is usually linked to one of the other three triggers—a relationship dispute, a transition, or a loss. Whatever the source of your loneliness, it is critically important that you build strong relationships. Without them, you are excessively vulnerable to negative feelings, including depression, anxiety, hopelessness, and worthlessness.

Trigger Five: Negative Thinking

While some people consider our emotions and our thinking to be separate functions, many experts believe they are two sides of the same coin. How we think can affect the way we feel, and the way we feel can affect the way we think.

For example, if you came from a family that placed a very high value on success rather than on relationships, you might believe *To feel good about myself, I must be successful at everything I do.* If so, when you encounter failure, you are likely to feel worthless. In that emotional state, you might say to yourself things like: *I can never do anything right* (overgeneralization); *Why should I ever try again? Nothing will ever work out the way I want it to* (negative fortune-telling); *I've never done anything worthwhile* (selective recall of the past); and *I'm a nobody* (negative labeling). All these thoughts will exacerbate your negative feelings. Plus, as you get more emotionally distraught, your negative feelings will direct your thinking to focus on negative things about yourself, about others, and about the future while selectively ignoring anything positive in your life. And, of course, the more you think about how much you have failed at life, the worse you will feel, thus perpetuating a vicious cycle of painful emotion and negative thinking.

To make matters worse, destructive thinking patterns can lead to behaviors that cause others to act in ways that confirm your negative beliefs and heighten your toxic emotions. For example, when people get depressed, they often feel that no one really likes them. So they can be defensive and irritable, full of complaints and pessimistic, when they get around the ones they love. Not surprisingly, others are turned off by this kind of behavior, which leads to their disapproval and withdrawal, which confirms the depressed person's pessimistic, negative mind-set.

Anger and anxiety have similar self-defeating patterns. First, anger. When you are angry, you focus on how you have been wronged, and you may think in black-and-white terms: *He always thinks about himself first. He always treats me like scum. I've never really liked him because he's so self-centered.* You selectively attend to that person's faults and ignore his or her strengths. This only intensifies your anger and leads you to be even more critical and negative. Not surprisingly, your negativism will be reacted to negatively by the other person, which confirms your negative view of him or her.

Second, when you are anxious, the tendency is to focus on the signs of danger and rejection and to ignore any signs of safety and security. In relationships, you might take the smallest sign of disapproval as a sign of total rejection. This might lead to clinginess or angry attacks, both of which lead the other person to become more rejecting and disapproving. And the cycle continues.

Now let's consider two of the most common types of negative thinking: all or nothing and jumping to conclusions.

The first type, all-or-nothing thinking, occurs when you see things in either-or, black-and-white categories. Take Katie, for example. She seems to always have a foot just inside a panic attack, especially since she's started dating Jimmy. Her relationship style leans more toward the ambivalent category, so she is especially sensitive to signs of rejection. She perceives any sign of disinterest from Jimmy, even a yawn at midnight, as rejection. When anxiety and anger kick in, Katie's thinking becomes more rigid. She starts pressuring Jimmy for more attention, which may lead him to become irritated and to withdraw. This only intensifies Katie's fears, so she turns up the heat. And the cycle continues.

Jumping to conclusions happens when we act like we can read other people's minds. For example, listen as Susan talks about her very close friend Mandy: "I know Mandy hates me. She never wants to talk to me again. And you know what? I think she's crossed the line this time. She's really hurt me."

"What happened?"

"I just had an argument with my sister on the phone. Mandy was at my place and getting ready to leave. When I hung up the phone on my sister, I was really steamed—she drives me crazy! Then Mandy says, 'What's up with her?' I told Mandy, 'I don't want to talk about it right now.' She shot back, 'Fine! I have to go anyway.'"

"Susan," we said, "help us understand what about that conversation upset you so much that you feel like Mandy has 'crossed the line.'"

"She was basically saying, 'I hate your guts. I never want to talk to you again. You're stupid, and I don't want to hear about your problems ever again.'"

"What do you mean she basically said, 'I hate your guts, and I never want to talk to you again'? Did she actually say this?"

"No, but she might as well have. It hurt all the same."

Susan was mind-reading. Why? Partly because of her past. Susan has been rejected and disappointed by people who have treated her like they didn't care, like they really didn't want to hear about her problems. Plus, she had just broken off an emotional conversation with her sister, so she was already feeling rejected. Seeing Mandy as mean-spirited and rejecting fit Susan's mood at the moment. Notice how she concluded that Mandy didn't care about her problems even though Mandy asked what was upsetting her. First Susan selectively ignored this, and then she wrote it off as, "She didn't really care. She was just trying to make me feel like she cared."

Another type of jumping to conclusions is called fortune-telling.[4] We do this when we assume the worst and make negative forecasts about how people will behave. The result is relational paralysis: we stop working on relationships because we are convinced they will never work out.

As we met with Susan, we helped her see that perhaps Mandy didn't really mean anything negative by her terse comment, "Fine. I have to go anyway." She may, in fact, have been a little angry because *she* felt her helping hand was being rejected. We tried to get Susan to go to Mandy and patch things up, but Susan was convinced that Mandy would criticize and reject her: "There is no use in trying. She'll just throw it back in my face that I'm too sensitive. I'm sure she's written me off now that I haven't talked with her for a couple of weeks."

Susan's fortune-telling was keeping her stuck in a state of turmoil. She was convinced that her past experiences would repeat themselves. Unfortunately, she was playing an important role in these repeats of earlier rejection. She was convinced, for instance, that Mandy had completely rejected her, but her belief was based on faulty perception, not reality. And because Susan had convinced herself that the conflict couldn't be worked out, she wouldn't even try to reconcile with Mandy. Nor would she consider information about relationships that might disprove her old set of relationship rules *(I can't count on others. They believe I'm fundamentally flawed. They will always let me down.)* Thus she had created in the present an exact replica of the past. And in the future she will undoubtedly use her experience with Mandy as yet another example of how people have let her down.

EMOTIONAL ATTITUDES

Another type of thinking that can intensify negative emotions is rooted in the basic assumptions we have about our feelings. We call this our *emotional attitude.*

As we noted earlier, some people have very negative attitudes about negative feelings. Remember Joe? He considered sadness, for example, as a sign of weakness. So when he felt sad, he became self-critical: *What's wrong with me? I need to toughen up. If I let myself get down, I'll never get back up. People shouldn't wallow in their problems; they need to pull themselves up by their bootstraps.* Criticizing himself for feeling sad eventually led him to feel an out-of-control anger. When he almost lost his job and his marriage, he tried to bury the anger, which led to panic attacks. And for a man like Joe, anxiety was the ultimate sign of weakness, so next he heaped guilt and shame onto himself. Then depression set in. Joe's emotional attitudes got him into deep trouble.

Are you like Joe? How do you feel about your feelings? Do you think negative emotions in yourself or in others are unacceptable? To what degree? Since emotions are as basic to our existence as hunger, thirst, and the need for air, it would be calamitous for us to deny them or, worse, to flog ourselves for having them. Learn from people with anorexia who criticize themselves for getting hungry and tell themselves they are weak if they give in and eat what others consider a normal meal. For anorexics, the result is physical deterioration. Likewise, cutting yourself off from your primary emotions will lead to an emaciated emotional and spiritual self.

Other people, however, may confuse their secondary emotional reactions with primary ones. These secondary emotions are the ones we want to help you target and eliminate. And, paradoxically, the best way to rid yourself of secondary emotions is to face your primary ones. As Carl Jung pointed out, the source of all unnecessary emotional pain is the avoidance of legitimate emotional pain. But people trapped in emotional storms can't see that the way out involves identifying, accessing, and working through their primary emotions.

SIX STEPS TOWARD CALMING YOUR EMOTIONAL STORMS

Learning to recognize and eliminate secondary emotions so that you can deal with primary, healthy emotions requires hard work, and we believe that four elements are necessary: a desire to change (*vision*), a commitment to see the process through (*intentionality*), a healthy investment of time, determination, and effort (the *means*), and, finally, *courage*. It's not easy to loose yourself from experiences that have been deeply ingrained in you, but God will supply the grace and the power for that to happen.[5]

Below we will describe a six-step process we teach our clients to help them learn to calm their emotional storms. The goal is not only to teach you to calm your intense, out-of-control, destructive feelings but also to help you transform the way you *look* at your feelings. Instead of making them your enemy or having them as your master, you can make them your servants.

Step One: Identify the Primary Feeling

As we discussed above, primary feelings are designed to help you resolve problems. For example, Phyllis came to see us because she was feeling so much anger when she was around her children. She was always irritable and grumpy when her kids were playing and having fun. As we talked about this more, we learned that she was actually filled with fear. About a year before, her son had been happily riding his bike—and crashed right in front of her. He'd had a helmet on, but he'd still required several stitches in his mouth. Since then Phyllis had been on edge, always on guard, afraid that one of her kids would get hurt while they were playing.

A key first step for Phyllis was to see that her anger was a secondary emotion and that her fear was primary. Her son's accident had shattered her assumption that being a careful, watchful mother could *always* keep bad things from happening to her children. She was now afraid that something else could happen and that she would have to stand by helplessly and watch it happen—just like the bike accident. Her fear was understandable, but she had resisted this emotion and replaced it with anger, which made her feel more powerful. Unfortunately, the anger was a wedge between her and her children. "My kids can't stand to be around me," she said. "But I can't help it. I don't know what's wrong with me."

We helped Phyllis access the primary fear she had of her children being seriously hurt or killed. We also helped her realize that this fear was based on a very healthy longing or desire: that her children be safe from harm's way. Any good mother desires this, and it showed that she cared about her kids and their safety. This perspective helped Phyllis validate her more primary emotion of fear.

Step Two: Connect Primary Emotion to a Triggering Situation

We've looked at different situations that trigger strong emotions. When those strong emotions come—when you feel rage, fear, and anxiety, among others—first label them appropriately. Then identify what triggered them. Were you cut off on the highway? Did your spouse try to mother you? What happened? Here are tips on what kinds of events trigger which emotions:

- Anger springs from situations where you've been wronged or mistreated. You're not being treated fairly, and you focus incessantly on that, replaying the event in your mind over and over again.

- Fear surfaces when you or someone you love is in danger. The danger can be physical (fear of getting killed in a car accident or having a heart attack) or emotional (being criticized, ridiculed, or abandoned).

- Sadness is connected to the loss of someone (a loved one or a close friend) or something (a dream or, in the case of failure, a part of the self).

Step Three: Target Negative Thinking

We've described how negative thinking can intensify negative moods, and that's one reason why it's important to tell ourselves the truth. As Paul said, "Whatever is true, whatever is noble, whatever is right, whatever is pure, whatever is lovely, whatever is admirable—if anything is excellent or praiseworthy—think about such things" (Philippians 4:8).

Take Paul's advice to heart. Whenever you catch yourself in the act of negative self-talk, you've taken the first step toward repairing your destructive thinking pattern. The process usually involves three more steps.

1. Now that you've caught yourself, ask yourself, *What am I telling myself about my situation that is not true or accurate?* Be brutally honest in your response. Blaming someone else for your own inability to do what needs to be done does you no good.

2. Find a new way to look at the situation, a way based more on truth than on emotion.

3. Practice looking at the world from the new perspective. Test the new belief.

Susan, for example, could have told herself, *Okay, maybe Mandy doesn't hate me. It is possible that I read something into the situation.* Then, to solidify this new perspective, Susan would have to test it. She'd have to talk to Mandy: "I'm sorry about the other day. I just felt like you weren't interested in me." Mandy would then have the opportunity to share her perspective and, ideally, help Susan see how she had injected past experiences into the present.

Another possibility for Susan would be stepping outside of her own feelings and putting herself in Mandy's shoes for a moment. Perhaps Mandy had also felt rejected, as we suggested before. Susan could go to her and say, "I want to apologize. I'd just gotten off a difficult call with my sister. I was angry, and I think I took some of it out on you. Talk to me."

Step Four: Behave Differently

Although many counselors believe lasting change only comes by working from the inside out, we're suggesting a complementary method—changing from the outside in. Let's explore this method for a moment.

People who fear criticism—and that could be you—often avoid social settings. To facilitate change, we suggest you go into a social situation like the company picnic or a friend's party. Each time you take a social risk—say hello to someone, ask a question, strike up a conversation—your anxiety will diminish a bit. When you throw yourself into social situations you're afraid of, when you challenge yourself to open up and take part, you help yourself learn that people are warmer and more supportive than you expect. And if you do happen to meet a cold fish, the world keeps turning and you survive unscathed. Just consider being a cold fish the cold fish's problem—because it is—and keep going.

This approach works for other changes as well, so seek out whatever triggers your unwanted behavior. Do exactly the opposite of what you feel. Sure, doing so takes courage, but change has never been for the faint of heart. Each time you assault your fears, your anxiety, or your sadness, your action generates new information that can help you revise your negative thinking patterns.

Now for a surefire way to launch yourself out of depression: get busy. Get your head and body moving. And that's not at all what we want to do when we plunge into depression's depths. Instead we sit. We stare at the tube. We perfect the art of procrastination. We disengage. We may not get dressed, brush our teeth, shave, or put on makeup. The more we do nothing, the more time we have to stew about whatever threw us into the hole in the first place. As we often say, the sofa is the greenhouse of depression. But when we get up and get going, the adrenaline starts pumping, our brains start looking around for better ways to do whatever we're doing, and our depression fades. It may happen slowly at first, but when we're persistent, it'll eventually fade away.

As we get up and get going, our activities just may lead us to cross paths with others, and those folks can help us laugh and enjoy life again. And if you happen to do something good for yourself while you're out and about, that can further help change your negative, self-defeating thoughts. Finally, if while you're doing something good for yourself you manage to extend that kindness to others—well, nothing attacks depression better than a "thank you" from someone.

Maybe you see why, when we work with folks who are depressed, we begin by getting them active.[6] We help them plan small activities (taking a fifteen-minute walk, putting the dishes into the dishwasher, vacuuming the living room, etc.) for every day of the week. The more things they do, the more positive they feel and the more positively they see themselves. And the emotions start spiraling upward. The better they feel, the more they feel like working, and the work we have them do helps them deal with some of their fundamental relationship issues, which may have triggered the depression in the first place. The more they feel positive about the work they've done and the more good feelings that have resulted from that work, the more work they want to do. Depression soon becomes an unwanted memory.

Step Five: Use Problem-Solving Techniques

Our negative moods can cause us to feel helpless and make us feel like there's nothing we can do to change the bad situation we're mired in. And the more passive we become, the more hopeless we feel. Nothing gives us a greater sense of being able to deal with our environment or our situations than working to solve the problem. But sometimes our relationship styles keep us from doing that.

Those with an avoidant style often just want to detour around their problems, especially those involving close relationships. As a result, their problems only mount. Those with an ambivalent style become so overwhelmed with emotion that they believe problem-solving techniques just won't help, and they become absolutely passive. The trick for people in both these groups is to look at the situation they're in, possibly define a problem that's a workable chunk, and then devise a plan that will solve the problem or at least make the situation more manageable. When we come up with such a plan, we put depression and hopelessness on notice: *We're taking control, God willing, and we're going to climb out of this hole.*

We want to introduce you to Amy, one of our clients, and how she might use problem-solving techniques in her life. Amy's attachment style is ambivalent, so instinctively she fears rejection and clings to those close to her whom she thinks might be getting ready to bolt on her. Her husband doesn't like being smothered, so when she does cling to him, he withdraws into a project at work. The deeper he buries himself, the angrier she feels because of his rejection. She feels abandoned and helpless to do anything about it, which makes her feel even angrier. She cries out, "I know he loves work more than me. He always has. And there's nothing I can do about it." Really? Let's take a look.

First, Amy could stop saying there's nothing she can do about it. There *was* something, but we knew she was afraid to try anything because she didn't want to be rejected again. So we suggested that she first go to the Lord and ask for courage. *Pray*, we said. *Ask God the Father, through the work of His Holy Spirit, to help you realize that you have power in this situation.* We also encouraged Amy to ask God for wisdom.

The next step for Amy was identifying the problem. We told her to ask herself, *What is really bothering me? Why is it a problem?* This step seemed easy for Amy. She quickly answered, "He works all the time." People with ambivalent relationship styles use "always" and "never" phrases to get themselves off the hook. You see, those phrases make the problem unsolvable. We couldn't accept her answer.

So we asked Amy to restate the problem more honestly in a way that might be a little riskier. "He doesn't want to spend any time with me," she said. That was better. Then we suggested that she come up with some possible solutions. *Be creative here*, we nudged. Amy's first response was that she had already tried everything, but of course she hadn't. In fact, she'd avoided a whole set of possibilities—and for good reason. She was afraid.

All of Amy's responses so far had come from that fearful part of her, that part that wanted to grab on to her husband and not let him leave, that part that approached him with angry negatives and with sharp criticism, a paradoxical but common strategy for ambivalents. Now Amy had to explore that part of herself that needed the courage she had just prayed for. Well, by God's grace, Amy *did* gather up her courage, and we were proud of her. She asked hubby for a date—and he said yes! She lined up a baby-sitter and planned the entire evening. She put all her irritation about his work schedule aside and chose to have a good time with him.

But she also took another important step. Even though it had become Amy's enemy, that project at work was important to her husband. Getting it done right and on schedule would mean kudos at work, maybe a raise later, and certainly a more agreeable and satisfied husband at home. So Amy decided to support him in his effort. During their evening out, she told him, "I know I haven't supported your work on the project as much as I could. In fact, I know I've been more a hindrance than a help. I want to apologize, and I want you to know that you can take all the time you need to make sure you get it done on time. And if I can arrange things at home to make working there easier and more pleasant for you, I'll do it."

Her husband was openly appreciative. Then, over the next few weeks of the project's duration, Amy followed through. She knew her husband loved sun-brewed tea, so she made sure he had a good supply of it as he worked in his home office, and she made sure his area was clean and quiet. And to her delight, before the project was over, he was working in the living room with her. Occasionally he even stopped work and made Amy the hot herbal tea *she* liked.

Next came one of the most important steps in any problem-solving process: checking the results. We instructed Amy to ask herself these questions: *Did my plan work at all? Could it work better? What should I change?* When she assessed the results, she could make changes and work the new plan.

Amy was overjoyed with the results. Her hubby seemed more willing to spend time with her, and he was actually behaving more warmly. She loved it when he made her tea. But there were still times when her negative instincts took over. What should she do when that happened? Set about solving the new problem. Starting with prayer, she would work her way through the steps again and come to a solution.

Amy also brought her husband in on the process. She told him about the emotional work she was doing and why she was doing it. Then she told him that if she ever reverted back to her old habits, he was to call her on it, maybe saying something like, "Honey, I don't like the criticism. I think you're getting angry, and there's no reason to."

Something wonderful happened when Amy did this. Her husband began to search his own behavior and see how his busyness had stirred up Amy's negative feelings. He saw that she lashed out because she was angry about his distance. So he moved toward her, not away. He learned to slow down and listen to her. Now they work together to make their marriage stronger.

Step Six: Plug in to Healthy Relationships

To truly deal with our heart-level emotions, we have to seek out close, support-ive relationships that allow us to take risks and grow. The preceding five steps are key to taming emotional storms, but they don't take you all the way. You need healthy relationships.

Relationships can be a means of healing and transformation. That's why you've just *gotta* muster the courage to risk plugging in to relationships—including already established relationships. You fathers may need to plug in to your rela-tionship with your children. You wives may need to plug in to your relationship with your husband.

It's time to break free of what has come to be the acceptable level of pain in relationships that are bringing more grief than joy. It's time to choose a differ-ent way of relating even though the prospect may be a little frightening. It's time to have loving, lasting relationships with those we hold dearest. It's time for a new way to live.

10
LOVE, SEX, AND MARRIAGE

Working Out Our Most Intimate Relationship
WITH SHARON HART MORRIS, PH.D.

*Therefore shall a man leave his father and his mother, and
shall cleave unto his wife and they shall be one flesh.*
—GENESIS 2:24 KJV

I (Tim) was a graduate student doing one of my first counseling sessions, and
it wasn't going all that well. Tom and Cindy, a couple in their twenties, sat on
the sofa opposite me talking over some pretty weighty relational matters, and
they were getting tenser by the second. Jaws were tightening, eyes were narrow-
ing, and phrases were getting shorter and penetrating like bullets. Suddenly
Cindy reached her limit. She stood up and screamed at Tom, "All I've ever
wanted is for someone to love me. Is there anything wrong with that?" Then she
ran from the room.

Tom immediately looked at me—and I looked at him. His eyes grew wide.
For the first time ever, he had *heard* her; he could see what was happening.

"If you love her," I said, "go get her."

MADE FOR CONNECTION

Remember Adam wandering around the Garden of Eden by himself? Well,
God saw that it wasn't good for man to be alone. So He caused a deep sleep to

175

fall on Adam, and He created Eve from Adam's flesh and bone to be his companion and helper. Clearly, God designed us for intimacy. In fact, He created us for the most intimate of intimacy, to be united with our spouse as one flesh.

Since we were created for such a relationship, God lodged the longing for it in our hearts. When we are free of the external and internal influences that cloud our true desires and drive us to become islands, we realize that we truly crave to be seen, known, understood, and valued. We want to have someone kiss our face, hold us close, and make us feel cared for. In a word, we—like Cindy—want to be *loved*. It's the dream of every bride and the hope of every groom.

But I Don't Feel Connected

Yes, feeling loved is the dream and hope of everyone who says, "I do," but married couples don't always feel close and connected. Every marriage, to varying degrees, will go through low periods—times when we don't always feel respected or cared for by our spouses. Since each of us has our own share of human frailties, we husbands and wives intentionally and, more often, unintentionally cause one another pain. And this happens whether or not we have a secure relationship style.

On your wedding day, when your love for one another was vast and immeasurable, you gazed into one another's eyes and undoubtedly saw love and acceptance for who you are. Neither of you imagined a marriage of strife and emptiness, but if you are like most people, your marriage hasn't been everything you'd hoped. You've discovered that you two are very different in many and often irritating ways, and your spouse hasn't always been thoughtful or emotionally accessible.

You probably haven't been all that emotionally accessible either. You haven't always been as kind and considerate as you could have been either. Through the years, you've hurt each other. You've disappointed each other, let each other down, stepped on each other's feelings, and occasionally, when trying to protect your heart, lashed out and said things you later regretted. You've long wanted your mate to understand you and all those hurts you've felt, but there's little time to talk. And when you do talk, you end up criticizing one another and defending yourselves, and you leave the room feeling judged and overwhelmed. And when you *do* leave that room, you both feel painful resentment and fear that all the love and acceptance you once felt have met the same fate as the *Titanic*.

So—what causes all this trouble and friction in marriage? Some people blame it on things like crowded schedules, money pressures, communication problems, and midlife crises. Others target differences. She might be gregarious, he might be thoughtful; he might be plagued by fears, she might boldly push the envelope. They might have differing political opinions or biblical priorities. Every one of these differences—and more—can spark an argument, and every one can bring trouble and friction to a marriage.

Difficulties in marriage also arise out of unresolved relational hurts. Arguments and misunderstandings flare up and die, but you never deal with the issues that caused all the flames in the first place. Then as the battles rage, those battles and the wounds they cause become issues in themselves, seriously marring the marital landscape. When you feel hurt and your feelings go unnoticed, your wounds—many of which probably started out as paper cuts—become deep and raw and produce pain that just doesn't go away. People can't live like that for long.

As emotional pain becomes unbearable, both spouses will try various fixes. A wife might try to repair the hurts by pointing out all that's wrong with her husband. Her intentions are pure; she hopes hubby will see his faults and change. A husband generally defends himself and then points out his wife's faults, hoping, as she did, to promote change. Usually their hope is in vain. In fact, these failed attempts to draw each other closer usually cause the spouses to push each other even further away. The wife becomes hurt and angry; the husband, frustrated and resentful.

Eventually, when the unresolved pain becomes absolutely unbearable and any hope of reconciliation dies, each spouse emotionally disconnects: "He/she just doesn't know me. We just can't talk about the deep emotional stuff. He/she isn't able to understand me—and hasn't for a long time. No matter what I do, it doesn't make a difference. I'm always walking on eggshells. It's best just not to care." The two are left empty, exhausted, and feeling very far apart.

THE KEY TO A LOVING, LASTING MARRIAGE:
STAYING EMOTIONALLY CONNECTED

When spouses no longer feel safe, secure, or significant, or—even worse—when they become emotionally bruised, even bloodied, and can see only more wounds in the future, they distance themselves from the threat. They quite reasonably decide, *You go your way, and I'll go mine. Take all the shots you want. They'll never hurt me again* (but they do). *I'm far away. They'll all fall short of their mark.*

Now emotionally disconnected, the two unite only around chores or family matters. They may live side by side and sleep side by side, but they're definitely separate individuals, each seeing the other as part of the problem with the marriage. But they don't *want* to be disconnected. They want to once again be as they were in the beginning: "You used to be so understanding, so tender." As their emotional separation grows, one spouse usually expresses anger while the other just shuts down. Both stay guarded and protective—and not at all connected to the other. What exactly causes this kind of fatal damage?

It's not differences between spouses (she's a night person; he shines in the morning). It's not the battles they engage in either. Interestingly, studies show that it is not *what* couples fight about or the fact that they *do* fight that threatens the marriage. (Actually, what couples argue about at the beginning of their marriage they usually argue about for the duration.[1]) The key to the success and longevity of marriages is not *if* but *how* couples fight. The crucial factor is being able to remain emotionally connected during and after their fights. In fact, a recent study showed that couples who perceived their spouses to be emotionally available, accessible, and responsive reported having happier and healthier marriages.[2]

Worth Fighting For

Before we write another word, we need to say that your marriage, no matter how difficult it's been, is *not* beyond the reach of God. He *can* turn your marriage around. Or, if your marriage isn't on life support, He can provide a tune-up. Whatever the current state of your marriage, we believe that you can strengthen your love by applying the principles outlined in this chapter. So we encourage you to step back from—not out of—your marriage and work to rebuild your relationship on a different, much firmer, foundation. As we've said, no marriage is beyond God's healing hand.

And God's healing can bring a marriage in which both of you are seen, understood, and loved by the other within a nurturing, secure bond that allows your hearts to turn passionately toward each other as your marriage finds new life. Fostering such a close, deep, and secure connection with one's spouse is a process that can take a lifetime. So hang in there. Don't lose heart. Some of the healthiest marriages we know have weathered some pretty severe storms.

THE RELATIONSHIP STYLE'S IMPACT ON THE MARRIAGE

As you might guess at this point in the book, marriage is governed by a curiously strict set of relationship rules that sprout from our experiences with parents, caregivers, and those closest to us as we grow. Together, these rules shape how we view ourselves and our own worth as well as whether or not we see relationships as safe. This web of rules and ways of being that arise from our past connections with people forms a relationship style. This style is strongly formed as we're nurtured, or not nurtured, by our caregivers and then shaped by our relationships over the course of a lifetime.

You bring into your marriage certain ways of viewing yourself, the ability of others to love you, and the safety of the world around you. This set of beliefs informs you how safe it is to trust your partner with yourself. This style, which began to develop when you were young, comes to life each day as you relate to your spouse. Looking at your marriage through the lenses of the different relationship styles can help you make sense of your own reactions as well as the reactions of your spouse. And you may finally realize that your partner is not out to get you, is not weird, and is not just too bizarre to be understood.

Five Key Aspects of the Marriage Bond

What is it about a marriage that accentuates the impact of a person's relationship style? To help answer that question, let's look at what sets marriage apart from other close relationships.

First, spouses *seek out* their partners for comfort and closeness. Their hearts ask each other, *Will you be there for me when I reach for you? Will you be emotionally as well as physically accessible when I need you?*

Second, when our partners respond with sensitivity and care, they become *safe havens* to which we can turn for comfort and love.

Third, the relationship then serves as a *secure base* from which we can enter the world with assurance and confidence and to which we return at the end of the day knowing that we'll be understood and cared for.

The fourth aspect of the marriage bond is that *when the bond is threatened or when we perceive that our partner is not there for us, fear and anxiety are triggered, and the fighting begins.* These behaviors, even the arguing, are aimed at restoring the bond, retrieving our spouse's attention, repairing the disconnection, and restoring closeness.

Fifth, after failed attempts to restore or reestablish the bond, *the loss of the connection causes grief, sorrow, and, finally, an emotional disconnection.* It's not a peaceful or joyous disconnection but rather one that guards a spouse's deep emotional being. All the while, the spouses are yearning for reconnection, for "someone to love me."

The Secure Relationship Style in Marriage

In relationships based on a secure bond, spouses have a reasonably confident assurance that the other spouse will be there for them no matter what. They ascribe the best motives to each other and are able to place any misunderstandings, forgetfulness, and disappointments in a positive, or at least a neutral, context as they interpret their mates' intentions in light of who they know those persons are. They shake off sarcasm and even hurtful remarks, and they are honest and open when they are disappointed. After a hurt, they might say to themselves, *Oh, he's just tired and has had a long day. Sure, he's grumpy, but I know he doesn't mean it. I'll let him know that his mood is hurtful, but I'm confident that he has my best interest at heart.*

Sometimes the hurts are very real, of course. But people with a secure relationship style are better able to tolerate them, and after a fight, they bounce back and emotionally reconnect. In fact, they often catch themselves mid-fight and admit, "I really don't want to be doing this. What I said was unkind, and I'm sorry." Then, instead of leaving the room with the hurt still alive and well, they usually take their apology to the next level. They wrap their arms around each other and restore the intimacy to their relationship.

The Ambivalent and Disorganized Relationship Styles in Marriage

Persons with an *ambivalent style* vacillate between being drawn to relationships and fearing being hurt by them. These people perceive themselves as not all that lovable and find it hard to believe their spouses will love them as they want to be loved. They have every confidence that if presented with someone worthy of being loved, their spouses would gladly oblige. They just don't perceive *themselves* as being lovable or worthy. These partners fear that if their spouses really knew them, they would just up and leave. Terrified of being found unworthy and even more terrified of the abandonment that would result, these spouses cling ferociously to their partners and accommodate their partners' every wish. They shy away from making decisions and speaking their own minds, and they desperately aim to please their spouses, but no matter how much they work at the relationship, they usually feel that they've fallen short of winning their spouses' love and attention. In fights they say things like: "I don't know why you married me. I'm just not a good wife to you. I can't do anything right. I wouldn't blame you if you left me for someone else."

In a similar vein, those with a *disorganized relationship style* believe that even if their spouses did love them, the spouses would be unable to meet their needs. They fear that their partners will eventually hurt and disappoint them. They desperately long for closeness, so they pursue and cling to their spouses. But fearing that those spouses will be unable to love them, they suddenly retreat and turn inward for comfort. When all seems well between them and their partners, they come across as warm, understanding, and trusting. But just when closeness looks possible, something threatens the bond and they pull away in fear of being hurt. They have no safe haven, no place to go to feel loved and emotionally safe. Trouble in these marriages elicits an array of emotions ranging from fits of rage to a sense of empty hollowness.

Spouses with disorganized and ambivalent relationship styles are anxious about their marriage. They experience greater stress during marital fights, and arguments stoke up greater anger and hostility toward their partners. After fights, these anxiously attached spouses view their partners less favorably. Disagreements sour their perception of love, commitment, respect, openness, and the supportiveness of their spouses. Since anxiously attached spouses feel unworthy of love, they don't expect emotional support from their partners. They fear they won't have the close connectedness they long for, which, in turn, makes it difficult to trust their spouses to provide comfort and support.

For example, Gregory has the ambivalent relationship style, and he feels and thinks exactly this way. His mother died when he was ten, and afterward his dad was so overcome with grief that he was unable to give Gregory the comfort and support the lad needed. Now, as a husband, Greg longs for a deep, sustained connection with his wife. To that end, he argues for time together but fears she won't really be there for him when they *are* together. He believes his fears are confirmed when her attention wanders away from him toward her hobbies and family.

For instance, when she calls him while he's away on a business trip, before she has said two words, he'll ask if she has called her mother yet. If she says, "Yes, just before I called you," he goes ballistic. "If you really loved me," he crows, "if I was really important to you, you'd have called me first. No matter what I do, your mother will always come first."

Greg sees his wife's actions and reactions through the lens of this belief: *You will eventually not be there for me.* He scans the horizon for incidents that prove she's redirected her attention and interests elsewhere and that she is failing to love him the way he needs. He always questions her intentions and doubts her honesty when she tries to explain. No matter what she says or does, he believes she will eventually fall short and not be there for him.

The Avoidant Relationship Style in Marriage

Spouses who are avoidant, who fear being hurt by others, make absolutely sure they remain self-sufficient and in control. Staying aloof, they avoid intense emotions and dodge any conversation that may elicit strong feelings or any emotional closeness. Their relationship belief is simple: *Nearness means getting disappointed and hurt. It's best to stay disconnected, distant, and disengaged from emotional involvement. Loneliness is better than agony.*

With this belief guiding their thoughts and actions, they keep their hearts in neutral. At night they scan the channels to keep their minds occupied and their hearts unavailable to pain. In an argument, they tend to be more avoidant, colder, and less supportive. Afterward, they don't feel much anger and don't necessarily see their partners less positively. Usually, in order to experience closeness and affirmation, avoidants marry anxiously attached people who frequently search for and cling to their mates. Not knowing what else to do, the avoidant spouses respond by remaining self-contained and regulating their partners' high emotional level.

PURSUE-WITHDRAW:
A PATTERN THAT KEEPS YOU DISCONNECTED

As two people attempt to love one another, their relationship styles and way of dealing with closeness and disconnections can create some powerful and unhealthy relational patterns. The typical pattern of hurting couples is "pursue-withdraw." One spouse, reacting to disconnection in the relationship, pursues the partner. In response, the partner withdraws. This withdrawal keeps the hurt alive and causes the pursuing spouse to pursue further, which causes the withdrawing partner to withdraw more. This pattern doesn't allow either spouse to understand and empathize with the other.

Here's an example: Remember the bad day Ronnie Blaire had back in chapter 4 because of her husband? While she was waiting for her husband to come home from work, her neighbor, Emily, knocked on the back door. Red-faced, fists clenched, she blurted out, "I just can't believe that man!"

Eyes wide, Ronnie asked, "Who? Your husband? Have a seat. I'm waiting for Matt. You'll enjoy the fireworks. I'm one mad lady."

"You don't know what mad is," said Emily angrily. "I'm fuming! And Tom won't get away with it this time. He's definitely going to hear how I feel—loudly and clearly. Why'd I marry him, anyway? We're just too different. And he's clueless. He just doesn't care. That's it, really. He just doesn't care."

"I'm not quite that mad," Ronnie said tentatively. "I mean, I'm mad, but I'm not going to explode or anything. I just want Matt to understand what happened today so he knows how I feel."

"So he can ignore you once more?"

"He won't ignore me. That's the neat thing about him. I mean, if *he* were mad, I'd want to know what I did. And when I'm mad, he wants to know what he did. We each have our perspective on things. He'll think about what's happened. And I bet, when all the dust settles, we'll both work to make things better."

"Is the sky blue in that fairyland you live in?" Emily grunted. "How can you even think everything's going to work out? Eventually it all comes crashing down. And why? Because men just don't have the emotional capacity to understand us women—understand with their hearts. Boy, are you ripe for getting slaughtered. Naive, that's what you are, Ronnie. You're going to end up getting hurt. Hurt bad."

Before she could say another word, Tom's SUV growled to a stop in the driveway. Emily's ears perked, her eyes narrowed, and she stormed out the back door.

Emily greeted her husband with a glacial glare. Tom knew that look—and the next one when her brows made sharp cliffs over those narrow eyes, her cheeks flushed, and her lips puckered and stiffened. She folded her arms defiantly and held her whole body rigid.

Tom knew he was in deep trouble, and he knew from experience that nothing he could say would make any difference. But it wasn't in him to just fold, so he tried to defend himself. Emily let him get a few words out, and then she attacked.

As her accusations became louder and harsher, Tom retreated into his shell. Over the years he'd found this was his best strategy—to shut down until she cooled off. They both knew the cycle: She pursues him, he withdraws, and they skulk around the house in silence for several days. Then something requires them to talk—the dishwasher explodes or a children's event brings them together. So they talk, but nothing about their relationship or Emily's explosion is resolved. And neither feels safe in this pattern of pursue and withdraw.

Emily always has her antenna up to get a read on her connection with Tom, and of course when she senses Tom's protective shield getting into position, she pursues Tom even harder. She's sure he'll stay close to her once he sees her broken heart and her longing to be connected. So, armed with anger, criticism, and contempt, she charges over the hill to decimate what she sees as Tom's indifference. But her effort ends without a gentle reunion of hearts. Instead both of them stay hurt, resentful, and emotionally disconnected. Why? Because instead of becoming vulnerable and sharing their longings and fears, they bludgeon each other with their frustration, misdirected anger, and resentfulness. Had they confronted each other with controlled, purposeful anger and solvable complaints—and had those complaints been aimed at creating an environment in which they felt comfortable sharing their hopes and feelings, their hearts and their empathy—they would have fostered change and emotional connection.

The Emotions That Fuel the Pursue-Withdraw Cycle

Anger is a natural response to finding someone we love unavailable when we need her or want him. When couples have secure relationship patterns, though, their anger is accompanied by the hope of restoration, and anger touched with hope can bring healthy change to a relationship. This anger signals the partner that hurt has occurred, and it is communicated in hopes that change will strengthen the marital bond.

Spouses with secure relationship styles not only *recognize* but also *regulate* their thoughts and emotions, controlling, for example, what they say and how they say it. They also recognize their secondary emotions, such as anger and resentfulness, and dig past them to access deeper primary emotions, such as sadness, hurt, and fear. Judiciously expressing these softer primary emotions usually elicits empathy and connects the spouses more closely. After all, secure people admit their longing and their need to be understood and accommodated, and their secure spouses accurately hear their partners' emotions and generally don't take the complaints personally. They're usually able to face the conflict assured that resolution will come.

On the other hand, couples with ambivalent, disorganized, or avoidant relationship styles are often caught in the pursue-withdraw cycle. They express anger and frustration explosively; they defend and criticize contemptuously. Their secondary emotions, anger and frustration, are vaulted to the primary position and expressed with harsh and accusatory voices. They don't entice their mates to listen, understand, and empathize. Instead, they shield themselves, bury their primary emotions, and drive their partners away. Underpinning these secondary emotions are often the fear of being abandoned, left alone, or disrespected and the fear of being found unworthy or unlovable. But those fears aren't expressed. Instead, anger, disappointment, frustration, and resentfulness are often the only emotions insecure couples share with one another. These emotions keep defenses up, and they cut, rather than establish, healthy emotional connections.

The Stories Behind the Reactions

As we shared earlier, primary emotions are often closely connected to the stories behind the strongest reactions and feelings. Whenever there is an overreaction to a relatively minor incident, pause to look past the reaction and try to discern your spouse's true motivation. What is the story behind the pain that's driving the overreaction? If the reaction is unusually harsh and critical, what primary emotions might be boiling underneath?

Those questions helped Henry figure out his wife, Tracy's, overreaction. Henry came home from work and tossed his sports coat over the back of a chair. Loosening his tie, he gave Tracy a quick peck on the forehead and shared a joke he'd heard at lunch. But Tracy didn't laugh; in fact, her lips remained ruler-straight and tight. She didn't care that Henry was making an effort to reach out and connect. Instead, her abandonment antenna went up. "So, was that pretty little secretary of yours at lunch with you? Was that *her* joke?"

Henry rolled his eyes and sighed wearily. Anyone with any sensitivity at all could see his heart take in the welcome mat for the evening. But Tracy didn't care a whit about his welcome mat. In her mind it was welcoming the wrong people, so she kept pushing and probing for evidence that would confirm her fear that Henry would eventually leave her.

Tracy had overreacted, a signal that something bigger was going on. That was Henry's cue to look for the story behind her overreaction. When he did, he discovered that Tracy was deeply bothered by his friendships with other women because, when she was growing up, her father had often cheated on her mother. His infidelity had devastated her mother and ruined many special times between Tracy and her mother, times that began happily but ended in tears over her husband's betrayal. Also, consumed with his affairs, Tracy's father often stood her up when they had scheduled father-daughter times. These betrayals left Tracy, like her mother, distrustful to the core.

Realizing Tracy's sensitivity, Henry now monitors his behavior. Whenever he can, he avoids even the slightest appearance that he might be straying. And when a situation inadvertently occurs that might be so construed, he lays himself open for any questions Tracy might have and, without protest, proves his innocence.

For her part, Tracy recognizes and takes responsibility for her own insecurity. She realizes these feelings aren't Henry's fault, so she does her best to look at every situation through the lens of trust. When she just can't do that, she's open and honest, and she asks questions without being accusatory. Because Henry answers her questions, she has been able to teach herself that she's *not* in emotional danger.

Tracy also reaches out for her husband by sharing core primary emotions rather than criticizing his behavior with anger and contempt. She "owns" her hypersensitivities and makes an effort to absorb Henry's words of assurance. As her trust in him grows, he becomes more willing to both express empathy and further change his behavior. The relationship begins to feel safer, and the connection becomes a place of respect and trust.

Tracy's relationship style begins to shift toward the secure style as she becomes more certain that Henry will be there for her and respond to her needs in a caring way. In response to Tracy's more secure style, Henry no longer hides from his emotions or needs to be self-sufficient. As Tracy proves to be increasingly trustworthy with the feelings Henry shares with her, he allows himself to be more vulnerable, carefully letting her know when she has hurt him. Eventually, instead of recoiling or attacking each other when they are in conflict, they listen, understand, and respond tenderly toward one another. Slowly Henry and Tracy are transforming their marriage into a safe haven.

That's Your Problem, Not Mine

"Okay," you might say, "you're making my point. My spouse's problem started long before I married him. So it's *not* my problem. Why doesn't he just get over it on his own?"

In one sense, you're speaking truth. Perhaps the problems in your marriage are primarily your husband's or your wife's. They spring from relationships that have nothing to do with you. How her parents treated her, for instance, has nothing to do with how you treat her now. So why should you have to work on changing and growing when you're not the one with the problem? Why can't your spouse be the one who does all the changing?

The answer is that, as wives or husbands, we need to consider our mates' lives and their ability to relate healthily with those who are important to them. In fact, Scripture tells us we need to live *for* them (see Ephesians 5:21–33), which makes our spouse's problems our problems. Besides, if we truly are one flesh, how can our spouses have issues reverberating so deeply within them and we *not* consider those same issues our concern? Your job as a Christian partner is to do what you can to bring understanding and healing to your relationship. Which means you're to hold each other in your hearts and listen attentively and gently to the stories behind the hurts and pains. In the safety of our acceptance and empathy, our mates can more aptly correct the misconceptions that produce their fears.

Now, we know you may be asking, *What about God?* And you're right; *you* can't fill what only *He* can fill. But God wants to work *through you* to make your spouse more like Him! That's your role, and it's a big responsibility. When your spouse repeatedly experiences your understanding and your caring responses, both of you will find your relationship styles gravitating toward more secure patterns. And as they do so, a trusting and caring relationship atmosphere will result, and both of you can learn to trust and reciprocate love in a meaningful way.

How to Begin Fostering a Close Connection

So what can you do to foster a close connection with your spouse? How do you get started, and what should you expect as the process continues? We're so glad you asked!

Be Willing to Be the First to Change

"Why should *I* change first?" we hear you ask. "I'm tired of giving and never getting anything back."

Husbands and wives often ask this question the instant we suggest this course of action, and they do so because they know that *change* means *vulnerability*, and *vulnerability* means *risk*. And taking risks is what got them hurt in the first place. We know that. We understand that the last time you put your heart out there, it was stomped on. And now you're thinking that doing it again, loving again, can be downright scary.[3]

So why *should* you risk change? Because *you* are the only one *you* have control over. And because your marriage is too important to simply abandon. The vow you made before God is too binding to let anything—least of all pride, resentfulness, and fear—keep you from making every effort you can to fulfill it. Change can also improve your emotional and even your physical health. But as important as all these reasons are, if your changing first wouldn't help your relationship, the reasons wouldn't matter. But your taking the first steps usually *does* work. And if yours is one of those rare relationships where it doesn't, at least you'll be able to look the Lord right in the eye and tell Him you did your best. So let's look at some of those initial changes you can make that we believe will bring you a closer bond with your spouse.

Pack Away Your Radar System

We all have radar systems, and we use them to protect our hearts. Our radar is always on, always scanning the horizon for signs that our spouses are about to let us down. And whenever a blip appears on the screen indicating that they just don't care—if our spouses aren't being considerate or if they give out one of those telltale sighs—we complain bitterly, criticize their intentions, and attack. Or we simply withdraw.

Those with avoidant relationship styles may nervously scan the horizon for signs of relational warmth heading their way. Perhaps dinner by candlelight?

"If the electricity's working, why candles? And what's that smell? Bug spray?"

"It's my perfume, dear."

"It'd make a good bug spray." Avoidants instantly become defensive or busy. "Which reminds me, I gotta spray for termites in my great-grandfather's wooden leg. It got him through the Civil War. I don't want it to not survive our attic."

Or the avoidants scan the horizon for any behavior that confirms their mates' unreliability. "I can't find the termite spray. I've told you repeatedly to keep that sort of thing on hand. Are you trying to sabotage my inheritance?" Or, to be a little more realistic, "Did you do what I asked you to and mail those bills?"

Those with the ambivalent relationship style scan the horizon for proof that their spouses will abandon them and they'll be left alone. Instead of manufacturing wedges between them and their spouses as the avoidant person does, though, the ambivalent person looks for evidence that wedges are already in there: *He doesn't call on time. She talks with friends more than she talks with me.* These blips appear, and in the mind of the ambivalent perceiver, they undoubtedly represent incoming missiles intent on doing grave harm.

Shut down the radar. Pull the plug, and the instant you find your instincts telling you something you just don't want to hear . . .

- Quiet your heart.

- Allow your intellect to override your instincts and do what you think a secure person would do. If you're avoidant and a warm fuzzy is "incoming," accept it. Enjoy it. If you're an ambivalent and you sense abandonment on the way, choose instead to assume that the best, whatever it is, is about to occur, and react to it positively.

- Disorganized persons drink from both of those cups periodically, so they need to be sure to open their hearts, not retreat, especially in the face of intense emotions. They must also remember that their feelings, especially their anger or fear of rejection, are just temporary even though they may feel like they'll last an eternity.

No matter what's going on, ask yourself, *Are my fears based on fact or on what I think might just possibly be happening?* More often than not, it'll be the latter. And, as we've said before, when you find that you're reacting to a radar blip, choose to react like someone who's secure in his or her relationships.

But now, having made this change and packed away your radar system, so what? As an avoidant person, do you feel you're destined to endure unwanted closeness for the rest of your natural life? Or, if you've always had an ambivalent or disorganized relationship style, are you thinking you'll still end up abandoned? Before you put that radar system on the curb for Goodwill, we want to remind you that your spouse knows whenever you are on radar watch, and to guard against the coming accusations, he or she becomes defensive or withdraws. So your watchfulness is always rewarded. You always find something—incidents, attitudes, tones of voice, omitted information—to confirm your fears and bring your spouse the confrontation he or she had expected. Maybe, as an avoidant, you merely glance at the stack of bills you had asked your mate to mail, and before you can say anything, your spouse fires a salvo. Instead of saying in a calm, matter-of-fact voice, "I was busy today. The bills aren't due until Friday. I'll make sure I send them out tomorrow," your spouse tightens up and lets you have it with, "Oh, don't start that with me. You just don't trust me, do you? Fine! Then *you* mail 'em."

Now that you're trying to change, though, don't blast each other. Instead of hovering over the unmailed envelopes, daring your spouse to respond, just pick them up. "I'll mail these on my way to work tomorrow," you could say. "You're working so hard. Let me take a little of the load." And you mail them on the way to work tomorrow without another word.

There. Wasn't that better?

"I Grace You"

Are you not so sure you can make this kind of change? The secret to making the change is simple: see your spouse as God's son or daughter—someone Jesus loved enough to hang on a Roman cross for.

Your mate is one of God's children, a fellow worker in His kingdom, so he or she is worthy of your respect. Also realize that you, too, are one of God's children and that God has given you to your spouse so He can work through you to accomplish a number of goals. Not the least of which is to help your mate to become more like Jesus. Which means you need to be like Jesus too. And to do that, your behavior needs to exemplify all that is meant by this one word: *grace*. And, simply put, grace means getting—and giving—what we don't deserve.

Grace *heals*. No, we're not forgetting that you have repeatedly been wronged. We understand that you have every right, in a worldly sense, to retaliate or shut down emotionally. But that's not living a relationship in grace. The hallmark of grace is forgiveness, and one aspect of forgiveness is the attitude, *I'm giving up my right to retaliation—my right to hurt you back.* Your spouse has given you every justification for withdrawing or fighting, but you're going to just let it go. You're going to cancel that debt.

But forgiveness is more than just canceling debts. Real forgiveness also includes reestablishing an appropriate relationship. We're not talking about being foolish, but about having enough courage to be vulnerable and take risks. Share those parts of yourself—those risky opinions, those secret feelings—you've locked up.

Be willing to say, "I forgive you. I *grace* you." Say it often. Do it as an act of obedience to God's command—and then watch how it nourishes your relationship.

Accept Offers for Connection from Your Spouse

One researcher found that couples who were happy and stayed happily married were able to accept each other's "bids for connection."[4] We see this when both spouses are going about their business of living and one of them tosses out a comment, tells a joke, asks a question, or shares an interesting point, and the other responds in a caring way, taking the opportunity to move closer. Distressed couples don't pick up on these bids from their spouses and miss those opportunities to connect.

So when your spouse cracks a joke or tells a story, respond as if it came from your best friend. When you do, you'll see more bids for connection coming your way. Often, being intentional about small ways of connecting can revitalize your marriage and foster a sense of closeness.

Relationship rituals also create a sense of connectedness and safety. They are such gestures as

- Kissing your spouse before you leave for the day

- Seeking out your spouse when you come home from work to give him or her a warm smile

- Sharing a joke of the day

- Connecting for a fifteen-minute recap of the day over dinner each night

- Holding each other close (kissing allowed—and encouraged!) for five minutes before falling asleep

- Scheduling regular date nights

Don't let yourself get too busy or be too tired to do things like this regularly!

Pray Together

Review what we discussed about God and you in chapter 8. The information there can help you create a closer, more loving connection in your marital relationship. Now we want to place an added emphasis on prayer.

Prayer demands vulnerability, and that's one reason why it is so hard to pray together. But do it anyway—not only because it's a meaningful spiritual discipline but also because it has a powerful impact on your connection to your spouse. Prayer softens your hearts, turns your focus toward God, and makes each of you more willing to be refined by God's gracious touch. It produces a powerful spiritual life with Christ in each of you and brings that life into the marital relationship. And that truly strengthens the husband-wife bond.

Claim the Connection You Were Created For

When difficulties arise—and they do in every marriage—couples too often become emotionally disconnected. The disconnection raises the fear they will never be able to emotionally reconnect, so they divorce. In many cases, we look at the situation and think, *Oh, if only they had stuck with it a little longer!*

So we urge you to remember that all marriages have seasons, times when connection is easy and times when it seems impossible. Holding on to your commitment, being dedicated to growth, and working through the disconnected times can result in a richer, sweeter marriage, one that lasts a lifetime.

Also know that retracing your relational history (start with your family of origin), reviewing your marital story, responding to your spouse with empathy, making your relationship a safe haven, and learning to accept love from one another—these steps will set you on a new path of loving and being loved. And that's what God has always wanted for you.

11

Parenting Secure Kids

Deep down inside a child's inner world are a multitude of needs,
questions, hurts, and longings. . . .
The busy, insensitive, preoccupied parent, steamrolling through the
day, misses many a cue and sails right past choice moments
never to be repeated or retrieved.
—Paul Tournier

Cody, a Little League center fielder, stood in the hot afternoon sun while the batter waited anxiously for the next pitch. It came, and a line drive exploded high over the pitcher's head, a line drive that had Cody's name written all over it. But Cody just wasn't ready for it. Everyone—coach, team, and a crowd of gasping parents—watched in horror as he not only missed the ball but stumbled around, confused and disoriented, as if he didn't even know where the ball was. Later, in the dugout, his coach asked him what had happened. Sheepishly, eyes locked on his shuffling shoes, Cody admitted that he just hadn't been paying attention. "I was looking in the stands for my dad. He promised he'd be here."

Here's Lookin' for You, Dad and Mom

Like this little outfielder, all kids want to see their parents in the stands. In fact, they need their parents to be there. Not just for baseball games, soccer tournaments, spelling bees, and Christmas plays, but for evening meals, bedtime books, scrapes on the knees, and to provide warm, comforting arms after bad dreams. Kids want their parents there for the good and bad, the highs and lows, and every moment in between.

When parents are there for their kids, the kids grow up knowing they're loved, and they'll believe that others are available and trustworthy. Finally, and most important, they'll know that God is loving, responsive, and always there for them too.

As an added bonus, when parents are there for the common, everyday interactions with their children, the kids learn how to deal with their emotions and the emotions of others. They learn how to solve social problems and how to focus their efforts on worthwhile, meaningful goals.

We hope we're being clear: parenting is neither for the selfish nor the faint of heart, its responsibilities are staggering, and its rewards are sometimes dubious, at other times heavenly. Above all, we want to say that parenting is a high, if not the highest, godly calling. And one thing is sure: as a parent, you're always having an influence—either good or bad.

Doing What Should Come Naturally

As we talk about parenting in this chapter, our goal is simple—to help you see that, in many ways, the parenting we describe reflects the natural order of things and comes easily to those with secure relationship styles. One parent, who considered but chose not to use a more "cookie-cutter" parenting approach with her newborn daughter, put it this way: "It just doesn't seem right to let my baby cry and cry when she's hungry. She needs me to comfort her now. It can't be healthy to just let her cry and thrash around in her crib at night. She needs me *to help her learn how to calm down.*"

In this chapter we'll show you why that mother is right in following her instincts. We'll walk you through what we call the T-factors—Temperament, Time, Teaching, Touch, and Tenacity—five critical ingredients in parenting, ingredients we hope will become important techniques in your parenting repertoire.

These five behaviors are important not only because they will help develop secure relationship styles in your children but also because you will grow emotionally and spiritually as you use them. But before we get to the T-factors, we want to help you enter into the mind-set of the kind of parenting we're talking about. This mind-set consists of four guiding principles: vision, training your child in the way of love, emotional learning, and sensitivity.

These guidelines are principles that help organize your parenting style. A great advantage of principle-based parenting is that "when you see the 'why' [of what you do as a parent], you are likely to do the 'how.'"[1]

Vision

We must always parent with a vision in mind. The Scriptures tell us, "Where there is no vision, the people perish" (Proverbs 29:18 KJV). Our vision or goal for parenting will organize and direct us even when we're beset by stress and turmoil.

As we've said, parenting is not for the faint of heart. It's stressful at best, and it's not uncommon to feel absolutely lost at times, befuddled, confused, and even betrayed by God. Even with the most well-behaved, easygoing kids experiencing the normal transitions of life—from crawling to walking, from diapers to underpants, from preschool to elementary school, from human to teen (just kidding!), from high school to college, from calm seas to unexpected storms— it's never easy to figure out what kids actually, truly, really need from you. Through all these parenting times, vision helps you stay the course.

A football coach's game plan is an example of vision. It describes, often in undecipherable shorthand, how the coach's team is going to decimate the other team. It details plays, plans, and what-if scenarios. And if something unexpected happens, if a key player is injured or an opposing team member plays the game of his career, there's enough planning and detail in the coach's plan to help him get his team back on track.

Or, if football's not your thing, consider the good teacher. She doesn't just show up for class, hold her finger in the air, and, based on wind direction, decide what to teach. She has a lesson plan. Within that plan is a step-by-step overview of the topic, a breakdown of what each class meeting will cover, the specific homework that'll be assigned, and the teaching aids to be used. She might also list every student's learning style. Clearly, she's ready for just about anything.

But vision has a broader perspective as well. It's not just about what you do in the present moment; it's also asking yourself, *How do I want my kids to remember me when I'm gone?* A college professor from our past had a cozy, book-lined office. We all found that office a fine, quiet place to work—except for one distracting thing: the human skull he kept on the second shelf right above his desk. Why did he keep a human skull where he could always see it? "It helps me remember what's really important" was his answer.

You may not have such a decorative ornament on your mantel reminding you of what's really important. If that's the case, you might try imagining your own funeral. Picture your child being asked to comment honestly about the kind of parent you were. What would you want your child to say?[22] That's the big-picture perspective of what's really important.

Training Your Child in the Way of Love

When the religious zealots of His day asked Jesus which commandment was the most important, Jesus replied, "'Love the Lord your God with all your heart and with all your soul and with all your mind.' This is the first and greatest commandment. And the second is like it: 'Love your neighbor as yourself.' All the Law and the Prophets hang on these two commandments" (Matthew 22:37–40).

Effective parenting prepares children to follow these two commandments. The scripture that says, "Train up a child in the way he should go" (Proverbs 22:6 NKJV) is about laying the foundation for our children to walk in the way of Christ and keep His commandments. And, as Jesus said, the whole law rests on these commandments of love: loving God and loving your neighbor as you love yourself. So training your children is about training them to love and to be loved.

And in the course of helping your children love and be loved, they need to

• Believe they are worthy of love—God's and yours

• Believe relationships are warm, pleasurable, satisfying, and safe

• Believe they can trust others to respond appropriately and promptly to their needs

- Have the ability to regulate and manage their negative emotions

- Have the ability to live within limits

- Have the ability to deal with frustration, loss, and failures and to actually grow stronger from such experiences

- Have the ability to solve social problems effectively, using words rather than aggressive behavior or social withdrawal

We hope these beliefs and abilities will become an integral part of your vision for your children and that you keep them in focus as you deal with your kids. As often as is practical, reflect on how you're relating to them and whether you're making progress toward these seven goals.

Emotional Learning

It's relatively easy to teach kids about truth at an intellectual level during Sunday school class or in a kids' Bible study, but if the lesson is not reinforced during times of emotional intensity, it is probably not learned. Such a situation will reveal whether your child can behave in a balanced, emotionally healthy way when chaos and pressure break out. It's primarily within the volcano of emotional stress where children really learn about themselves and others.

So guard against becoming *re*active and instead be *pro*active parents. And remember that the lessons we want our children to learn are often best taught during times of emotional intensity.

Sensitivity

Sensitive parents are *attuned,* or *keyed in to,* their children's needs—which might be quite different from their children's wants. Then those parents take the next step and *promptly and effectively respond to those needs.* And when they're not intuitive about their children's needs, they take the necessary time and energy to understand them. Also, as best they can, sensitive parents get behind their children's eyes and see the world from their perspectives.

Developmental Awareness

Sensitive parents know that their children's needs change as they develop. A three-month-old infant needs different nurture and support than a one-year-old, and those needs are, in turn, different from what a three-year-old needs. Sensitive parents understand that their children must learn how to do just about everything: how to calm themselves when upset, how to deal with frustration, how to delay gratification, how to handle social conflict, and how to motivate themselves to do what they just don't want to do. Sensitive parents teach their children how to work through and overcome life's challenges.

Creating a Comfortable Child

Sensitivity is about helping your child achieve comfort, whether it's physical, emotional, or spiritual. As one expert explains, "Adult sensitivity is any pattern of behavior that pleases the infant and increases the infant's comfort and reduces its distress."[3]

When a three-month-old is fussy, a sensitive parent helps the child reach a state of comfort. In contrast, insensitive parents ignore the child and let him or her "cry it out." Sensitive parenting assumes that children cry when they are uncomfortable and need soothing. When these parents then respond promptly and appropriately, children learn how to calm down and to believe that their felt needs are considered important. They learn that they're valuable, worthy people and that others are responsive. They grow up believing, *I can trust others to be there for me in times of need.*

Insensitive parenting assumes that fussy children are misbehaving or being manipulative and trying to get their own way. Those parents figure that the best way to eliminate bad behavior is to ignore it or punish it.[4] However, this parenting approach usually backfires. The children don't learn to calm down, and they become extremely vulnerable to negative moods later in life. Moreover, their view of themselves and others is generally negative. They might conclude, "There must be something wrong with me. I'm not worthy of love. And I can't count on others when I need them."

Children raised by insensitive parents are more likely to have behavioral problems, fewer intimate relationships with peers, and a less-than-intimate relationship with a future spouse. They are also more likely to turn for comfort to things—possibly resulting in addictions—rather than to people or, ultimately, to God.

The Zone: Finding Balance

The right combination of support and challenge promotes healthy personality development. That's one reason why we believe good parenting is much like good coaching. A good coach works *with* you to help you build the necessary skills. He or she doesn't assume you possess the skill naturally and then criticize you when you mess up. A good coach supports your efforts and then positively challenges you to do better: "Way to go! Now I'm going to throw the ball a little faster. Make a level swing. That's it. Go *through* the ball."

Insensitive parenting stems from a one-size-fits-all mentality. For example, insensitive parents might require a rigid feeding schedule. Some babies may adjust to this pretty quickly. However, if an infant doesn't eat enough and then gets hungry before the next scheduled feeding, he or she will probably spend some time crying. The insensitive parent may take this opportunity to teach the child natural consequences: if you don't eat, you go hungry. All the infant knows is that he's hungry and no one is feeding him. To him, his parents are unavailable.

What About Spoiling?

But if you respond to every little need children have, aren't you going to end up spoiling them? The answer is "No!" Sensitive parenting is not indulgent parenting. But remember that you're responding to your children's needs, not their wants.

Granted, discerning the difference between needs and wants becomes more difficult as children grow older. But a "dance" eventually develops between the two of you.[5] You become so attuned to your baby's needs, and so able to decipher needs from wants, that you respond naturally. In contrast, insensitive parents ignore intuition and replace it with rigid schedules, time clocks, and calendars. These parents typically lose touch with what their children really need. Over time, confusion over their needs and their wants intensifies, and in the end, both parents and baby become extremely frustrated with each other.

The "spoiling theory" is based on the false assumption that if you are sensitive, warm, and responsive to babies, if you feed them on cue, hold them when they cry, and help provide comfort, you'll cause them to become clingy, dependent, moody, and demanding. Since no one wants that kind of child, the spoiling theorists have worked to replace sensitive parenting with detached parenting. Of course they don't call it this. They even go so far as to use marketing schemes that imply that their detached form of parenting is "wise" and God-endorsed. But we warn you that such detached parenting—replacing babies' feeding cues with rigid schedules, letting babies lie in their cribs for long periods trying to cry themselves to sleep, ignoring babies' cues to be held, and interpreting such cues as manipulative attempts to get attention—is destructive to children.

And this isn't just our opinion. The scientific literature teems with well-designed research studies that show parental insensitivity leads to insecure kids—to clingy, dependent, moody, irritable, demanding, and aggressive children. On the other hand, sensitively raised children become secure and are more independent and emotionally stable. They have better relationships, better academic performance, more obedient behavior, and greater moral sensitivity.

What About the "Hovering Parent"?

People sometimes confuse sensitivity with hovering, but those two approaches to parenting are quite dissimilar. Hovering parents (usually they're moms) confuse their own needs with the babies' needs. Such parents tightly control everything their babies do, from when they feed to how, when, where, and for how long they play. These parents often interfere with what the children are doing and may even snatch them up and move them while they are in the middle of some activity. In essence, a hovering parent is "highly interfering, [having] little respect for her baby as a separate, active, and autonomous person whose wishes and activities have a validity of their own."[6]

Jennifer was a hovering mom, although she wouldn't have called it that. Mildly depressed and very irritable, she complained vigorously to us about her toddler, whom she described as irritable, clingy, and demanding. "Nothing satisfies him," she said, exasperated. "I try everything to please him, but nothing works." Knowing we had to see mother and child together to help her, we invited her to bring Alex, her baby, with her.

We filmed them while they played together on the floor. And as they did, we saw that Jennifer's facial and vocal expressions ignored Alex's expressions. She treated him as if he were merely an extension of herself. She didn't attend to him as a distinct person who had moods, a will, and preferences.

Nowhere were her efforts more visible than when she wanted him to play with blocks. She shoved them right into his face. When he pulled away, she grabbed his hand and tried to make him pick up and stack the blocks. Alex resisted. He had no desire to play with blocks, and the more he fought her, the more Jennifer's frustration mounted.

At one point when Alex turned away from Mom to explore other toys nearby, she said, "Why are you trying to get away from me, Alex?" She grabbed his arm and pulled him onto her lap. "Come, sit in Mommy's lap, and let's play tickle. You always like that."

But Alex resisted and became even fussier. Defeated, Jennifer gave us a look of frustrated helplessness. "See?" she said. "I can't get him to do anything, and nothing makes him happy. Nothing!"

Our stomachs tightened. This was an uncomfortable scene. Although Jennifer thought she and Alex were just having a playtime, she was turning it into a wrestling match as she imposed her will on a reluctant Alex. In subsequent sessions, we went over the film with Jennifer. Seeing herself working with Alex allowed her to be more objective about her intense need for control.

For example, we studied the block-playing section and the time when she pulled him up onto her lap to play tickle. "We know you genuinely want Alex to have fun here, and that's great. But even as young as he is, he's a person, and he wants to do what he wants to do," we explained. "He's not all that excited about being controlled."

We pointed out how Alex had tried to explore other toys and she had stopped him. "Jennifer," we asked, "what did you feel like Alex was trying to do here?"

"I don't know," she answered. "I guess he was trying to go off and do his own thing."

"And then you tried to pull him into your lap for a game of tickle, right?"

"Yeah, I was hoping to get him interested in me."

"What would have happened if you had followed Alex over to those toys and joined in with whatever he was doing?"

"I'm not sure. I guess that would have been fine. But I really didn't want to be chasing him around the room. I wanted to sit there and play a nice quiet game of blocks."

"But what about Alex? What do you think he wanted?"

"Certainly not what I wanted. It's always like that. He drives me crazy!"

It took awhile before Jennifer completely understood. As a controlling, hovering parent, she just couldn't see how her behavior frustrated Alex. The more she controlled, the more he resisted, which led her to control him more. We tried to increase her awareness of Alex's feelings, desires, and intentions, but she still mowed over him like weeds.

We had a breakthrough with Jennifer when we brought up her relationship with her own mother. "One word describes my mom—meddlesome! Actually, two words—meddlesome and interfering. No, three words—meddlesome, interfering, and intrusive. Make that four words—meddlesome, interfering, intrusive, and prying. I couldn't get away from her. I still can't. Her hobby is to tell me how to live my life. She drives me nuts."

We weren't all that surprised. Relationship styles pass from generation to generation like hair color unless they're consciously and intentionally changed (again like hair color). Jennifer and Alex's relationship was the mirror image of Jennifer's relationship with her mother. We finally helped her change her methods with Alex by helping her get in touch with her feelings about her mom's intrusive control.

As we helped Jennifer work through her thoughts and feelings about her mother—no easy task!—we had her bring Alex back in several more times. We filmed each ten- to fifteen-minute play session and reviewed the film with Jennifer afterward. As time went on, she became more sensitive to Alex's feelings and learned to follow his lead. As she did, their playtime became less of a wrestling match. She learned to enjoy motherhood, and by her last session with us, Jennifer had taught us a lot about how parenting styles, whether good or bad, are frequently an extension of how we were parented.

How Your Relationship Style Affects Your Parenting Style

Relationship styles color not only our own lives but also the lives of the most important little people we know: our relationship styles strongly influence how we parent our children. Let's see how.

Parents with Secure Relationship Styles

As we've said, parents with secure relationship styles are more apt to be sensitive to their children's needs. From the minute the baby is born they respond quickly and appropriately to his or her cries for comfort. They know their babies aren't being manipulative or controlling. They just need whatever they need, and their tears merely signal discomfort.

As their children mature, secure parents continue to respond. But even with all this good parenting going on, the kids, like all kids, get upset from time to time. And when they do, secure parents set limits on how the kids express those feelings, and they coach the children on how to ultimately deal with their emotions. Secure parents also understand, and aren't threatened by, their children's need for autonomy. They actually encourage their kids' independence by, among other things, letting the youngsters take controlled risks, like going to a friend's house for the night or going roller-skating with a friend's family. Secure parents want their kids to grow up with a certain sense of independence, but they also remember that their kids are still just children, and they remain available for them in case the going gets a little rough.

Parents with Avoidant Relationship Styles

Parents with insecure relationship styles aren't quite so sensitive. In fact, they might lack sensitivity altogether. For example, parents with an avoidant style are generally annoyed by their babies' bids for comfort. This annoyance often drives them to adopt parenting styles that prematurely encourage independence—and they can let their children cry for hours. Avoidant parents may hold their children only when there's a specific reason to do so, like when they're feeding them or changing diapers; they seldom get pleasure from cuddling and cooing with the little ones.

These avoidant parents may be controlling, especially over how emotions are expressed. And as their children mature, these parents ignore, criticize, and even reject their children's bids for comfort. They typically don't coach their children's emotions—and for good reason! To the avoidants, emotions aren't to be coached; they're to be repressed, or suppressed, but certainly not expressed. Negative feelings aren't allowed at all; happiness is demanded. Around these parents, you've gotta be happy—and keep those negative feelings to yourself.

The children of avoidant parents learn that if they need comfort, they're on their own; they certainly can't count on anyone else to be emotionally responsive. All this stems from the fact that avoidant parents really—and we mean *really*—want their children to be autonomous and independent. And that may be why they don't supply much of a secure base for the kids when the kids are upset and in need of comfort.

Parents with Ambivalent Relationship Styles

As you might expect, parents with ambivalent relationship styles are inconsistent. Sometimes they attend to the little munchkins, and sometimes they're aloof and unavailable. The children learn that, to get Mom's attention, they must be hugely dramatic. Ambivalent parents are also controlling, but not in the same way as avoidant parents. Instead of reining in their children's emotional expressions, ambivalent parents fence in their children's attempts at autonomy and independence. These parents reinforce their kids' neediness and dependence and ignore or even punish their attempts at independence.

Parents with Disorganized Relationship Styles

As we've seen, people with a disorganized relationship style have a lot of unresolved loss or trauma in their lives. As parents, they may reject and control their children's negative emotions like avoidant parents do or, like ambivalent parents, they may be chaotic and fearful when their children behave independently. In either case, their trauma and loss usually intrude on their parenting and lead to times when they explode, intimidating and frightening their children.

Or these parents, particularly the moms, may immerse themselves in abusive relationships where the children might see them being threatened or beaten. In severe cases, disorganized parents may have been abused as children, either by their mothers or fathers. Unfortunately, those who have been abused as children and have deep and unresolved trauma tend to repeat this abuse in some way with their own children.

THE T-FACTORS

We've looked at the mind-sets of sensitive parents, we've discussed how parents' overarching goal should be to train their children to love and be loved, and we've reviewed how relationship styles affect parents' relationships with their children. Now we want to get practical, and the T-factors are designed to help. T-factors are simple concepts you can use to help promote secure relationship patterns in your children, and you probably already use some of these concepts naturally.

If you're not yet a parent, we believe the T-factors will give you a sound parenting framework. If you're already a parent and your children seem happy and well adjusted, the T-factors will help keep you and the kiddos on track. If you and your kids are struggling, the T-factors should help you work your way toward a secure relationship style.

T-Factor One: Temperament

Lori is a labor-and-delivery nurse. She tells us from experience what we all know intuitively—that each child, right from birth, is different. She'll tell you that such differences are subtle but, to the trained eye, observable. As the days and months progress, these differences become more pronounced, reflecting the formulation of the child's individual temperament.

Our temperament comprises the most basic aspects of our personalities. It includes such traits as our activity level, our attention span, our ability to settle into patterns like eating and sleeping, our basic mood quality (whether we're laid-back and easygoing, uptight and tense, or fussy and irritable), our ability to adapt to new situations, and our tendency to stick with difficult projects. Each child is born with a certain temperament, and by a very early age, most children can be classified into one of four categories:

- *Easy kids* are pretty even tempered; they're laid-back. They easily get into feeding and sleeping patterns and adjust well to new situations. Their attention level is good, they're not too bouncy, and their mood is generally positive and stable.

- *Difficult kids* are often grumpy and fussy. They tend to retreat from new situations, and they are hard to get onto a predictable schedule. They are easily distracted, and their activity is often too intense for the situation. Their mood is generally negative.

- *Slow-to-warm-up kids* are less active, and they have difficulty warming up to new situations and people. Their moods are usually negative, especially in those new situations, but when the situation becomes more familiar, they can be more pleasant and engaged.

- *Mixed temperament.* Not all kids fit neatly into one of these three categories. Some have a unique blend of two or three.[7]

Since temperament involves lifelong traits, you may see not only your kids but also yourself in one of these descriptions, and it's important to note how well your temperament matches—or doesn't match—your child's.[8] The more mismatched you are, the more easily difficulties arise.

"Oh no!" you suddenly cry. "My child and I are completely opposite. Now he's doomed to an insecure relationship style."

Not so. Researchers have found that what *really* matters is how well parents adjust to their child's temperament. If you and your children have mismatched temperaments, or if you both have difficult temperaments, you can set behavioral limits and make sure your children always know that you love them. But when parents insist on changing their children's temperament through criticism, punishment, and rejection, problems hover on the horizon like black storm clouds.

Here's a quick example: Terri has a slow-to-warm-up temperament while her five-year-old Jacob has a mixed temperament. Morning finds him leaping out of bed, scrambling downstairs in an upbeat mood, and being a veritable whirlwind of activity. Terri, on the other hand, needs three cups of strong, black coffee and a tomb of silence to get her brain jump-started. As Jacob swirls around her each morning, a whirling dervish of movement and chatter, Terri wants to explode.

But, by God's grace, she manages quite well. She could easily criticize Jacob for being too "wound up," too energetic, too chaotic. But she knows all this activity is just his temperament, just the way he is in the morning. The last thing Jacob wants is to anger Mommy, but he finds it very difficult to be anything but what he is—and Terri doesn't ask him to be. Instead, she accepts him for who he is. She cloaks her words in warmth and kindness, always aware of what her child needs and how he views his world.

T-Factor Two: Time

In case you haven't noticed, parenting requires lots of love, and giving love takes lots of time. That's one reason we tell parents that kids spell love *T-I-M-E.*

Some parents, however, make a distinction between *quality* of time and *quantity* of time. They say, "What kids really need is *quality* time." What they're really saying is, "I don't have much time for my children. But when I do, I want us to have lots of fun."

But important, relationship-defining moments generally don't arrive according to any schedule. They occur when they occur. To actually have quality time with your kids, you have to spend a lot of ordinary time with them, time when you develop trust, learn their language, and come to understand their ways. You have to make an investment. Quality moments with your children happen during many hours of little moments: talking about your children's day—their triumphs and their losses—after school, sharing dinnertime conversation, reading stories at bedtime, getting drinks of water in the middle of the night, and listening to the stories of bad dreams the next morning. Moments like these mean so much to kids, so let every word you say, every cock of your head, every movement of your brow, tell them, *I like you. In fact, I love you. And because I do, I care about every bit of you: curly hair, freckles, and all.*

Bottom line: Kids need *both* high-quality and high-quantity time. They need *you* in healthy doses. Big presents and extravagant escapades pale in comparison to you.

And when we say you need to be there for your kids, it's not enough to be there physically if your mind is a million miles away or if your presence seems more judgmental than supportive. This lesson was brought home to us when a father came to see us with his grown son. The son was working through abandonment issues, and early in the session he told his father, "Dad, you were never really there for me."

Without a heartbeat's hesitation, his dad broadsided him: "That's not true! I went to every baseball game you ever had. I sat in those bleachers, burning under that hot sun. I watched every inning of every game. I even went to most of your practices."

"Yeah," his son responded, "you were there physically, but your head was miles away. You never talked to me about what I was doing—no, that's not true. You gave me a super hard time every time I messed up. But if I did well, you said nothing. And when *I* talked to *you* about the games, your brain was off wallowing in one of your business deals. Dad, I needed you, and you weren't there for me."

The moral of this story isn't all that subtle: listen to your kids when you spend time with them. You may think you can get away with only being physically present, but you can't. Kids know, just as you know when someone you're with is there in body only.

And when all of you is not there, kids conclude that you really don't care about them. They see you there in the stands, talking into your cell phone and pecking away on your Palm Pilot, and they think *I'm not as important to you as other things you do. And since I'm not important to you, my own parent, I must not be important to anyone.*

Of course, there is another side to this coin. Some parents are overly invested in their kids. Parents who were neglected as children might, for example, over-compensate with their own kids. They might feel the need to constantly enter-tain their children. Curiously enough, even though the parents themselves create this situation, it's the parents who eventually feel put upon and begin to resent their children.

Your gifts of time to your children require boundaries, guilt-free bound-aries. You—like all parents—need "down time" away from the kids. You need to have conversations in your own home with your spouse and with other adults without the kids interrupting. Now, the kids won't like this. Their natu-ral tendency is to be the center of all activity, but don't let them interrupt. This time is crucial. If you're going to have the physical and emotional energy for your children, you need time to charge your own batteries with other adults.

So each day make time for just you and your spouse to talk. It's okay for the kids to be there, but tell them they can't interrupt. Stick firmly to this bound-ary. And as they learn to honor this boundary, your time with your spouse will become increasingly meaningful and renewing.

Another battery-charging activity is a good old-fashioned date. Go out to a movie, or a play, or miniature golfing, or bowling, or out on the lake, or wher-ever a good time is to be had, and *have* it—at least twice a month. And while you're out there knocking those pins down or taking in the silver screen, don't talk about the kids. Talk about them during the week, but not during your date night.

Also, make time to take care of yourself. Exercise, read a new book, write in your journal, watch a favorite movie, enjoy a cup of coffee with a friend. Taking a few minutes for yourself can energize you to spend hours of good time with the kids. And if you sense yourself struggling or find yourself losing control, use your away-from-the-kids time to heal—with that book you're reading or that cup of coffee shared with a friend.

Finally, you may be trying very hard to do the right things with your kids, but you just don't seem to know how to do it. Seek help. Don't be bashful; don't be self-conscious. Don't see getting help as a weakness. To know that you need help is actually a strength, and the help you get is an investment—in your kids. And what a worthwhile investment that is.

T-Factor Three: Touch

We were taught in grad school that kids need eleven touches a day, but at least one expert says that a hundred touches a day would be better.[9] We agree! From high fives and wrestling matches to strokes of the hair, squeezes of the hands, and good-night kisses—find ways to touch your kids. Those of you with babies, hold them, gently and lovingly, not just functionally. Snuggle them, rock them, soothe them with soft singing, and, above all, enjoy them. Within the safety and warmth of your arms children learn that relationships are nurturing and secure.

Of course, just like the other factors, the need to touch your children may be hampered by your relationship style. Perhaps you have an avoidant style, and you just don't care much for physical intimacy. If so, holding and nurturing your children will be a challenge. But it's critical to meet this challenge because you as well as your children need to learn the value of touch.

In contrast, those with the ambivalent relationship style may want to touch their kids all the time. If you have an ambivalent style, your need to touch and touch and touch may cause your children to pull away and try to protect their private space. Respect that. Although it may be difficult, moderate how much touch you give them. Remember, physically touching your children should never be a substitute for hugs you ought to be getting from your spouse. Kids don't need to feel responsible for hugging you to make you feel better.

Finally, some children are repulsed by certain kinds of physical touch, and the reason is sensitive skin, not some deep-seated psychological problem. If your children suffer from this malady, attempts to snuggle and comfort them feel like they're being scraped by sandpaper. They naturally shrink away from it. So pay attention to your children's cues and adjust your behavior accordingly.

Search for which type of touch feels good to your children and then touch them in that way every chance you get.

T-Factor Four: Teaching

Deuteronomy 6:6–9 challenges us parents to teach our children God's truth at home, in the car, when you tuck them in at night, and when they wake up in the morning. One reason is that His truth provides safety.

Another one of the most important lessons children need to learn is how to handle negative emotions, not just ignore them or push them aside. Advice like "Just get over it" and comments like "You shouldn't feel that way" do little good. Instead, we need to set limits on how our children behave when they're upset; we need to teach them ways to manage their feelings and solve their problems. When we do this, we create a secure base from which our children can deal with negative emotions, and a host of good things begin to happen.

For example, research shows that kids who have secure relationships with their parents and have learned how to deal with negative emotions form strong, positive relationships with other emotionally healthy kids.[10] These relationships help buffer them from academic, behavioral, and drug problems. We have also seen that kids who can regulate their negative feelings are more open to the gospel and more willing to involve themselves in spiritual activities. After all, most kids act up when they are overwhelmed by anger or depression. If you teach your children how to deal with negative feelings, you will prevent a large percentage of possible behavioral problems.

T-Factor Five: Tenacity

Tenacity is sticking to something; it's remaining persistent in the face of stress. Tenacity is also the unalterable commitment to being a good parent. You may fail at times, and glaringly so, but tenacity brings you back to your vision, your commitment, and your heart-centered longing to see your children grow up healthy and whole.

Tenacity helps create a resilient family structure, one that generates warmth with clear boundaries and realistic and constructive limits. Following these three principles can also help you create a healthy and stable family environment:

1. *Commitment to a healthy belief system.* Help your children learn to grow from adversity. Teach them to see both the positive side of negative events and the potential for growth into stronger persons that those negative events offer. Furthermore, as Christian parents, we can help our children see the world from a "top-down perspective,"[11] to look at situations in light of the kingdom of heaven and to remember that this life is preparation for the life to come. That's the lesson Jesus taught during the Last Supper (see John 13). Sensing His disciples' fear and concern for what was to come—the cross—Jesus spoke the wonderful reassurances recorded in John 14:1–6: Our hope is heaven, God's place of safety—a place where we will be harbored in His love forever.

2. *Setting boundaries.* Boundaries are the rules and roles that form the underlying structure of our families. These rules for behavior need to be firm, but not *too* rigid. Discipline, not punishment, is essential for healthy parenting and enforcing family rules, and discipline must be appropriate, immediate, consistent, and never administered out of anger. Roles are about who does what—who washes the dishes, takes out the garbage, manages the finances, and makes decisions about discipline. When boundaries become blurred, problems result. If, for example, the rule is "Treat one another with respect," but a parent screams irrationally at a child for spilling milk, the inconsistency creates a problem. Kids don't understand how the rule applies: *Why do I have to be respectful and my parents don't?*

Another boundary violation occurs when we expect our kids to meet our emotional needs. This is obvious, for example, when Mom keeps children home from school because she is lonely and depressed. Or the violation can be subtle—a parent not allowing her nine-year-old to verbally express anger or disappointment. One parent we worked with would actually tell her daughter she couldn't express her anger because "it puts me in a bad mood." When we explored this with the parent, she told us that she expected her child to be upbeat all the time. We helped her see that it is a parent's job to help a child learn how to express and cope with negative feelings. This mom was giving her child the message that it was the child's job to take care of her parent's moods.

3. *Open communication.* Family members need to feel comfortable talking with one another—and this means talking about good stuff and difficult stuff. Healthy family communication is honest, clear, and direct, and its goal is understanding one another. Of course family members don't always agree, but they do work to see things from each other's perspective. This effort helps kids learn to empathize with others, and empathy is a building block for living by the Golden Rule.

Open communication also allows each family member to express negative feelings appropriately and facilitates the family's working together to solve problems, whatever their source. If, for example, little Johnny and little Tammy are angry at one another, instead of packing them off to their separate rooms, you sit them down together. Then you help them express their feelings openly but respectfully, identify exactly what the problem is, and come up with some reasonable solutions. Then you try out the solution. If the solution doesn't work, the family goes back to the drawing board.[12]

THE MOST IMPORTANT THING . . . ISN'T A THING

The family represents our core relationships in life. Sadly, much in today's world is working against this God-ordained institution. But one thing is certain—God gave you your child, and He wants to work through you to make that child more like Him. God has a neat plan for each of your kids. Be an instrument of God's love and an agent of hope in your child's life journey and don't provoke him or her to wrath (see Ephesians 6:4 NKJV).

To a sensitive, secure parent, success is that little nose pressed up against the windowpane waiting for you to come home or that smile that comes from center field when your eyes make contact from your seat in the stands.

P.S. Cody's dad *was* there.

12

BREAKING FREE!

A Prescription for Making Changes That Heal

Never give up!
—WINSTON CHURCHILL

Yogi Berra once said, "When you come to a fork in the road, take it."

Well, life has a nasty habit of presenting us with forks in our emotional roads. Actually, they're crossroads, and they present us with some hard choices: either we continue on as before, or we make changes that are sometimes painful and almost always frightening. At these times all the lights can go on, and we can suddenly see things very differently. These fork-in-the-road choices can come suddenly and out of the blue and be completely life changing. Ever been there?

Sam's fork in the road came when his father died, and he realized he'd never made peace with the man. Johnny's came one day when his wife, Julie, screamed, "I'm leaving you! This time for good." Bob was at his crossroads when he awoke one morning with the realization that he didn't know his wife, Maria, who had slept there next to him for years. And Tammy knew she was at a crossroads as she held the gun her young daughter had used to commit suicide.

When these life-changing experiences come, the major choice we face is whether to walk the pathway of healing or the pathway of continuing pain.

Ed was forty-five when he arrived at his crossroads, and he chose to continue on in pain. In need of open-heart surgery to prevent the inevitable, he rejected his wife's and his children's pleas and decided not to have it. A while before, he'd seen his brother, sore and wired back together, right after his open-heart surgery, and Ed had vowed never to subject himself to the same ordeal. Two years later, at forty-seven, Ed died from a massive, preventable heart attack.

The nearer Sally got to her fork in the road, the greater her emotional pain became. Her father had passed away years before, and immediately afterward her invalid mother had demanded every minute of her time. Now her mother had been moved into a nursing home, and for the first time in years, Sally had time to think and feel—and what surfaced was a mixture of guilt and anger. And the more she thought, the more guilt and anger she felt. She wanted to hide, to run somewhere where she wouldn't be reminded of what she saw as her failure.

But then a concerned neighbor told her about Jesus, and Sally immediately understood that His warm, open arms were waiting to comfort her and take her burdens. At that moment, she courageously decided to confront her painful feelings of guilt and failure. Accompanying the neighbor to church, she found a support group for people suffering unresolved loss. Sally began experiencing God's love and comfort as she bathed in Christ's fount of infinite grace.

Have you recently come to a fork in life's road and found yourself stopped dead in your tracks? What do you see as your choices? If you haven't come to one of these life-changing forks in the road, we can pretty much guarantee that you will. And what will your response be? What process could you use to decide how to respond?

When you stand at a crossroads, the first step is—to quote Shakespeare—"Know thyself." Facing the truth about ourselves is a threatening and tough assignment. It's far easier to live in denial and just go on with life as it is. But the first step to knowing which path of life to take is to look honestly at ourselves and at what brought us to where we are. This kind of truth sets the stage for us to be set free—free to know God's peace deep in our souls, free to mature into all that God wants for us, free to embrace all that life holds for us, and free to love and be loved again. That is what this chapter is all about.

Soul Hunger

Many of us have an enormous soul hunger for change right now. Despite our comfortable, abundant lifestyles, we are all too aware of our personal, spiritual poverty. After all, doesn't every one of us hunger for the freedom from our pain and suffering that can come from God's healing touch? Don't we long for the lasting and truly satisfying peace of God to be lovingly poured into our souls by the God of peace? And isn't an intimate relationship with our heavenly Father both the key to contentment whatever our circumstances and the everlasting treasure that never rusts and can never be stolen?

The world's big deception is that we can enjoy freedom, peace, and contentment apart from a personal relationship with God through Jesus Christ. Buying into that lie, we cram our lives with anything and everything we think might give us purpose, value, and meaning: things like money, sex, power, status, shopping, sports, retirement dreams, costly toys, clothes, diamonds, insurance policies and annuities, and friends who sparkle when they walk. And we foolishly believe that these possessions and behaviors mean we're on the right track. Yet those people who don't have a relationship with God and who honestly evaluate their lives when they're at a crossroads often admit how empty, shallow, and purposeless life is.

Sooner or later life trashes our trophies. Sometimes we come to the painful realization that our promotions, big house in the suburbs, speedboat, swimming pool, hot tub, and big-screen TV don't give us what we *really* want; they don't grant us peace, spiritual comfort, or satisfaction.

When wisdom finally takes root in our hearts, we discover that what really matters is who we love and who loves us. You see, eventually we all face tragedy and loss. No one goes untouched. Such loss hits all of us. And when that pain that shakes us to the core comes, we find ourselves at a potentially life-changing crossroads, one that challenges our most fundamental beliefs. Some people invite God into the crisis, and by His grace and resting in His peace, they work through the tough times. Tragically, other people hunker down, cloak themselves in denial, and live in deception, carrying on as if all is well.

So ask yourself the following questions, one or more of which will probably apply to you today: Is it time to prepare myself so that I'll be ready and able to choose the right, the healthy path when tragedy comes my way? Have I been trapped for too long in the pain of my past? Isn't it time to make peace with a past I regret? What choice will I make right now—to heal and truly live or to continue on in pain? Will the path I'm about to choose lead to freedom and renewed life—or will it lead to bitter loneliness and a living death?

These aren't easy questions. So take time to listen for God's still, small voice calling to you. Become aware of His presence beckoning you to a closer relationship with Him. He will be a haven of safety, a sheltered harbor for your heart. Choose Him . . . and you'll be choosing life!

Finding the Freedom to Love and Be Loved

Remember Sam from the beginning of the chapter? He found himself at a crossroads soon after his father died unexpectedly. The entire family was stunned by his death, but it took Sam a little longer to deal with it.

Sam, the eldest son, had recently turned fifty, and he'd had a long history of run-ins with his dad. Their disagreements over the years had run the gamut: Vietnam, drug use, politics, career choices, religious commitments, and, finally, how Sam chose to raise his children. His dad had always held Sam to some pretty high standards of behavior, and Sam had never seemed to measure up. As Sam got older, the emotional wound caused by the antagonism between them grew, and because neither Sam nor his dad initiated the crucial talks necessary to aid healing, the wound festered and became excruciating. One method Sam employed to deal with the pain was to deny that the rift existed; another was to fill his life with possessions and experiences that might eventually soothe the nagging ache of his soul wound.

It wasn't that Sam and his dad never talked. They did—about sports, local business, and hunting; they even went golfing together. But even though they spent hours together on the links, they both adhered to an unspoken but powerful family rule: thou shalt *not* talk about issues that hurt. To bring up any subject that touched their personal wounds, ignited family conflict, or made anyone in the family uncomfortable was just not done. So they pretended that buried feelings of anger and resentment didn't exist. And they fashioned a family myth: if we don't talk about issues, they just go away.

As we said in chapter 7, untold stories are bound to be repeated. And that's what happened to Sam. Determined that his kids would have a different life than he'd had, Sam was devastated when he realized the same rift that had separated him and his dad now separated him from his seventeen-year-old son Jason. And when he tried to reconnect with Jason, he was rebuffed. Jason was just not interested in a father-son relationship. After all, Jason saw his dad as someone who really wasn't in touch with what was happening in his life. Besides, now he had relationships with all the guys at school, relationships energized by all those pressures to look good and act cool. He also had relationships with just about as many girls at school, relationships that required even more attention than those with the guys. To add a desperate father to the "to do" list was just more hassle than this young man wanted to bear.

Sam took stock of Jason's anger and the guilt he felt about his relationship with his son, and he wondered if the two of them would ever be close. As Sam examined this issue, he realized that he had always had trouble with relationships. Not just with his deceased father and closed-off son, but with everyone. Sam came to see that he was intimate with no one and that there wasn't a single person he trusted without hesitation, and he immediately blamed himself. Although he usually made fun of those who went to see counselors, Sam— feeling completely ashamed and worthless—decided to do just that. He was finally going to tell his story, his whole story.

FINDING A NEW LIFE:
A JOURNEY TOWARD HEALING AND HOPE

Today Sam enjoys new intimacy in his relationships. God's love has set him free to experience peace about his dad and to love his son the way he'd always wanted to. Sam's journey to healing involved a journey with God, and we've seen some amazing transformations in him.

And no wonder. The journey we'll describe is designed to bring God-imbued healing into our injured souls and apply it to the wounds in our hearts.

This journey helps us deal with powerful, long-buried feelings from within warm, safe, supportive relationships. And as we process these feelings, we revise our relationship rules, those core beliefs we hold about ourselves and others.

These revised relationship rules replace our old ones so that our new behaviors promote closeness and intimacy. And as we grow closer to one another, we move closer to God and begin to live our faith in new, more courageous ways. We learn to stop hiding; we give up on isolation. Instead we learn to break out of our fantasy world and live totally in the present, in the now—not in the past or future, but right here and right now.[1]

You can take the same journey Sam did. The path has been trod by a great many people over the centuries. Based on our own clinical experience and the work of quite a few pioneers in the field,[2] we've identified five distinct stepping-stones on this path that leads right to healing. These steps work for nearly any person who has been wounded in a relationship, and that's just about everybody.[3]

Step One: Remember Your Story

To remember history can be a great blessing—or a great curse. Today's Jews certainly call it both. When referring to the Nazi Holocaust, they darkly but sincerely chant, "Never forget!" To forget invites repetition. However, remembering this tragedy in their history bathes the Jews with bitter images and devastating pain, both of which can erode the spirit and continue to scar the psyche. So, taking George Santayana's famous statement to heart: "Those who forget the past are doomed to repeat it," we want to help you remember your story.

Now you may be thinking just the opposite: *I can't get my story out of my mind. I don't want to keep dwelling on what happened.* We don't want you to dwell on what happened either, but we do want you to talk about it to someone you trust and get it out in the open. This kind of remembering is empowering; this type of personal recollection has a corrective nature all its own.

So, as you formulate your story, do the following:

- *Recall the facts.* Describe specific painful events in play-by-play fashion. If you're angry because your father "let you down," point to specific events that typified what he did. How old were you? Where were you? What was the situation? Who was there? What exactly did he do that hurt you? What resulted from the hurt? Talk about the event like a newspaper reporter would.

- *Retrace the path of the pain.* When you describe the facts, the past comes alive in the present. (But realize that the past has always been alive— covered up, but alive. If you still carry its pain, the past hasn't passed.) As you describe the wound, you may find yourself tangled with emotion and discussing the event in the present tense as if it were happening now. You may tell your story with flushed face and a raised voice, but once you've released the painful events through words, you can know healing for your soul wound. Your wounded self is no longer cloaked in denial.

Now keep working with the story. Remember and *feel* the feelings involved in that episode. Were you angry? If so, what about? Were you afraid? How afraid? Terrified, maybe? What did you think was actually going on? What did the event signify for you? What did you want to happen that didn't? How did you respond? How did you want to respond? How did you feel as you responded? How did others respond? How did this incident affect you? How does the incident affect you now? How do you feel, right now, as you revisit the event?

As you answer these questions, your whole story begins to emerge. And as you translate your life experience into a story, you place it out in the open so that those who are helping you heal can better understand you and what brought you to this point. Describing what happened to you also helps you gain control of the event. Once it's told as a story, your experience has a beginning and an end. It's no longer some unrestrained, all-consuming, never-ceasing, impossible-to-deal-with turmoil. It's now limited by meaningful words, and you *can* deal with it.

By the way, the job of those helping you along this journey is quite simple: *help facilitate the story* and encourage it when the storyteller becomes hesitant or fearful.

Step Two: Recognize Your Pain and the Need for Healing

Professional counselors often say, "You can't treat what you don't see." That's why remembering your story and recognizing your pain are necessary steps, and we think you'll see why as we guide you through this part of the journey.

• *See purpose in the pain.* Pain has a purpose. In fact, the pain we feel as we tell our story has several important purposes. First of all, as we said in chapter 9, accepting primary pain is validating. Up to this point, your emotional life may have been shrouded in guilt and shame as a result of believing that you were wrong for feeling as you did. Giving yourself permission to feel primary pain tells you that you were right to feel as you did.

In addition, when we acknowledge our pain and vulnerability, we become more aware of our need for God. Jesus said, " 'Come to me, all you who are weary and burdened, and I will give you rest' " (Matthew 11:28). To go to Him with our burden requires us first to acknowledge that we have one and then that we're tired of carrying around the pain. When we finally lay that burden at the cross, we find He's our soul's great Comforter, our refuge from life's storms. We also experience the truth God spoke to Paul: " 'My grace is sufficient for you, for my power is made perfect in weakness' " (2 Corinthians 12:9).

It follows that when we disavow our raw emotions, we deny that Christ is powerful enough to help us deal with them honestly, and our denial pushes Him away. If we push Him away enough, we come to experience Him as a distant, uninvolved, even uncaring Engineer of the universe. We become emotional atheists, denying the reality of God's ability to touch our hearts and heal our deepest wounds.

• *Validate your anger and mourn your losses.* When you have been wounded, anger swells—and this anger is appropriate. But you want to get past it, and the best way to do so is to first own it and then validate it. You can say to yourself, *I was wronged, and it's okay for me to be steamed about it. I needed you to be there for me and you weren't.* Then give yourself permission to grieve over what you lost or never had, to feel sorrow, to cry, and then cry out to God, who will be a great consolation. True sorrow is an aspect of spiritual brokenness that especially attracts the Holy Spirit, who comes into the life of the sufferer with divine comfort and power.

Step Three: Reframe the Meaning of Your Story

Soul wounds trigger intense, painful emotions, and too many people deal with this pain by burying it. When we do this, these emotions—and the beliefs they foster about self and others—are mummified, locking us into negative, rigid views of how relationships work and how we should behave.

For example, Sam's anger toward his father left him feeling wronged and victimized. He had difficulty achieving intimacy with his own son—and with others—because he feared being misunderstood and criticized. So he kept himself distant. But no matter how far away from others he put himself, *he* was always right there with himself, and he was his own worst critic. He would constantly berate himself for even the slightest shortcoming or failure. To try to outdistance that internal voice, he pushed himself unmercifully to always do more, earn more, achieve more. But, as you can imagine, he was never satisfied with how much he did, earned, or achieved. He never heard the voice say, *Enough. You're okay!* Instead he used his father's words to flog himself. Sam carried the part of his father he resented most right there with him everywhere he went.

Then, when Sam found himself with a son of his own, he overcompensated and refused to push Jason at all. Furthermore, since Sam spent so much time trying to satisfy the endless demands of his own internal critic, he had little time or emotional energy for Jason, which resulted in Jason's growing apart from his father. After all, he'd been wounded too; he felt his dad didn't love him. He believed he could do nothing that would interest his father, so he learned to depend on himself for emotional support, just like his dad. In spite of Sam's good intentions, his story had repeated itself in his relationship with Jason.

So, for Sam, *reframing* involved understanding his story from a new perspective. He could see he was a workaholic and that he struggled to connect with others, especially his wife and children. He could see his anger toward his father and how he had internalized his dad's harsh, self-directed criticism. And now he could see *why*. After all, Sam could have turned against his dad, but he didn't. Instead, he turned the anger on himself and, in a perverse way, the strategy worked. It preserved the relationship with his dad. His dad would have never understood Sam's anger. He would've seen it as rebellion, as weakness. So

Sam held in his anger as a way of maintaining some kind of closeness with his dad. The price of this denial, however, was that of an internal anger that criticized and was never satisfied.

By reframing his story, Sam could see that his response to his dad's chronic disapproval was his way of adapting, at the time, to a difficult situation. And, as we said, it worked. In spite of the anguish and frustration, Sam was married with children. He had a good job, and he was successful at it. His heart was in the right place. He *wanted* to connect; he wanted to be a successful parent and a loving husband. In a way, it wasn't his fault that he had no idea how to break free from the bonds of the past and make it happen.

The objective of reframing your story is to see yourself, and your past, in a different light. Where before you generally saw just your weakness and frailties, now you're able to see your strengths as well—among them, your tenacity, your will to survive, and your desire to thrive. More importantly, you'll begin to see how God has worked in your pain to woo you closer to Himself and to bring healing moments throughout your journey.

So, as you tell your story, ask yourself questions: How did I react to the pain of my past? Did my way of dealing with the pain back then get me through? In what ways am I a different person, perhaps even a stronger, wiser person, because of what I've gone through? What has God revealed to me about Himself during these times of turmoil? Did I turn away from Him? If so, why? What kept me from turning back to Him or from turning to Him in the first place? Is God calling me now? Or, a better question, in what ways is God calling to me now? Do I still want to turn away, or do I want to change my life? Is my fear a sign of weakness or an element of self-preservation?

These questions and others like them set the stage for change. They help us see, first, that our present situation is largely a reaction to fear and hurt and, second, that although what we used as a strategy worked then, *it doesn't work now.* For example, Sam's protective self decided that when he hurt, his only option was to look to himself for comfort. This isn't a healthy relationship style, but children, conditioned by a difficult parent to believe we're essentially unlovable and unworthy, can come to believe that the only available comfort is self. Or we may have learned that the only way to find someone to love us is to be a doormat, allowing others to take advantage of us and molding ourselves to meet their expectations. This strategy may have worked for us as children; it may have kept us from getting hurt too badly. But now it's time for a change.

Reframing also helps us see the healthy strivings that lie just beneath the surface of our unsuccessful behaviors.[4] Sam could see that his distancing from Jason was, in part, rooted in a healthy desire not to harm Jason as his dad had harmed him. But distancing wasn't the best way to get what he wanted. In fact, it produced the very outcome he wanted to avoid. But now that Sam can more clearly see his healthy goal, he can explore healthier options and begin to break free from the shackles of his past.

Now, some might say that reframing your life's story is just denial in the form of positive thinking. There certainly is positive thinking involved (finally!), but there's no denial. Instead, effective reframing only begins once you've broken through the denial. It looks past the pain and leads you to understand how you've matured and what you've gained through your experience.

Remember Joseph of the Old Testament and how he reframed the abuse he had suffered at the hands of his brothers? Many years later he looked them in the eyes and said, "You meant evil against me; but God meant it for good" (Genesis 50:20 NKJV). You may not be able to say anything this positive about the harmful incident(s) in your past, but you can identify what you've gained because of having gone through that painful experience.

Step Four: Repair Your Story—and Your Damaged Relationships and Emotions

Now comes the longest and most involved of the five steps. To repair means to restore by putting together or fixing something that's been broken or torn. And insecure relationship styles result in broken stories. As you might have discovered in the reframing part of the healing journey, your style may have worked in the past. But now your story only creates more pain—over and over again. So . . .

Understand and Halt the Vicious Cycles

You've heard the old saying "If at first you don't succeed, try, try again." It's good advice, of course, but what about when what you "try, try again" keeps making matters worse? Well, then you grab onto a different saying: "The definition of insanity is doing the same thing over and over and over again and wishing for a different result." Okay, a broken story is not the same as insanity, but a broken story *is* a perfect illustration of the vicious cycle of insanity.

Here's another example of a vicious cycle. I (Gary) had cancer when I was in my mid-twenties, and fighting it required the removal of the lymph nodes along my spinal cord. The operation left a scar extending from my sternum down past my belly button, and the surgeons needed every inch of that opening. Through it they removed all my intestines in order to get to the lymph nodes. Then, when the cutting was done, they stuffed them back inside and sewed me up. By all measures the operation was a success. But there was pain. A lot of it. I needed the pain reliever with codeine that the doctors prescribed.

But I wasn't home for more than a couple hours before the pain returned, and this time it was more severe. I called the doctor, who said to take more of the pain reliever. Which I did. When the pain returned, it was again far worse than it had been before. And now I was getting increasingly nauseated. Within a couple of days, I landed back in the hospital. Why? The drug was designed to deaden my pain, but the doctors found that the codeine was causing my intestines to shut down—which caused *more* pain! So the more I took, the worse I felt. A vicious cycle.

In the same way, our insecure relationship styles are designed to protect us from pain in our youth. But when these styles are played out in our adult relationships, they can cause more pain, unnecessary pain. The repair process involves breaking the vicious cycle. To do so requires two important steps. First, you identify the elements of your story that are broken.

For example, if you have an avoidant relationship style, your story's vicious cycle probably goes something like this: (1) You believe others are basically incapable of meeting your emotional needs. (2) You believe that you can take care of yourself and that you really don't need anyone else to provide comfort and support during times of distress. (3) You deny your feelings of vulnerability and your longing for connection. (4) Your philosophy is "suck it up, quit whining, and pull yourself up by your own bootstraps."

Sure, this formula has worked for you in the past, but now it's not. Your loved ones are angry with you, and they complain that you are uninvolved and consumed with work. The more they complain, the more pain you feel—pain you deny. You deny your longing for their support, and you feel angry and resentful when criticized. So you say to yourself, *That just proves I can't rely on people to be there for me,* and you pull away, retreating more and more into fantasy, work, success, or possessions—your addictions. This brings you back full circle. This vicious cycle, this self-defeating pattern of behavior, reveals the brokenness of your story.

We saw this cycle at work in Leah, a woman who came to us for help with her feelings of depression and anxiety. Her insecure style played itself out in a number of her close relationships. One was with Marisa, a friend at church. In an unusual step for Leah, she and Marisa talked about everything, even some of her deepest feelings about her childhood, her children, and her marriage.

What made this intimacy with Marisa so unusual was that Leah had come out of a childhood that promoted a more insecure relating style. Leah had a fairly strong relationship with her father, a sensitive and warm man. But he was a passive influence on her life and allowed Leah's mom to rule the roost. A stern, humorless woman, her mother was far too busy to listen to her children discuss something as insignificant as feelings. Priding herself on being practical about every aspect of life, Leah's mother had taught her daughter an important relationship rule: *Don't get too close, and when you're upset, don't talk about your feelings. It will only cause trouble. People, especially women, don't need to hear about your pain. They have enough to do without having to listen to you whine.*

Marisa seemed the exception to this rule. Leah saw that relationship as going quite well. But for persons with broken stories, even good relationships don't go well for long. Leah's friendship with Marisa ran into difficulty when stress crept into Leah's home life. Her husband began to travel out of town more than she liked. Her parents lived eight hours away, and she had no family in town who could help. This left Leah at home with four children, feeling abandoned and resentful toward her husband—and ashamed and guilty . . . because she was embarrassed about feeling abandoned and resentful. After all, he was just trying to earn a living and provide for her and the four kids.

It didn't take much for Marisa to sense her friend's distress, and she offered to help. But Leah refused her help. Unable to believe that anyone could possibly be truly concerned about her well-being, Leah was sure Marisa's offer originated only from a desire to fulfill some warped sense of "Christian duty."

Understandably feeling snubbed, Marisa found herself getting angry with Leah. Especially when Leah, warned by caller ID, stopped taking Marisa's calls altogether. Leah just didn't want anyone feeling sorry for her. Instead, she decided to feel sorry for herself. She withdrew into her own world and lay on the couch all day while the kids were in school, her head buried under a quilt.

After Leah's husband's business returned to normal and Leah's home life settled back into its familiar groove, she called Marisa. The instant Marisa realized who she was talking to, her voice became icy. She was clearly upset, and for good reason. Leah had cut off her gestures of friendship without warning or explanation, and there are unwritten rules among friends about behavior like that.

Now Leah was at a crossroads. She had a choice to make here: She could have simply said, "You sound upset. Did I do something?" And Marisa would have told her what the problem was, and Leah would have managed an explanation and apologized, and their relationship would have had the breath of life breathed into it. Unfortunately (and predictably, we might add) Leah's relationship style took over, as it does for all of us in times of stress, and interpreted her friend's attitude as yet another warning that flashed: REJECTION-REJECTION-REJECTION. Leah said to herself, *See what happens when I get close to other women? They dump me every time. Why do I even try?*

Leah had no idea why Marisa was upset. The only explanation Leah's relationship style allowed to filter through was that Marisa was angry because Leah had had a bad week and her less-than-attractive emotions had seeped to the surface.

Breaking this vicious cycle involves two important steps: revising relationship rules and replacing defensive behavior with courageous loving.

• *Revising relationship rules.* As we said earlier, relationship rules are core beliefs about ourselves and others. Although we aren't always fully conscious of these beliefs, they are a powerful influence on our behavior. For example, Sam's relationship rules included "I can't really trust others" and "I have to depend on myself for support and comfort." Of course these rules had a negative impact on his behavior, resulting in chronic work, lots of self-criticism, and a retreat from intimacy—because how can you be intimate with someone you don't trust?

At a fully conscious level, all Sam knew was that people were hostile toward him and that he received very little satisfaction from relationships. But as he traveled the journey we've outlined so far, he saw how his distancing and excessive devotion to work triggered that resentment from others. Then he was able to see the rules that had been governing his behavior and understand how they directly influenced how he related.

Likewise, Leah's relationship rules affected how she related to her female companions, especially when she was under stress. In session, we asked, "Leah, why do you think Marisa was so cold and distant when you talked to her?"

"I don't know. I guess because she just doesn't like me anymore."

"Any idea why she would just stop liking you?"

"Well, I've been in a bad mood lately. Nobody likes me when I get upset; it's best I just stay to myself when I get like that."

You can see Leah's relationship rules at work here shaping her conclusion that Marisa didn't like her because she was upset—even though Marisa had had no way of knowing why Leah was distressed and retreating. But we're happy to report that, like Sam, Leah traveled the journey we've outlined here and saw how she interpreted the present through the lens of the past.

Now that both Sam and Leah could see their relationship rules at work, their task was to change them, to revise their faulty assumptions about others, and to realize they are prone to distort the reality of the present to fit the experiences of the past. But—as you may know—change is a two-steps-forward, one-step-back kind of process. And it's a tedious and often painful journey.

• *Replace defensive behavior with courageous loving.* Genuine, godly love is not for the faint of heart. It requires courage; vulnerability always does. Besides, it was because of your vulnerability, those many years ago, that you got hurt in the first place. That's why you may have developed an insecure relationship style back then—for defense and to minimize your vulnerability so that the ones you loved and who claimed to love you wouldn't hurt you again.

But we hope that by now you realize that healthy relationships are not only crucial to a happy, vital existence but that they are possible for you. And if you believe this, then you probably want to change the way you relate, right? Again, this change requires courageous loving as well as a change in those defensive behaviors, perhaps even doing away with them altogether. A change in how you relate to people also requires that you become vulnerable again and risk being rejected, criticized, and used. We don't mean that you lie down and become a doormat but that you learn to love honestly and boldly.

In Sam's case, we asked him to increase the time he spent with his family—to just be with them, listening, watching, and understanding. Sam started by spending the first thirty minutes after he got home from work talking to his wife about his day. He touched on the high points and the low ones. Before long he was talking about his hopes for work, for a promotion, and how he wanted to change things there. He told her about his boss and some of the people he worked with. Before long, his wife started opening up. Vulnerability breeds vulnerability as trust breeds trust. Soon they were both talking about their feelings—what they liked and what they didn't. They began to talk about themselves as a couple. They talked about their future, their hopes, and their dreams. Sam was learning the value of listening to others and allowing others to listen to him.

We had worked with Sam to help him actively listen to his wife. He didn't tune her out anymore. He tried to understand her, and when he didn't, he asked questions to show that he really wanted to understand because he did. And as he listened, he found his wife interesting. Even funny. It was truly delightful the first time they laughed together. It had been so long, yet it felt so comfortable.

By connecting to his wife and others, Sam's relationship belief that only he could provide himself with comfort and support began to change. He also found that the more he understood his wife, the more she understood him, and when she didn't, she asked questions until she did. And the more she understood, the less she criticized him. In fact, she began to encourage him. Even when he did what she hated most, left his underwear on the bathroom floor, she picked it up. She only mentioned it that night when they finally fell into bed. "You seem preoccupied tonight," she told him. "You've been pretty good about throwing your dirty clothes in the hamper, but you didn't tonight. Is something wrong?"

Yes, there *was* something wrong. There were rumors of layoffs at work, and Sam was scared. As he told her his worries, she placed a warm, reassuring hand on his arm and just smiled at him. That was all. No words, but at the moment he felt absolutely safe. Not safe from bad things happening at work but safe because he knew that, no matter what happened, they'd get through it together. The cycle had been broken. Sam was repairing his story.

Step Five: Reconnecting

As we've said before, we believe that God created people to be in relationship. Thus, the ultimate destination in this healing journey is to build better, more enduring relationships—relationships that are rich, satisfying, and intimate, that help you grow stronger, that fill you with a sense of purpose and meaning, that inspire you to act with grace and mercy to the world around you, and that strengthen your spiritual awareness and enhance your ultimate relationship: your relationship with God.

Of course, such relationships have conflict and even smatterings of pain. But healthy relationships ultimately grow as a result of conflict. In fact, the participants in the relationship actually begin to see conflict as an opportunity for growth. After all, when the offender is repentant, has sincerely apologized for his or her wrongdoing, and has promised to turn from his or her damaging ways, reconciliation and forgiveness are possible. But even when repentance doesn't occur and reconciliation isn't possible, we should still extend our forgiveness. In this section, we want to suggest that reconnecting starts with forgiveness.

When we've been betrayed by someone we trusted, an injury results, a wound that bleeds anger and resentment that can be directed toward either the offender or oneself. To forgive, to move on and grow, we need to work through these feelings, and we can choose from three paths when we stand at a crossroads that requires forgiveness.[5] Two are destructive; only one actually leads to resolution and reconnection.

The first destructive path is *denial* or *self-blame*. On this path we either tell ourselves the injury didn't really happen or, acknowledging that it happened, we blame ourselves for the injury. For example, if your parents were unavailable to you as a child, you might tell yourself and others that they were really great parents. Like Arnold did back in chapter 5. For years he denied he even had any soul wounds, and he dealt with his pain through an addiction to possessions, success, and power. Ultimately, because Arnold buried his story, he repeated it in his own family. Other people, as a result of burying their stories, might fall into emotional numbness and depression.

Whereas denial paves over the wound and pretends it doesn't exist, self-blame says, *There is a wound, but I'm at fault.* Someone might say, for instance, "My parents were never there for me, but if I had a kid like me, I wouldn't be there for him either." Once again, the wounded person can't bear to place the blame where it belongs. Self-blame carries with it the heavy burden of responsibility.

The second destructive path is *bitterness*. In this case our emotional feet get mired in the event, and no matter how hard we try, we can't move on from it. We keep reliving the event, continually asking ourselves, "Why me?" This incessant search for an answer that never comes leads to intense anger and smoldering resentment. Replaying the event comes from both our need to understand the world we live in and a need for justice. But since there's no acceptable reason for someone to hurt you and there's no godly way for you to seek justice, you're left trapped in the past. Just like the path of denial, the path of bitterness eventually leaves you feeling hopeless and depressed. (By the way, we find it interesting that the avoidant style is rooted in *denial* and the ambivalent style is stuck in *bitterness.*)

The third and constructive option is the following path to forgiveness:

1. *Place blame appropriately.* Don't act like the injury didn't occur, don't blame yourself, and don't make excuses for the offender. Simply be honest about what happened and how it hurt you.

2. *Grieve.* When you grieve, you appreciate what was lost. Grieve, for instance, over your lost ability to trust. Then allow yourself to experience the feelings that came with that loss. You will probably vacillate

between feelings of sadness and anger and as you acknowledge what you wanted and needed but didn't receive.

3. *Empathize.* Empathy is the ability to see the world from another person's perspective, and the ability to empathize helps us to cooperate, to act with compassion and mercy, and to restrain aggressive impulses. Empathy is critical to forgiveness because it helps us look at offenders in a different light. We try to understand their history, background, and life experiences, not to excuse their behavior, but to try to understand what could have motivated them to do what they did.

When working with Sam, for example, we learned that Sam's father's father also had died young, when Sam's dad was only thirteen. As the oldest son, Sam's father had to keep the family business going and provide for the family. He had done so, but he had never had the time or the support to grieve his father's death. Besides, his feelings probably only got in the way of the adult job he was doing, so he worked hard and was hard on himself. This approach got him through.

By understanding his dad's own history, Sam realized that his dad wasn't just a mean ol' man who incessantly pressured Sam to perform. He had been hardened by a life that required him to do a difficult job for which he was ill prepared—and he did it the only way he knew how, by always pushing himself harder. He had done the same with his son.

Now before we move on, we want to remind you that there's another side to empathy: as you come to understand what's behind the other person's sin, you realize that you have sinned against others too, that there are people out there who deserve to be angry with *you*, and that you need to be forgiven too. Denying this reality puts you in the same class as the self-righteous unforgiving servant in one of Jesus' parables (see Matthew 18:23–35). The king forgave this servant an enormous debt, but then this servant demanded from one of *his* servants the immediate repayment of a relatively small debt. When his servant begged for mercy, the forgiven but unforgiving servant refused to grant mercy and had the man cast into prison. Obviously the unforgiving servant lacked empathy. He refused to see what it was like to be unforgiven, so he could not extend forgiveness to his debtor.

Empathy was a powerful tool for Sam as he studied his relationship with his son. He realized how he had hurt Jason, and seeing this hurt allowed him to understand the anger and resentment that had built up in his son over the years. Sam desperately wanted his son's forgiveness, and that passionate desire helped him see how his own dad, if he were alive today, would want and need Sam's forgiveness. Sam wept bitterly. He felt differently toward his dad. He felt compassion.

4. *Forgive.* There are two parts to forgiveness. The first is being willing to get involved in the painful and difficult process of forgiveness. Then, once your softened heart is ready, you need to actually extend forgiveness—which may be easier said than done. You may encounter several roadblocks, and each is rooted in a misconception about forgiveness.

The three most common misconceptions about forgiveness are: (1) "If I forgive, it means that I'm condoning the act." No. Forgiveness begins with righteous anger, an acknowledgment that the offense was wrong and that it hurt you. (2) "To forgive means I must forget—and I can never forget." This is also false. Forgiveness does not mean you forget anything. You just give up the right to replay the event in your mind, and you stop wishing for revenge. (3) "If I forgive, I become a doormat; I'm saying it's okay for people to walk over me." This is also blatantly false. Forgiveness means you don't hold the injury against the offender any longer; it does not mean that you give him or her, or anyone else, a license to walk all over you.

5. *Consider reconciliation.* Remember that forgiving is different from reconciling. Forgiveness is a one-way process. It requires you to give up your anger and your desire for revenge. Reconciliation, on the other hand, is a two-way process in which the other person chooses to apologize for his or her wrongdoing and to commit to not doing wrong again. Even so, you want to be cautious and let that person earn your trust.

6. *Make peace with yourself.* Unyielding rage toward someone not only leaves you bitter and resentful, but it also locks you into a chronic pattern of self-doubt and self-criticism. Forgiving others frees you to forgive yourself for anything and everything and therefore frees you to truly

live. You learn to care about yourself in an honest and genuine way, and you learn to trust yourself and your ability to love others.

7. *Learn to trust again.* Soul wounds shatter our ability to trust others, and they lead either to isolation and emotional defensiveness or to excessive clinginess. But forgiveness helps free us up emotionally so we can risk closeness again. Since we're less afraid of being hurt, we are more willing to try again. Learning to trust isn't a speedy process by any means, but it is a potentially very rewarding one.

8. *Reconnect.* The final step comes when you plug into the world of relationships and allow yourself to love and be loved. If you're a parent, for instance, you reconnect with your children by honestly acknowledging your shortcomings, your distance, your criticism. If you are a spouse, you recommit to your marriage, and you become very intentional about loving your spouse and improving your marriage. If you are single or divorced, you commit yourself to no longer being isolated but to reconnecting with others—to healthy people who are able to love you in return. Bottom line, your message to all your loved ones becomes *Above everything else, I love you.*

WORKING YOUR WAY TO THAT
MORE WONDERFULLY FULFILLING PLACE

Well, you're here. You've reached the end. We've worked hard to give you a good look at relationships and the four styles that govern them. Our hope is that you've seen yourself within these pages and that, if your style isn't secure, you've decided to change. That's why in this last chapter we've given you a map that outlines a journey to healing.

If you feel comfortable working on your own, good. But if you don't, please seek help right away from your pastor or a professional Christian counselor. If you're not sure how to find one, give the American Association of Christian Counselors a call at 1-800-526-8673, or visit our Web site at www.aacc.net and we'll help you find someone you feel comfortable with.

As you work your way to that more wonderfully fulfilling place of safe and loving relationships, don't forget that God created you and me to be in relationship. Why? Maybe so that we would come to yearn for a healthy, intimate relationship with Him. After all, our relationship with God is the source and foundation of every good element of our lives, especially our relationships. Which means that concentrating on our relationship with God should be the principal focus of our lives.

Thankfully, if our relationship with God is healthy and intimate, if it compels us to love others in godly, selfless ways, it will also help us fashion healthy, intimate earthly relationships, particularly with our husbands and wives. And when our relationships are in order, they bring us fulfillment, safety, and comfort, and they fill our cup to overflowing with love and contentment. They also act as a firm foundation from which we can launch ourselves into the other aspects of our lives—our jobs, our churches, our hobbies, and our communities.

If you take on the challenge of change, you'll never regret that decision. Life is short. And if you haven't started the journey already, we hope you'll begin to change your life the instant you close this book. Know that God is with you every step of the way!

GLOSSARY

Ambivalent relationship style—Style based on fear of being abandoned, a sense of incompetence, low self-confidence, and the desire for a strong protector; these dependent people can be anxious, melodramatic, or angry.

Attachment—A special relationship, bond, or connection with another person(s) that is characterized by strong emotions and continues through time.

Avoidant relationship style—Style impacted by fear of intimacy, lack of trust in other people, and the consequent idea that one has to rely only on oneself; these people struggle with emotional connection, the disclosure of private thoughts and feelings, and with nonsexual touch; people with this style can be narcissistic, disconnected, or compulsively perfectionistic; addictive behavior and angry resentment toward God are disturbing tendencies.

Disorganized relationship style—Style of interacting that is greatly affected by dissociated pain, a shattered sense of self, untold stories of an unresolved past, and a compulsion to repeat the painful past; behavior can reflect both the ambivalent and the avoidant styles.

Dissociation—The ability to turn off thoughts, feelings, and even physical pain and move those experiences to some other part of the consciousness.

Emotions—The physical, gut-felt responses that fuel our behavior and motivate us to act. Emotions are important in relationships because they motivate us to seek closeness during times of stress.

Endogenous opioids—Chemicals released by the brain; God-given painkillers that are the brain's equivalent to heroin.

Hyperarousal—A state of physical alertness in which the body is ready to either fight or flee; a key feature of a person's response to trauma. The heart races, the pupils enlarge, hot or cold flashes occur, and the body is in a state of tension.

Power of reflection—The ability to describe our internal experiences.

Primary emotional reactions—Emotions that come in response to a situation in real time.

Proximity principle—The set point for a child's relationship thermostat. If a child believes Mom is close enough, he feels safe and secure, and he is willing to explore the world around him. If the child believes Mom is not close enough, he chooses whatever behavior is necessary for getting physically closer to her.

Relationship rules—Core beliefs about ourselves and others. Although we aren't always fully conscious of these beliefs, they are a powerful influence on our behavior.

The first set of core beliefs, or relationship rules, form the *self* dimension. It centers around two critical questions:

1. Am I worthy of being loved?

2. Am I able to do what I need to do to get the love I need?

The second set of beliefs form the *other* dimension. It centers around two other important questions:

1. Are other people reliable and trustworthy?

2. Are people accessible and willing to respond to me when I need them?

Relationship style—Behavior in relationships shaped by a two-part set of basic assumptions, conclusions, or core beliefs about one's self and others (see "relationship rules").

Replacement defense—A means of protecting oneself by replacing what is really wanted and needed (parental love) with something else (a love of things). A way of walling off emotions and not letting oneself feel so vulnerable and helpless.

Secondary emotional reactions—Emotions (stress, anger) that are experienced as one is trying to deny or repress primary emotions (fear, pain).

Secure Relationship style—A healthy way of interacting with and relating to people based in confidence about "who I am," confidence about one's effectiveness in the world, and trust in others. Secure people are emotionally strong, willing to seek and accept comfort from others, courageous about love and intimacy, and responsible for themselves.

ENDNOTES

Chapter 1. The Heart of the Matter: Relationships in Everyday Living
1. Ernest Becker, *The Denial of Death* (New York: Free Press, 1973).
2. Russell A. Barkley, *Defiant Children: A Clinician's Manual for Assessment and Parent Training*, 2nd ed. (New York: Guilford Press, 1997).

Chapter 2. Shaping Our View of Ourselves and Those We Hold Dearest
1. For a dynamic review of the history of attachment theory, see I. Bretherton, "The Origins of Attachment Theory: John Bowlby and Mary Ainsworth," *Developmental Psychology* 28 (1992): 759–75, and R. Karen, *Becoming Attached: First Relationships and How They Shape Our Capacity to Love* (Oxford, England: Oxford University Press, 1994).
2. John Bowlby, *Attachment and Loss*, vol. 1, *Attachment* (New York: Basic Books, 1969).
3. Adapted from J. Holmes, *John Bowlby and Attachment Theory* (New York: Routledge, 1993).
4. We realize that children are not actually asking questions in a verbal fashion. But they act as if they are. The point is that attachment is so basic that it develops even before our language systems develop.
5. Bowlby called this the internalized working model or relationship rules. See Bowlby, *Attachment and Loss*, vol. 1, *Attachment.*
6. This information is adapted from K. Bartholomew, "Avoidance of Intimacy: An Attachment Perspective," *Journal of Social and Personal Relationships* 7 (1990): 147–78.
7. While we use the term *disorganized* attachment style, other researchers refer to it as the *fearful* style.
8. Mary Ainsworth, M. C. Blehar, E. Waters, and W. Wall, *Patterns of Attachment: A Psychological Study of the Strange Situation* (Hillsdale, N. J.: Erlbaum, 1978).
9. Mary Main and E. Hess, "Parents' Unresolved Traumatic Experiences Are Related to Infant Disorganized Attachment Status: Is Frightened and/or Frightening Parental Behavior the Linking Mechanism?" in M. T. Greenberg, D. Cicchetti, E. M. Cummings, eds., *Attachment in the Preschool Years: Theory, Research, and*

Intervention (Chicago: University of Chicago Press, 1990), 161–82, and M. Main and J. Solomon, "Procedures for Identifying Infants as Disorganized/Disoriented During the Ainsworth Strange Situation," in Greenberg, Cicchetti, and Cummings, *Attachment in the Preschool Years*, 121–60.

10.   W. Pollack, *Real Boys* (New York: Henry Holt, 1998), 113.

11.   G Habermas and Gary Sibcy, "Religious Doubt and Negative Emotionality: The Development of the Religious Doubt Scale," 2001. Manuscript is currently under review in the *Journal of Psychology and Theology*.

Chapter 3. Soul Wounds

1.   Susan Johnson, J. A. Makinen, and J. W. Milikin, "Attachment Injuries in Couple Relationships: A New Perspective on Impasses in Couples Therapy," *Journal of Marital and Family Therapy* 27 (2001): 145–55.

2.   John Bowlby, *Attachment and Loss*, vol. 2, *Separation: Anxiety and Anger* (New York: Basic Books, 1973), 246.

3.   Ibid., 249.

4.   John Gottman, *The Marriage Clinic: A Scientifically Based Marital Therapy* (New York: W. W. Norton, 1999).

5.   Ibid.

6.   David Olson, "Circumplex Model of Marital and Family Systems: Assessing Family Functioning," in Froma Walsh, ed., *Normal Family Processes*, 2nd ed. (New York: Guilford Press, 1993).

Chapter 4. Equipped to Face Challenges and Take Risks

1.   Bowlby, *Attachment and Loss*, vol. 2, *Separation: Anxiety and Anger*, 246.

2.   Greenberg and Paivio, *Working with Emotions in Psychotherapy*.

3.   Developmental psychologists call this right combination of support and challenge the *zone of proximal development*. See L. S. Vygotzky, *Mind in Society: The Development of Higher Psychological Processes* (Cambridge, Mass.: Harvard University Press, 1978).

4.   John Gottman, *Raising an Emotionally Intelligent Child: The Heart of Parenting* (New York: Simon and Schuster, 1997), and John Gottman, L. F. Katz, and C. Hooven, "Parental Meta-Emotion Philosophy and the Emotional Life of Families: Theoretical Models and Preliminary Data," *Journal of Family Psychology* 10 (1996): 243–68.

5.   See Gottman et al., "Parental Meta-Emotion Philosophy."

6.   Those who study infant behavior call this *implicit relational knowing*. For a review of this concept, see D. K. Silverman, "The Tie That Binds: Affect Regulation, Attachment, and Psychoanalysis," *Psychoanalytic Psychology* 15 (1998): 187–212.

7. Richard Foster calls this "simple prayer." See his book *Prayer: Finding the Heart's True Home* (San Francisco: HarperSanFrancisco, 1992).
8. M. Scott Peck, *The Road Less Traveled* (New York: Simon and Schuster, 1978).
9. Viktor Frankl, *Man's Search for Meaning: An Introduction to Logotherapy* (New York: Simon & Schuster, 1963, 1984).
10. Gary Habermas, personal communication, 2002.
11. J. Holmes, *John Bowlby and Attachment Theory* (New York: Routledge, 1993).
12. For a discussion of what researchers call an "earned, secure base" for building and rebuilding relationships, see J. L. Pearson, D. A. Cohn, P. A. Cowan, and C. P. Cowan, "Earned- and Continuous-Security in Adult Attachment: Relation to Depressive Symptomatology and Parenting Style," *Development and Psychopathology* 6 (1994): 359–73, and J. L. Phelps, J. Belsky, and K. Crnic, "Earned Security, Daily Stress, and Parenting: A Comparison of Five Alternative Models," *Development and Psychopathology* 10 (1998): 21–38.

Chapter 5. The Hardened Heart

1. The "adult attachment interview" was first developd by attachment researcher Mary Main. See E. Hess, "The Adult Attachment Interview: Historical and Current Perspectives," in J. Cassidy and P. R. Shaver, eds., *Handbook of Attachment: Theory, Research, and Clinical Applications* (New York: Guilford Press, 1999), 395–433.
2. Allan N. Schore, *Affect Dysregulation and Disorders of the Self* (New York: W. W. Norton & Co., 2003).
3. A. N. Shore, "The Effects of a Secure Attachment Relationship on Right Brain Development, Affect Regulation, and Infant Mental Health," *Infant Mental Health Journal* 22 (2001): 7–66, and D. Siegel, *The Developing Mind: Toward a Neurobiology of Interpersonal Experience* (New York: Guilford Press, 1999).
4. N. Weinfield, L. Sroufe, B. Egeland, and E. Carlson, "The Nature of Individual Differences in Infant-Caregiver Attachment," in Cassidy and Shaver, eds., *Handbook of Attachment* (New York: Guilford, 1999), 68–88.
5. J. F. Masterson, *The Search for the Real Self: Unmasking the Personality Disorders of Our Age* (New York: Free Press, 1988), 90.
6. J. F. Masterson and R. Klein, eds., *Disorders of the Self: New Therapeutic Horizons: The Masterson Approach* (New York: Brunner/Mazel, 1995).
7. This aspect of the exiled self is true of those who actually come in for therapy. There is a subgroup of individuals who fit the criteria for schizoid personality disorder in the *DSM-IV* (*The Diagnostic and Statistical Manual of Mental Disorders*, 4th ed., published by the American Psychiatric Association). This subgroup is more emotionally hollow and interpersonally withdrawn than the folks we refer to as the exiled-self group. Because those in the *DSM-IV*

group are more impaired, they are less likely to identify with a desire to con-nect with others and are consequently less likely to respond favorably to any type of therapy.

8. For an overview of the characteristics of obsessive-compulsive personality dis-order see D. Robinson, *Personality Disorders: Explained* (Port Huron, Mich.: Rapid Psychler Press, 2000).

9. See chapter 3, "Soul Wounds."

10. Habermas and Sibcy, "Religious Doubt and Negative Emotionality." In per-sonal communication, Gary Habermas used the phrase *volitional doubt* to describe one's angry resentment toward God.

Chapter 6. Don't Abandon Me!

1. Irvin Yalom, *Existential Psychotherapy* (New York: Basic Books, 1980).

2. A. Beck, A. Freeman, and Associates, *Cognitive Therapy of Personality Disorders* (New York: Guilford Press, 1990).

3. S. Shea, *Psychiatric Interviewing: The Art of Understanding* (Philadelphia: W. B. Saunders, 1988), 355.

4. D. G. Perry, L. C. Perry, and P. Rasmussen, "Cognitive and Social Learning Mediators of Aggression," *Child Development* 57 (1995): 700–11, and Robinson, *Personality Disorders: Explained.* Both of these resources provide a helpful overview of the *DSM-IV* personality disorders. Keep in mind that per-sonality disorders are maladaptive extensions of personality styles.

5. L. Benjamin, *Interpersonal Diagnosis and Treatment of Personality Disorders* (New York: Guilford, 1993).

6. Fredrick Firestone, *Combating Self-Destructive Thought Processes: Voice Therapy and Separation Theory* (New York: Sage, 1997).

7. T. Millon, *Disorder of Personality: DSM-IV and Beyond* (New York: John Wiley & Sons, 1996).

8. Shea, *Psychiatric Interviewing,* 358.

9. Gary Sibcy, "Self-Reported Attachment Styles and Psychopathology in a Clinical Population" (doctoral diss., Union Institute and University's School of Clinical and Professional Psychology, Cincinnati, Ohio, 2000).

10. Beck, Freeman, and associates, *Cognitive Therapy of Personality Disorders.*

11. L. Greenberg and S. Paivio, *Working with Emotions in Psychotherapy* (New York: Guilford Press, 1997).

12. For a distinction between criticism and contempt in marital communication, see J. M. Gottman, *The Marriage Clinic: A Scientifically Based Marital Therapy* (New York: W. W. Norton, 1999).

Chapter 7. The Grass Is Always Dead on Both Sides of the Fence

1. Mary Main and E. Hess, "Parents' Unresolved Traumatic Experiences Are

Endnotes

Related to Infant Disorganized Attachment Status: Is Frightened and/or Frightening Parental Behavior the Linking Mechanism?" 163.

2. C. H. Kempe, F. N. Silverman, B. F. Steele, W. Droegmuller, and H. K. Silver, "The Battered-Child Syndrome," *Journal of the American Medical Association* 181 (1962): 17–24.

3. Bruce Perry, "Violence and Childhood: How Persisting Fear Can Alter the Developing Child's Brain, a special Child Trauma Academy website version of the neurodevelopmental impact of violence in childhood" (http://www.child-trauma.org/vio_child.htm). This information is also included in D. Schetky and E. Benedek, eds., *Textbook of Child and Adolescent Forensic Psychiatry* (Washington, D.C.: American Psychiatric Press, 2001), 221–38.

4. We are not proposing a new legal definition of abuse that would mean if you yell at your child one day, you need to call social services and turn yourself in. But we want to make a strong statement about how destructive certain kinds of parenting can be, and we want to help educate parents to be mindful of how they can prevent themselves from treating their children in these ways.

5. Bill Carmichael, *Habits of a Healthy Home* (Wheaton, IL: Tyndale House, 1997), 115.

6. William Bernet, "Child Maltreatment," in H. I. Kaplan and B. J. Sadock, eds., *Comprehensive Textbook of Psychiatry*, 7th ed., vol. 2 (New York: Lippincott, Williams and Wilkins: 2000), 2878–89.

7. David Finkelhor, *Sexually Victimized Children* (New York: Free Press, 1979).

8. John N. Briere, *Child Abuse Trauma: Theory and Treatment of the Lasting Effects* (Thousand Oaks, Calif.: Sage Publications, 1992).

9. Ibid.

10. Stephanie Brown, *Treating Adult Children of Alcoholics: A Developmental Perspective* (New York: John Wiley, 1988), 27.

11. Louis Breger, *From Instinct to Identity: The Development of Personality* (Englewood Cliffs: Prentice-Hall, 1974), 198.

12. Basal van der Kolk, "Trauma and Memory," in Basal A. van der Kolk, A. C. McFarlane, and L. Weisaeth, eds., *Traumatic Stress: The Effects of Overwhelming Experience on Mind, Body, and Society* (New York: Guilford, 1996).

13. Basal van der Kolk, "The Complexity of Adaptation to Trauma Self-Regulation, Stimulus Discrimination, and Characterological Development," in van der Kolk, McFarlane, and Weisaeth, *Traumatic Stress*, 193.

14. Ibid.

15. Daniel Siegel, *The Developing Mind: How Relationships and the Brain Interact to Shape Who We Are* (New York: Guilford Press, 1999).

16. Basal van der Kolk, "The Compulsion to Repeat the Trauma: Re-enactment, Revictimization, and Masochism," *Psychiatric Clinics of North America* 12 (1989):

389–411. Also posted on the Internet at http://www.cirp.org/library/psych/vanderkolk/.

17.   R. Pitman, S. Orr, D. Laforque, et al., "Psychophysiology of PTSD Imagery in Vietnam Combat Veterans," *Archives of General Psychiatry* 44 (1987): 940–76.

18.   We don't want to imply that all victims of trauma are addicted to tragedy and go searching for ways to get beat up or raped. But research shows that victims of childhood trauma are more likely to experience traumatic relationships and events during adulthood.

19.   A. Miller, *Thou Shalt Not Be Aware* (New York: Farrar, Straus, & Giroux, 1984).

20.   R. Firestone and Joyce Catlett, *The Fear of Intimacy* (New York: American Psychological Association, 1999).

Chapter 8. God and You—with George Ohlschlager

1.   Peter Kreeft, *Love Is Stronger Than Death* (San Francisco: St. Ignatius Press, 1992).

2.   Dallas Willard, *The Spirit of the Disciplines: Understanding How God Changes Lives* (San Francisco: Harper & Row, 1988), 98.

3.   Ibid., 9.

4.   Ibid., 156.

5.   Ibid., 163.

6.   Ibid., 172.

7.   Richard Foster, *Prayer: Finding the Heart's True Home* (San Francisco: Harper, 1992). This is only one of many types of prayer that Richard Foster so eloquently elaborates on in this classic book. We believe that all types of prayer facilitate our attachment with God. We discuss simple prayer because we believe it is the stepping-stone to other types of prayer. Also, simple prayer seems to most closely parallel the dynamics of an attachment relationship because in it we learn to immediately turn to God.

8.   Ibid., 11–12.

9.   Søren Kierkegaard, quoted in Foster, *Prayer*, 39.

Chapter 9. Taming Emotional Storms

1.   Greenberg and Paivio, *Working with Emotions in Psychotherapy*, 21.

2.   We adapted these triggers from G. Klerman, M. Weissman, B. Rounsaville, and E. Cheveron, *Interpersonal Psychotherapy of Depression* (New York: Basic Books, 1984). This book is a classic and is a must-read for any serious therapist treating depression and emotional disorders.

3.   Gottman, *The Marriage Clinic*.

4.   David Burns, *The Feeling Good Handbook: Using the New Mood Therapy in Everyday Life* (New York: W. Morrow, 1989).

5.   In Dallas Willard's *Renovation of the Heart: Putting on the Character of Christ*

(Colorado Springs: NavPress, 2002), he identifies three crucial elements involved in change: vision, intentionality, and means. We also believe a fourth element is crucial, and that is courage.

6. This technique is based on the most recent research on treating depression. It seems that people do change from the outside in. By getting depressed people active, their minds seem to be more open to new ways of thinking, and their self-esteem begins to snap back. See J. B. Persons, *Essential Components of Cognitive-Behavior Therapy for Depression* (Washington, D.C.: American Psychological Association, 2000).

Chapter 10. Love, Sex, and Marriage—with Sharon Hart Morris, Ph.D.

1. John Gottman, *Why Marriages Fail* (New York: Simon and Schuster, 1994).
2. Sharon Hart Morris, "Conceptualization and Development of 'Haven of Safety' Marital Assessment Scale" (doctoral diss., Fuller Graduate School of Psychology, Pasadena, Calif., 2000).
3. A word of caution: In abusive relationships, risking to trust again can be dangerous. Evaluate the emotional and physical safety of your relationship. If your relationship is peppered with emotional, physical, or sexual abuse, seek professional help. We would not ask you to risk your heart with a spouse who is abusive. On the other hand, sometimes a hurt heart can feel like it has been abused. Seek counseling to discern the difference.
4. John Gottman, *The Relationship Cure* (New York: Crown, 2001).

Chapter 11. Parenting Secure Kids

1. Russell Barkley, *Taking Charge of ADHD: The Complete, Authoritative Guide for Parents*, 2nd ed. (New York, Guilford Press, 2000), 6.
2. Stephen Covey, *The Seven Habits of Highly Effective People: Restoring the Character Ethic* (New York: Simon and Schuster, 1989).
3. Patricia Crittenden, *CARE-INDEX Coding Manual* (Miami: Family Relations Institute, 2001).
4. Some recent parenting programs call for a highly structured parent-centered approach to raising infants and toddlers. But the real origin of this approach began with the radical behaviorists of the 1940s and '50s. Such individuals as B. F. Skinner and J. B. Watson were not at all friendly to Christianity and to belief in God. They believed that children come into this world as blank slates—with no previous learning in the womb plus no genetic hardwiring. So they claimed that an infant's cry was merely a learned behavior, not a God-programmed behavior designed to cue parents as to its needs. The goal of the behaviorist was to manufacture children who were precociously independent and autonomous. Since crying ran counter to these goals, behaviorists assumed it to be a negative behavior that needed to be extinguished. Picking up the cry-

ing child and feeding it would reinforce the behavior and lead to a spoiled child, they said. Such a philosophy has been scientifically proven to be woefully inadequate and even harmful to kids.

5. Ainsworth, Blehar, Waters, and Wall, *Patterns of Attachment.*
6. Mary D. S. Ainsworth, "Maternal Sensitivity Scales," a mimeographed report (Baltimore: Johns Hopkins University, 1969), now available through a State University of New York at Stony Brook Web site: http://www.psychology.sun-ysb.edu/edu/ewaters/measures/senscoop.htp.
7. S. Chess and A. Thomas, *Know Your Child* (New York: Basic Books, 1987), and A. Thomas and S. Chess, *Temperament and Development* (New York: Bruner-Mazel, 1977).
8. Experts call this the goodness-of-fit model. See Thomas and Chess, *Temperament and Development.*
9. Dr. Grace Ketterman, personal communication, 2000.
10. J. M. Contrera, K. A. Kerns, B. L. Weimer, A. L. Gentzler, and P. L. Tomich, "Emotion Regulation As a Mediator of Associations Between Mother-Child Attachment and Peer Relationships in Middle Childhood," *Journal of Family Psychology* 14 (2000): 111–24.
11. Gary Habermas, personal communication, 2000.
12. Froma Walsh, *Strengthening Family Resilience* (New York: Guilford Press, 1998).

Chapter 12. Breaking Free!
1. Living *in* the now should not be confused with living *for* the now. To live *in* the now is to accept your experiences and appreciate what you have. It heightens your sense of responsibility and helps you make effective choices. Living *for* the now is self-centered and impulsive. It actually causes you to feel a lack of responsibility and leads to poor choices.
2. Our thoughts on this subject have been influenced by Dan Allender, Larry Crabb, John Gottman, Leslie Greenberg, Susan Johnson, and Donald Meichenbaum.
3. Keep in mind that, just because you don't feel like you have been wounded, doesn't mean you haven't been. Many people come from families where the rule is not only do you not talk about painful events but you also do not remember them.
4. D. B. Waters and E. C. Lawrence, *Competence, Courage, and Change: An Approach to Family Therapy* (New York: W. W. Norton, 1993).
5. David Stoop, *Real Solutions for Forgiving the Unforgivable* (Ann Arbor, Mich.: Servant, 2001).

SELECT BIBLIOGRAPHY

Ainsworth, Mary D. S., M. C. Blehar, E. Waters, and S. Wall. *Patterns of Attachment: A Psychological Study of the Strange Situation*. Hillsdale, N.J.: Erlbaum, 1978.

Barkley, R. *Defiant Children: A Clinician's Manual for Assessment and Parent Training*, 2nd ed. New York: Guilford Press, 1997.

Bartholomew, K. "Avoidance of Intimacy: An Attachment Perspective." *Journal of Social and Personal Relationships* 7 (1990): 147–78.

Beck, A., and A. Freeman and Associates. *Cognitive Therapy of Personality Disorders*. New York: Guilford Press, 1990.

Becker, E. *The Denial of Death*. New York: Free Press, 1973.

Bell, R., and M. D. S. Ainsworth. "Infant Crying and Maternal Responsiveness." *Child Development* 43 (1972): 1171–90.

Benjamin, L. *Interpersonal Diagnosis and Treatment of Personality Disorders*. New York: Guilford, 1993.

Bettelheim, B. "Individual and Mass Behavior in Extreme Situations," in *Surviving and Other Essays*. New York: Knopf, 1979. (Original works published in 1943.)

Bowlby, J. *Attachment and Loss*. Vol. 1, *Attachment*. New York: Basic Books, 1969.

———. *Attachment and Loss*. Vol. 2, *Separation: Anxiety and Anger*. New York: Basic Books, 1973.

———. *Attachment and Loss*. Vol. 3, *Loss*. New York: Basic Books, 1980.

Breger, L. *From Instinct to Identity: The Development of Personality.* Englewood Cliffs: Prentice-Hall, 1974.

Brennan, K. A., and J. K. Bosson. "Attachment-Style Differences in Attitudes Toward and Reactions to Feedback from Romantic Partners: An Exploration of the Relational Bases of Self-Esteem." *Personality and Social Psychology Bulletin* 24 (1998): 699–714.

Bretherton, I. "The Origins of Attachment Theory: John Bowlby and Mary Ainsworth." *Developmental Psychology* 28 (1992): 759–75.

Briere, J. N. *Child Abuse Trauma: Theory and Treatment of the Lasting Effects.* Newbury Park: Sage Publications, 1992.

Brown, Stephanie. *Treating Adult Children of Alcoholics: A Developmental Perspective.* New York: John Wiley, 1988.

Carter, C. S. "Oxytocin and Sexual Behavior." *Neuroscience and Biobehavioral Reviews* 100 (1992): 204–32.

Dodge, K. A. "Social Cognition and Children's Aggressive Behavior." *Child Development* 51 (1980): 162–70.

———. "Attributional Bias in Aggressive Children" in P. C. Kendall, ed., *Advances in Cognitive-Behavioral Research and Therapy.* Vol. 4. New York: Academic Press, 1985.

Dodge, K. A., and C. L. Frame, "Social Cognitive Biases and Deficits in Aggressive Boys." *Child Development* 53 (1982): 620–35.

Drossman, D. A. "Physical and Sexual Abuse and Gastrointestinal Illness: What Is the Link?" *American Journal of Medicine* 97 (1994): 105–7.

Drossman, D. A. "Chronic Functional Abdominal Pain." *American Journal of Gastroenterology* 91, no. 11 (1996): 2270–81.

Finkelhor, D. *Sexually Victimized Children.* New York: Free Press, 1979.

Firestone, F. *The Fear of Intimacy.* New York: American Psychological Association, 1999.

Firestone, R., and Joyce Catlett. *Combating Self-Destructive Thought Processes: Voice Therapy and Separation Theory.* New York: Sage, 1997.

Fonagy, P. "Attachment in Infancy and the Problem of Conduct Disorders in Adolesence: The Role of Reflective Function." Plenary address to the International Association of Adolescent Psychiatry, San Francisco, 2000.

———. "Attachment, Reflective Function, Conduct Disorders, and Violence." Paper presented to the American Academy of Child and Adolescent Psychiatry's Mid-Year Institute on Integrating Psychotherapy and Psychopharmacology in the Treatment of Children and Adolescents: A Practical Approach. Puerto Vallarta, Mexico, 2000.

Fonagy, P., M. Steele, H. Steele, G. S. Moran, and A. C. Higgitt. "The Capacity for Understanding Mental States: The Reflective Self in Parent and Child and Its Significance for Security of Attachment." *Infant Mental Health Journal* 12 (1991): 211–24.

Fraiberg, S., E. Adelson, and V. Shapiro. "Ghosts in the Nursery: A Psychoanalytic Approach to the Problems of Impaired Infant-Mother Relationships." *Journal of the American Academy of Child Psychiatry* 14 (1970): 387–421.

Frankl, Viktor. *Man's Search for Meaning.* Boston: Beacon Press, 1963.

Gottman, J. M. *Raising an Emotionally Intelligent Child: The Heart of Parenting.* New York: Simon and Schuster, 1997.

———. *The Marriage Clinic: A Scientifically Based Marital Therapy.* New York: W. W. Norton, 1999.

Gottman, J. M., L. F. Katz, and C. Hooven. "Parental Meta-Emotion Philosophy and the Emotional Life of Families: Theoretical Models and Preliminary Data." *Journal of Family Psychology* 10 (1996): 243–68.

Greenberg, L., and S. Paivio. *Working with Emotions in Psychotherapy.* New York: Guilford Press, 1997.

Habermas, G., and Gary Sibcy. "Religious Doubt and Negative Emotionality: The Development of the Religious Doubt Scale." (2001) Manuscript is currently under review by the *Journal of Psychology and Theology.*

Hazan, C., and D. Zeifman. "Pair Bonds As Attachment: Evaluating the Evidence," in J. Cassidy, P. R. Shaver, eds., *Handbook of Attachment: Theory, Research, and Clinical Applications.* New York: Guilford Press, 1999.

Hess, E. "The Adult Attachment Interview: Historical and Current Perspectives." J. Cassidy, P. R. Shaver, eds., *Handbook of Attachment: Theory, Research, and Clinical Applications.* New York: Guilford Press, 1999, 395–433.

Holmes, J. *John Bowlby and Attachment Theory.* New York: Routledge, 1993.

Johnson, S. M., J. A. Makinen, and J. W. Milikin. "Attachment Injuries in Couple Relationships: A New Perspective on Impasses in Couples Therapy." *Journal of Marital and Family Therapy* (2001).

Kaplan, H. I., A. M. Freedman, and B. J. Sadock, eds. *Comprehensive Textbook of Psychiatry.* 2 vols. Baltimore: Williams & Wilkins, 1980.

Karen, R. *Becoming Attached: First Relationships and How They Shape Our Capacity to Love.* Oxford, England: Oxford University Press, 1994.

Kempe, C. H., F. N. Silverman, B. F. Steele, W. Droegmuller, and H. K. Silver. "The Battered-Child Syndrome," *Journal of the American Medical Association* 181 (1962): 17–24.

Lochman, J. E., and L. B. Lampron. "Situational Social Problem-Solving Skills and Self-Esteem of Aggressive and Nonaggressive Boys." *Journal of Abnormal Child Psychology* 14 (1986): 605–17.

Lyons-Ruth, K., and D. Jacobvitz. "Attachment Disorganization: Unresolved Loss, Relational Violence, and Lapses in Behavioral and Attentional Strategies," in J. Cassidy and P. R. Shaver, eds., *Handbook of Attachment: Theory, Research, and Clinical Applications.* New York: Guilford Press, 1999.

Main, M., and J. Solomon. "Procedures for Identifying Infants As Disorganized/Disoriented During the Ainsworth Strange Situation." In M. T. Greenberg, D. Cicchetti, E. M. Cummings, eds., *Attachment in the Preschool Years: Theory, Research, and Interventions.* Chicago: University of Chicago Press, 1990.

Main, M., and E. Hess. "Parents' Unresolved Traumatic Experiences Are Related to Infant Disorganized Attachment Status: Is Frightened and/or Frightening

Parental Behavior the Linking Mechanism?" in M. T. Greenberg, D. Cicchetti, and E. M. Cummings, eds, *Attachment in the Preschool Years: Theory, Research, and Intervention*. Chicago: University of Chicago Press, 1990.

Masterson, J. F. *The Search for the Real Self: Unmasking the Personality Disorders of Our Age*. New York: Free Press, 1988.

Masterson, J. F., and R. Klein, eds. *Disorders of the Self: New Therapeutic Horizons: The Masterson Approach*. New York: Brunner/Mazel, 1995.

Miller, A. *Thou Shalt Not Be Aware*. New York: Farrar, Straus, & Giroux, 1984.

Millon, T. *Disorder of Personality: DSM-IV and Beyond*. New York: John Wiley & Sons, 1996.

Nass, G. D., and M. P. Fisher. *Sexuality Today*. Boston: Jones and Bartlett, 1988.

Olson, D. H. "Circumplex Model of Marital and Family Systems: Assessing Family Functioning." In Froma Walsh, ed., *Normal Family Processes*, 2nd ed. New York: Guilford, 1993.

Pearson, J. L., D. A. Cohn, P. A. Cowan, and C. P. Cowan. "Earned- and Continuous-Security in Adult Attachment: Relation to Depressive Symptomatology and Parenting Style." *Development and Psychopathology* 6 (1994): 359–73.

Peck, M. Scott. *The Road Less Traveled*. New York: Simon and Schuster, 1978.

Perry, D. G., L. C. Perry, and P. Rasmussen. "Cognitive and Social Learning Mediators of Aggression," *Child Development* 57 (1986): 700–11.

Phelps, J. L., J. Belsky, K. Crnic. "Earned Security, Daily Stress, and Parenting: A Comparison of Five Alternative Models." *Development and Psychopathology* 10 (1998): 21–38.

Robinson, D. *Personality Disorders: Explained*. Port Huron, Mich.: Rapid Psychler Press, 2000.

Rosenfeld, A. A., C. C. Nadelson, and M. Krieger. *Journal of the American Academy of Child Psychiatry* 136 (1979): 791–95.

Sandler, L. "Issues in Early Mother-Child Interaction." *Journal of the American Academy of Child Psychiatry* 1 (1962): 141–66.

Shea, S. *Psychiatric Interviewing: The Art of Understanding.* Philadelphia: W. B. Saunders, 1988.

Shore, A. N. "The Effects of a Secure Attachment Relationship on Right Brain Development, Affect Regulation, and Infant Mental Health." *Infant Mental Health Journal* 22 (2001): 7–66.

Sibcy, Gary. "Self-Report Attachment Styles and Psychopathology in a Clinical Population." Doctoral diss., The Union Institute and University's School of Clinical and Professional Psychology, Cincinnati, Ohio, 2000.

Siegel, D. *The Developing Mind: Toward a Neurobiology of Interpersonal Experience.* New York: Guilford Press, 1999.

Silverman, D. K. "The Tie That Binds: Affect Regulation, Attachment, and Psychoanalysis." *Psychoanalytic Psychology* 15 (1988): 187–212.

Slaby, R. G., and N. G. Guerra. "Cognitive Mediators of Aggression in Adolescent Offenders: 1. Assessment." *Developmental Psychology* 24, no. 4 (1988): 580–88.

Sperry, L. *Handbook of Diagnosis and Treatment of DSM-IV Personality Disorders.* New York: Brunner/Mazel, 1995.

Stoop, David. *Real Solutions for Forgiving the Unforgivable.* Ann Arbor, Mich.: Servant, 2001.

van der Kolk, B. A. "The Body Keeps the Score: The Psychobiology of Traumatic Experiences." In B. A. van der Kolk, A. C. McFarlane, and L. Weisaeth, eds., *Traumatic Stress: The Effects of Overwhelming Experience on Mind, Body, and Society.* New York: Guilford, 1996.

———. "The Complexity of Adaptation to Trauma Self-Regulation, Stimulus Discrimination, and Characterological Development." In van der Kolk, McFarlane, and Weisaeth, eds., *Traumatic Stress.* New York: Guilford, 1996.

———. "The Compulsion to the Trauma: Re-enactment, Revictimization, and Masochism." *Psychiatric Clinics of North America* 12 (1989): 389–411.

———. "Trauma and Memory." In van der Kolk, McFarlane, and Weisaeth, eds., *Traumatic Stress.*

Vygotzky, L. S. *Mind in Society: The Development of Higher Psychological Processes.* Cambridge, Mass.: Harvard University Press, 1978.

Waters, D. B., and E. C. Lawrence. *Competence, Courage, and Change: An Approach to Family Therapy.* New York: W. W. Norton, 1993.

Weinfield, N., L. Sroufe, B. Egeland, and E. Carlson. "The Nature of Individual Differences in Infant-Caregiver Attachment." In J. Cassidy and P. Shaver, eds., *Handbook of Attachment: Theory, Research, and Clinical Applications.* New York: Guilford Press, 1999.

Willard, D. *The Spirit of the Disciplines: Understanding How God Changes Lives.* San Francisco: Harper and Row, 1988.

Yalom, Irwin. *Existential Psychotherapy.* New York: Basic Books, 1980.